Pan American World Airways
Aviation History
Through the Words of its
People

James Patrick (Jamie) Baldwin, J.D.
and
Jeff Kriendler

International Standard Book Number 13: 978-1-60452-072-9

International Standard Book Number 10: 1-60452-072-8

Library of Congress Control Number: 2011943286

BluewaterPress LLC
52 Tuscan Way Ste 202-309
Saint Augustine Florida 32092-1850
http://www.bluewaterpress.com

This book may be purchased online at—http://bluewaterpress.com

Cover and Title Page Photo Credits

Cover design by Lesley Giles (Copyright © 2011 by Lesley Giles)

Title Page: Boeing 747 – Clipper Juan T. Trippe – Photo by Rolf Wallner. Jamie Baldwin was on board the aircraft at the time.

Contents

Dedication

To my wife, Lesley, for her support, and my late father and mother, who stirred my interest in the airline industry and in particular Pan American World Airways, and to Pan American enthusiasts around the world. I would also like to dedicate this book to the late Ron Davies, formerly Curator for Air Transport at the National Air and Space Museum in Washington, DC.

Jamie Baldwin

To my parents, Florence and Bob, who epitomized the glamorous days of air travel, shown below boarding a Clipper to London in the early 1950s, as well as to my daughter Catherine, who gave me inspiration to produce this anthology. In August, 2011 the Pan Am family lost a true pioneer with the passing of John Borger. I would also like to dedicate this book in his memory.

Jeff Kriendler

Preface

More than 80 years ago, Pan American Airways embarked on a remarkable course of daring, commitment and vision. No other airline opened—and shrunk—the world the way Pan Am did. No other airline in the history of commercial aviation took as many risks, blazed as many new trails, set a high standard for service or brought together so many people from every corner of the globe, passengers and staff alike.

To anyone interested in airlines and aviation, the history of Pan American World Airways can be considered the history of international airline transportation. This is no loosely worded generalization. The history of Pan American "firsts" has been well documented and indeed, a recent book by co-editor Jamie Baldwin, *Pan American World Airways – Images of a Great Airline*, highlighted these "firsts" along with major historical events in the life of the airline.

In this book, we are offering Pan Am's history in a different and most unique format: through the eye-witness experiences of the people of Pan Am – the pilots, the flight attendants, the station managers and other staff who participated in the history making events that arguably made Pan Am the greatest airline that ever was— and certainly the most renowned and celebrated.

On December 11, 1934, Pan Am's founder, Juan T. Trippe in a New York City speech stated:

> *"By each successive step, aviation is advancing to that potential ideal of a universal service for humanity. By overcoming artificial barriers, aviation can weave together, in closer understanding, the nations of the world, and lift for the peoples of the world those horizons which have too long limited the perspective of those who live upon this earth."*

These words are fulfilled in this book, an anthology of stories written by the people of Pan Am. They were there at the important and news-making events that shaped the airline's life. Many of these events made headlines around the world, such as the carnage at Tenerife or the Lockerbie bombing. And, with the recent fall of Muammar Ghaddafi, the name Pan American is still commanding space in news publications today. Other events, among so many, might have just been a small item in the local newspaper or were never reported at all.

There were those employees who went beyond the call of duty; others were simply doing their job and in some cases there was loss of life of their dear friends. The bottom line, big or small, heroic or otherwise, is that the events were important to the airline and its people. This is the story we have to tell: The historic achievements of Pan Am as experienced and lived by its greatest resource – its people.

Among the 71 essays gathered included are the writings of Bill Nash, a prolific journalist still at the age of 94, an aviation historian and great airman who leads off with tales of the flying boat era (page 1), taken from his many articles in Airways Magazine whose Editor and Publisher John Wegg has so kindly gave us permission to use. We have the personal recollections (page 4) of Kathleen Clair who worked at the right-hand of Juan Trippe for many decades. From Jay Koren, In Flight Service Director and Purser extraordinaire, and author of The Company We Kept, we learn about his experiences on the inaugural flights of both the 707 and 747 aircraft starting on page 10.

On November 22, 1963, flight attendant Kari Mette Pigmans related the joy – and then the utter despair – of being with President John F. Kennedy in Dallas just a few minutes before he was assassinated (page 24). On a happier day, Jill L'Epplatanier shares her fun trip (page 30) in 1964 when the Beatles first flew to the United States – on Pan Am of course. Through the years Pan Am carried many dignitaries and celebrities; Heads of State, TV and movie idols, politicians and sports heroes. However, the passenger flight attendants perhaps most enjoyed serving was Mother Teresa. Ron Marasco's tale of how Mother Teresa of Calcutta became Pan Am's patron saint will bring joy to our readers on page 105.

Always in the forefront of American diplomatic efforts to bring the world closer together, Pan Am forged commercial air service from the USA to the Soviet Union in 1968, and re-opened China in 1980 while, along the way bridging oceans and cultures from Latin America, Asia, Africa and the South Pacific. Our writers cover different aspects of Pan Am's expansive global reach and were a part of globalization before the word was coined. They write of their recollections of the reservation list for the First Commercial Flight to the Moon; of Black September, when a 747 was blown up in Cairo by extremists; a secret mission to Mogadishu; the merger of Pan Am and National; the sale of the Pacific routes and the Internal German Service; and the final flight.

The company's historic commitment to the US military – be it during World War II, the Berlin Airlift, the Korean Conflict, Vietnam or Desert Storm – is also told by several employees who were proud to be part of the mission to support Uncle Sam. There were many refugee evacuation flights, R&R charters, troop carriage, and air cargo lifts. The men and women of Pan Am lived history and in some instances, suffered the ravages of the dark side of it. As the "Red Menace" of the Cold War gave way to radical Islamic fundamentalism, Pan Am was a prime "bogey" and paid a heavy price for carrying the US flag on its aircraft tails.

Today, some 20 years after its last flight, the airline remains a national treasure. In his article "Pan Am: the Fall of a Legend" in 1991, Peter Wilkinson described Pan Am in its glory days, saying,

> "Pan Am had become part of the popular culture. In the 50's, Norman Rockwell illustrated Pan Am. Ernest Hemingway told *Look Magazine* writers: 'Pan Am and I are old friends....I feel as safe with Pan Am as I do any morning I wake up to a good working day.' Passengers tasted Caspian caviar and truffled Strasbourg goose-liver pate. Gentlemen freshened with Remington electric shavers before landing. A bridal suite was available to newlyweds. Pan Am hotels offered the same Sealy mattresses everywhere in the world. Pan Am called itself 'the world's most experienced airline', and no one could argue the point."

When Pan Am sold its European routes to Delta, New York writer and frequent flier Grace Hechinger wrote in the *Wall Street Journal* on November 21, 1991,

> "Pan Am Clippers were an early aviation symbols of glamour. They starred in exotic black and white movies with Humphrey Bogart in foreign lands winging off into the sunset. My last European flight on Pan Am stirred my nostalgia for a past when flying was fun and glamorous. I used to wear gloves and sometimes even a hat. You did not have to fly first class to feel special and coddled. Children got free gifts, which they showed off proudly for weeks after."

Pan Am was also a movie star, being portrayed in many films, such as *Casablanca, Midway, Bullitt, 2001: A Space Odyssey* and *Indiana Jones*. More recently, Steven Spielberg captured the essence of Pan Am crew members through Leonardo DiCaprio in his 2002 blockbuster movie *Catch Me If You Can*, which was turned into a Broadway musical of the same title in the Spring of 2011 and will tour the United States in 2012.

And in the Fall of 2011, ABC/Sony Pictures is airing a TV series---"Pan Am"---which their publicity team describes as "passion, adventure and espionage... They do it all – and they do it at 30,000 feet. The style of the 1960s, the energy and excitement of the Jet Age and a drama full of sexy entanglements deliciously mesh in a thrilling and highly original new series. Welcome to the Jet Age. It's 1963. World War II and Korea are history. A new kind of war, a Cold War, is underway. The world is poised on the brink of a cultural revolution, and everywhere change is in the air." The show is summed up with these words:

> "In this modern world, air travel represents the height of luxury, and Pan Am is the biggest name in the business. The planes are sleek and glamorous, the pilots are rock stars, and the stewardesses are the most desirable women in the world. Not only are these flyboys and girls young and good looking, but to represent Pan Am they also have to be educated, cultured and

refined. They're trained to handle everything from in-air emergencies to unwanted advances – all without rumpling their pristine uniforms or mussing their hair. These pre-feminist women form a powerful sisterhood, as they enjoy the rare opportunity to travel outside the country -- something most women in this age can only aspire to – and one of the few career options that offers them empowerment and respect."

In today's troubled airline industry, air journeys have become stressful due to invasive airport security, uncivil, unkempt and unappreciative passengers, and in some cases uncaring management and staff. The glamorous days of Pan Am-inspired flying are sorely missed but are re-kindled by the memories and tales of staff as told on these pages.

On December 4, 1991 Pan Am ceased all operations. From a tiny airline that operated a single route between Key West to Havana, it grew into the most powerful and prestigious in the world. Books and articles were written about it. Movies were made, and Pan Am starred on television. The people of Pan Am literally spanned the globe, with careers and postings that rivaled US State Department employees. Over the years the members of the Pan Am family numbered in the tens of thousands. We are fortunate to share with the readers of this book the stories of some of these people. Please read and enjoy them all and relive an era that will never be replicated.

Jamie Baldwin
Ormond Beach, Florida

Jeff Kriendler
Miami Beach, Florida

December, 2011

Those of the Pan Am family wishing to contact any of the authors of these stories are invited to email us at either jpbpa2@gmail.com or jkriendler@aol.com.

Acknowledgements

Putting together this book required the assistance of many people, and first and foremost, we would like to express gratitude and admiration to the members of the Pan Am family who devoted their time and writing talents--and photo images--to this book.

We would also like to thank Jamie Baldwin's wife, Lesley Giles for her critical assistance in the design and production of the manuscript. Her expertise and artistic abilities were invaluable to both of us.

Jackie Scott-Mandeville, daughter of the late R.E.G. Davies, to whom this book is dedicated, provided valuable assistance with editing. She volunteered for this task and we thank her for her suggestion and comments.

Jeff Kriendler would like to thank John Hill for writing such a compelling Forward, Harvey Bilt for his photographic support, Kelly Cusack, author and source of countless Pan Am images at www.everythingpanam.com, the University of Miami Richter Library Special Collections—Cory Czajkowski and Steve Hersh, the Pan Am Historical Foundation and John Wegg, publisher of *Airways Magazine*

Jamie Baldwin would like to thank Joe and Ardis Clark, publishers extraordinaire.

We take full responsibility for the contents in this book and any omissions.

Foreword

Great civilizations throughout the ages have used innovative transportation technologies to reshape the world. The stirrup provided Mongol horsemen of central Asia unprecedented maneuverability throughout Europe and the Middle East. The Romans built roads and operated a highway system on three continents, and England's shipbuilding extended the reach of a vast dominion when Britannia ruled the waves. For the United States in the Twentieth Century, one private company in particular saw to it that the airplane—that crowning achievement of the industrial age—would play a central role in defining what publisher Henry R. Luce called the American Century. That company was Pan American World Airways.

Air transport was the new frontier in the century's opening decades. Domestic over-land air service first showed promise in the fledgling airlines of the 1920s, although the speed, safety, and affordability of railroads would remain unchallenged for some time. Over-water flying, on the other hand, presented a more immediate and a greater comparative advantage over sea surface transport—ocean liners were at least two-thirds slower than trains and airplanes. It was out over the wide oceans where the airplane would take full possession of its transformative powers. The mastery of ocean air transport by the pioneering company destined to become the world's most experienced airline would unfold as a strikingly singular achievement.

Pan Am's modest beginnings flying the mail from Florida to Cuba in 1927 belied the enormity of purpose with which the airline was endowed at its inception. Initiated by Henry H. Arnold, implemented and led by the like-minded Juan T. Trippe as co-envisioned with his early colleague John A. Hambleton, backed by financiers such as C. V. Whitney, it developed an extensive route system throughout the Caribbean Basin and Latin America with startling speed. This ability to seize and hold the leading edge in a rapidly developing and increasingly competitive commercial aviation industry would become Pan Am's hallmark as it continued to blaze a trail in the sky during the next six decades.

By the early 1930s, the primary goal of reliably and repeatedly flying the oceans, and thereby introducing the world's first regularly scheduled international air service using heavier-than-air, fixed-wing aircraft, could now be plausibly considered thanks to Pan Am's Caribbean experience. That early success fed into the core mission of a global system and was the operational foundation upon which such an audacious leap forward would be realized.

Logically, the Atlantic would come first. Its 1,900 miles were certainly daunting and a North America–Europe aerial trade route was highly prized. Fate would intervene, however, for despite Pan Am's assessment of its own readiness to overcome the geographical and navigational challenges of the North Atlantic, it was man-made barriers that stalled such an attempt. Protracted diplomatic negotiations, primarily with the British, failed to resolve issues of landing rights and other reciprocal concessions.

Flying the Pacific, which of course had also always been anticipated in good order, suddenly took top priority. Trippe was keenly aware of the importance of being first and the power of momentum. He was not willing to idle while the Atlantic situation sorted itself out. Furthermore, if carefully planned and implemented in a timely manner, a clear jurisdictional pathway across the Pacific, that was for the most part free from the types of political entanglements encountered in the Atlantic, seemed to present a distinct possibility.

Realistically, however, the Pacific presented far greater physical degrees of difficulty. Not only in sheer distance covering the more than 8,000 miles of ocean, but also in navigation where tiny islands rather than a continental landmass would have to be found with pinpoint accuracy along the way. Even by breaking the Pacific span into segments with the use of five mid-ocean island bases, the longest leg—the 2,400-mile "Hawai'i Sector" from San Francisco to Honolulu—remained an unattainable distance for transport flying. If it could be reached, however, the entire world would fall within Pan Am's grasp as no wider water gap lay in the way of a global airline system. Thus the challenges of the Hawai'i Sector, the key to the aerial trade routes of the world, became Pan Am's ultimata.

And so the fateful, albeit controversial, decision was issued from the company boardroom—Pan Am would fly the Pacific to Asia through Hawai'i. Old World Europe would have to wait.

With the determination of this western course to the Far East came faint echoes of unfinished business when European explorers discovered that the continents of the western hemisphere impeded the way to the true Spice Islands. It carried over something of the United State's own history of westward momentum and its notion of Manifest Destiny. The logistical challenges of crossing the Pacific by air even revisited the remarkable journeys of seafaring Polynesians who braved these great distances in sailing canoes centuries before. This new Silk Road of the air would radically alter the rate of East–West exchange through a time warping backdoor to Asia. Moreover, the spectacle of such a monumental undertaking and the very figure of a giant, silvery aircraft lifting and carrying the hopes of a nation battered by economic depression brought all its dramatic weight to bear on the collective imagination through the attention of press and newsreel.

To build this aerial route required next generation technology in the class of aircraft, the state of navigation and communication, the operating standards of flight personnel, and extensive ground support. Pan Am devised a multiple crew concept and trained pilots, navigators, engineers, and radio operators for long-haul flying. These professional airmen acquired the highest skill levels in aviation yet achieved while their captains earned the company's own Master of Ocean Flying Boats certification. At the precise moment of critical need, Pan Am's Hugo Leuteritz developed a breakthrough proprietary radio direction finding system solving the extreme navigational demands. For the Caribbean service, airplane designer and manufacturer Igor A. Sikorsky and Charles A. Lindbergh, Pan Am's technical advisor, had devised the first of the airline's famous Clippers. The four-engine, long-range flying boat did not require a landing field as it took off and alighted only on water. Sikorsky's new Clipper, the S-42 model, was pressed into service to survey the Pacific route and modified to extend its range for the Hawai'i Sector. Midway, Wake, Guam, Manila, and eventually Hong Kong were all on the shorter legs and at each an airbase was created as at Alameda and Honolulu. The S-42 became the workhorse for the proving flights begun in April of 1935 while awaiting the next, larger M-130 flying boats being built by the Glenn L. Martin Company solely for Pan Am and its requirements. The successes of the S-42 flights dramatically showed that the Pacific was now flyable. Pan Am had shattered the barrier of the Hawai'i Sector.

By November, all three Martin M-130 flying boats were delivered and from them the China Clipper was assigned the first scheduled revenue flight; San Francisco (Alameda) to Manila. On November 22, 1935—a mere thirty-two years after Kitty Hawk and before bridges were even built across San Francisco Bay—the instantly famous China Clipper departed for Asia as Pan Am delivered the world's first regularly scheduled and sustained transoceanic commercial airplane service. The start of the Atlantic route followed in 1939, inaugurated by the Yankee Clipper, one of a fleet of even larger "Super Clipper" Boeing 314 flying boats, once again developed exclusively for Pan Am...the airline that had now become a household name.

Pan Am's milestone achievement in ocean air transport placed the United States squarely at the forefront of the air age and set the standard for long-range commercial flying. Its business model became the blueprint for an industry that would make the ancient dream of flight a reality for many millions as it altered twentieth century perceptions of space and time.

The flying boats, wonderful hybrids that had made the metamorphosis from sea surface to air travel, gave way to long-range, land-based airplanes. Pan Am's capabilities in ocean flying and the skills of its personnel became highly significant strategic assets leading up to, and during, World War II, and the airline served the national interest with great distinction. In the postwar era, it was Pan Am that was ready to both anticipate and induce the air travel boom and bring flying to within reach of the average salary earner by pressing forward with economy fare programs aimed at democratizing the airways, often over the objections of some industry leaders and government regulators.

The propeller-driven airliners were themselves phased out by the new jet engine transports, another class of airliner first successfully introduced once again by Pan Am—which would come to include the wide-body configurations. While the speed of jet travel was certainly attractive from a consumer standpoint, it was affordability that actually fueled exponential growth in commercial aviation. With the jet age came dramatic reductions in per-passenger operating costs that Pan Am then passed on to its customers.

Pan Am enfranchised the travel industry with a long list of subsidiary services, hotels, and specialized concerns. It came to symbolize the United States itself and its trademark was a beloved signpost to travelers around the world as its level of customer service was unsurpassed. Today, twenty-years after ceasing operations, Pan Am's legendary status retains an indelible place in history and remains a subject of great interest. The spirit and élan with which it carried itself are celebrated in literature, film, television, and on Broadway. A 75th anniversary event recently held in the San Francisco Bay Area to recognize the importance of the inaugural flight of the China Clipper drew more than one thousand participants. Today, more than two dozen Pan Am associations and social groups around the world remain active as former company employees continue to enjoy the bonds of friendship and satisfaction in their collective roles in having made Pan Am such an exceptional company. The Pan Am Historical Foundation retains a sizable membership as it continues to preserve and share the airline's important legacy. As the philanthropic organization of former Pan Am flight attendants, World Wings International conducts its charity work with thirty chapters in the United States, Europe, and Japan.

As is always the case, it is exceptional people that make an exceptional organization. Pan Am's success can be traced from the entrepreneurial initiatives of its founding visionaries in the 1920s through the work of each employee who joined its ranks throughout the decades. Their stories and first person recollections such as told in this book are the true historical account of Pan Am as experienced from the inside. Their contribution to the world in making Pan Am such a success and such an inspiring example of excellence is truly a gift that continues to give.

John H. Hill
Assistant Director, Aviation
SFO Museum

THE FLYING BOATS

By William Nash

Flying Pan Am's Boeing-314 Clippers

When I joined Pan Am in 1942, one of the first phrases that I learned was "flying by the seat of your pants" – an old adage used to describe proper flying techniques. Before high-altitude jets flew commercially, we had to fly through wide storms rather than over them. To do so, we developed a seat of the pants technique – literally– whereby our bottoms were being bumped, rather than slipping or sliding. (Increased bumping meant you were headed for a thunderstorm's core.)

Boeing 314 at anchor in San Francisco Bay

Today, we have the sophistication and luxury of jetliners to fly over many of those boiling storm masses, cabin pressurization for oxygen supply, and radar to show us the dangerous storm cells, enabling us to fly around the violent depictions shown on the weather radar screen.

1

When crossing an ocean in a Pan Am flying boat such as the Boeing-314, we navigated celestially using an octant. Every Pan Am pilot was required to learn two methods of star computations to lay a position on the chart. On a Boeing-314 we had a glass hatch atop the cabin through which we could "shoot stars". When the sky was partly cloud-covered, we plotted whatever navigational stars we could see. If the sky was overcast we could not use our octants, but could take drift sights.

In the daylight we could see wind streaks on the surface of the sea, shiny lines running 90 degrees to the waves. If we had cloud cover below as well as above, we would navigate by dead-reckoning, using the wind we thought we had. If clear below and we passed a ship we could see, we could compare our position with theirs.

Approaching a coast, such as much of the Atlantic shoreline, which could be a mass jungle, while receiving poor or no radio signals, we aimed at the shore off-course 30 degrees left or right of wherever we considered the destination most likely to be. When we arrived at the coast we then followed the shore to our destination. If we had flown straight at the destination and saw nothing, we would not have known which way to follow the coast.

During a typical 11-12 hour flight, we usually took turns resting every 4 hours in our crew bunks. The props turned at 1,600 RPM's and they vibrated violently. Consequently, it took some time to fall asleep.

During World War II on trans-oceanic flights, Pan Am crews had to learn how to decipher coded messages. At departure we received an envelope which was not to be opened until we were aloft containing the keys to the codes which were valid for only a certain number of hours and then changed.

The Boeing-314 crew consisted of a captain, first officer, second officer, third officer, fourth officer, first and second flight engineers and one Morse Code radio-operator plus varying number of flight personnel. Four or more male stewards were aboard, depending on the aircraft's configuration. The work on board was considered too strenuous for stewardesses. Hefty, large-capacity life rafts had to be handled and there were ponderous bunks to be prepared for sleeping.

The entire aircraft was First Class, and our flying boats often carried kings, queens, presidents and potentates. We were instructed to be pleasant with them if they addressed us, but not to seek out conversation. President Juan Trippe wanted us to be able to converse intelligently by keeping up with current events, and having a good knowledge of history and sensitive political issues.

Passengers enjoyed delicious meals that were prepared onboard and served in a 14-place dining room with black walnut tables in a silver and blue décor. The food was elegantly served in courses by stewards in white jackets, on pale blue table cloths with matching monogrammed napkins and china. Wine was always served and dinner was topped off with fancy desserts, fruits and cheeses, and a cordial of crème de menthe. Sometimes there was a captain's table. After dinner, the dining room was converted into a lounge where some passengers chose to relax while others went to their cabins to sleep.

The Boeing-314's were retired from Pan Am's service in 1946, after World War II. Not one survived, and only a few parts exist in museums, which to me, is very sad. Clare Booth Luce, a playwright, United States Congresswoman and Ambassador to Italy, returned to the US aboard a flight on the Boeing-314 and said "Years from now, we will look back upon Pan American's flying boats as the most glamorous, romantic air travel in the world".

To me, experiencing this phase of early commercial aviation was one of the best times of my life. Having had the opportunity to be part of a Boeing 314 crew was an outstanding adventure for a young man, and I still recall it well at age 94, and thrill to the memories of that great aircraft and the exciting era of world history, all made possible by my years with Pan Am.

Bill B. Nash was a pilot with Pan American from August 1942 to June 1977. He lives with his wife, Eva, in SW Florida.

JUAN TRIPPE'S ASSISTANT

By Kathleen M. Clair

Assistant to Juan Terry Trippe, Chief Executive Officer of Pan American World Airways

I joined Pan Am in 1948 and worked with the company until my retirement in 1980, always at the side of our leader, Mr. Trippe.

He was very quiet and soft spoken. He never issued an order, rather he would say "don't you think we should do this" and everyone did it on the double. He never used profanity; he never seemed to be in a rush. Honestly, he would keep the President of the United States waiting on the phone while he finished the call he was on.

Mr. Trippe always finished what he was doing before he started something else – he was very persevering. No matter how many turn downs he got from the government or others he would just start out on another tack five minutes later on the same subject, sometimes pursuing the same objective for 30 years. He wouldn't give up. One could say that he was tough, but in a quiet way. His day used to begin at around 7:30 in the morning and it was rare that he would leave before 8:00 at night.

When I first began working for Mr. Trippe, I would put five cigars in his pencil slot every morning and he would smoke them throughout the day. One day, he just stopped smoking them and they stayed there for years. He didn't say anything about quitting but he had just given them up, never mentioning anything. He smoked the inexpensive Robert Burns, and if one were offered to any of the men in the office, they would refuse because they didn't like cheap cigars.

Pan Am Archives

STAKING OUT THE WORLD

Trippe and his famous globe, about 1939. He used to stretch string between two points and measure it, and after that he would translate the inches into a flying boat's hours in the air.

4

When Howard Hughes had control of TWA, Mr. Trippe went out to meet with him at a secret destination to discuss a possible merger. His personal pilot, Al Ueltschi, flying a private plane, took him to a remote place in the California desert, along with his son, Charlie, who was about 12 years-old at the time. They were met by an old jalopy and were driven further out into the desert until they finally arrived at a little shed where Howard Hughes was waiting.

Nothing ever came of those merger talks because Hughes wanted a ridiculous price for his stock.

Through our office came hundreds of legendary people and, in my opinion, one of the greatest was Charles Lindbergh. He would use our office as his New York base when he visited. He was one of the most wonderful people I ever met, very self-effacing. You couldn't do anything for him. You couldn't dial a phone number; you couldn't type anything for him. Nothing – he did it all himself.

After the war he worked for Pan Am for a dollar a year. He refused to take a salary but he said that he would submit an expense report and on his first trip to Paris he came back and handed me a bill noting "here's my expense account".

It was a car rental bill for a Renault and I asked him, "Well, where's the hotel bill?" And he said, "Uh, uh, I slept in the Renault". He was used to twisting up in small places, you know. I remember that he would carry a pair of socks in his pocket and a razor in his other pocket and just go off. He didn't want anyone to recognize him when he flew, but he would sit up in the cockpit with the pilots and talk all night and answer any questions they had—and the pilots loved every minute of their personal encounters.

I remember so well when he was in New York's Columbia Presbyterian Hospital and he was told that he had only two weeks to live. He called Mr. Trippe to say goodbye and Mrs. Trippe told me that they talked for two hours and Mr. Trippe just sat in his chair. There were tears pouring down his face because both men had been through so much together from day one in the life of Pan Am.

Pan Am Archives

Lindberghs and Trippes

General Lindbergh wanted to die at his home in Maui and Mr. Trippe wanted to send him out on a Pan Am plane, but Lindbergh wouldn't allow it because it wasn't a Pan Am route and would be too costly. So Mr. Trippe arranged to have him flown on United Airlines where they curtained off the back section and he was there with Mrs. Lindbergh and their son Jon. An ambulance waited at every stop in case he died on the way but he made it and he lived about 10 days after arriving, looking at the Pacific Ocean he loved so much.

Perhaps my most vivid remembrance of Mr. Trippe was that he was a great patriot. A lot of people did not know this because he was very quiet about what he did. The government often called him for jobs they could not do politically and he always did them immediately, better than they ever dreamed it could have been done. One example: the Africa service during World War II.

Churchill and Roosevelt asked him to establish a route – this was all secret at the time – across the South Atlantic and across Africa to get supplies to Field Marshall Montgomery in the desert in Egypt. They gave him 90 days – he did it in 60.

Mr. Trippe started our Inter-Continental Hotels company at President Roosevelt's request because it was his Good Neighbor Policy at the time and he wanted hotels in Latin America so that when people went by air they had a place to stay.

Anytime the government asked him to do anything, which was often, he outdid himself. Pan Am trained Navy aviators how to fly the Pacific when the war came because Pan Am crews were the only ones who knew how to cross the Pacific at the time. Pan Am trained thousands of airmen, including some of Doolittle's crew for the Japan operation. It seems to me Pan Am never got credit for all the good things the company did.

I was blessed to work for Pan Am for most of my life, especially in the presence of such kind, gracious and patriotic Americans--Juan Terry Trippe and Charles Lindbergh.

Kathleen was Assistant to Juan T. Trippe from 1948 to 1980 and is active with the Pan Am Historical Foundation while residing in Manhattan.

Courtesy of the author

DEATH IN THE AMAZON

By Barbara Sharfstein

The Crash of Flight 202 In South America

Iapplied and was hired as a "stewardess" by Pan American World Airways in July, 1951, one month after reaching my 21st birthday and after graduating from college. About three months later, my friend from home and school, Pat Monahan, joined me and three other new hires in a rented house one block from the Miami Airport. We started our careers flying to South America and almost all islands in between. We agreed it was the most amazing, wonderful life imaginable. The types of airplanes we crewed were: Convairs, DC-4s, Constellations, and our all time favorite, the Boeing 377 Stratocruiser.

Toward the end of April, 1952, we were advised by scheduling that a Pan Am Stratocruiser was missing and one of our room-mates was aboard. It was my friend Pat. Only two of us were home at the time, including me -- the others were out flying -- but we waited by the phone for news every minute for three days. I was scheduled to leave on a 23-day DC-4 trip (making many stops and crew layovers) to Buenos Aires. On the third day and when I reached operations at the Miami Airport, I received the news the wreckage had been spotted from the air.

"Clipper Good Hope," N1039V, had crashed in the northern Brazilian Jungle on April 29th, killing nine crewmembers and 41 passengers. The official cause was the presumed failure of the number 2 propeller, causing the engine to separate from the airplane resulting in an out-of-control spin. The airplane hit the ground upside down killing all on board instantly.

I was trying my best to hold back the hysterics – but strangely enough, it never occurred to me to say I would not take the trip. The purser on the trip was Mr. Norm Reynolds (now deceased), a true character who was extremely supportive. He was a veteran of the China Clipper

Courtesy of the Author

Barbara Sharfstein (left) as a young Stewardess.

Humphrey Toomey (head bowed, behind cross), American leader of the official rescue team, conducts a burial service at t

What really happened when the huge luxury airliner fell in the
Brazilian jungle this spring? Who made hostages of the rescue
party? Why, even now, are investigators still dissatisfied with
their findings? Here, at last, are the facts in

The Jungle Crash of Flight 202

By HAROLD H. MARTIN and H. STUART MORRISON

RIO DE JANEIRO.

THE flight that Pan American World Airways calls El Presidente Especial is one of the luxury flights of intercontinental aviation, and the cities it links—Buenos Aires, Rio de Janeiro and New York—are the glamour capitals of the Western Hemisphere. It is the plane that the vice-president in charge of foreign sales takes when he leaves Manhattan to call upon his South American customers, with his brief case stuffed with order blanks and a fat expense account to fall back on. It is the plane that carries the rich beef barons from the Argentine and the coffee magnates from São Paulo, and Rio's diplomats, when they travel with their wives to New York to shop for jewels and for furs.

To a Latin, riding El Presidente on its 6000-mile flight confers a certain distinction upon the traveler, as the North American takes pride in going to Europe on one of the Queens or traveling to the West Coast on the Super Chief. For on El Presidente Especial all is done with elegance and grace. Flight stewards speak Spanish and Portuguese, and sometimes French and German as well as English, and the meals they serve aloft may run to as many as seven courses. Only the tenderest chicken and the juiciest filets are served, prepared hot in the plane's own galley, and before meals there are always cocktails—Martinis, very dry, or Manhattans—to whet the appetite. The dinner wine is champagne or a mild rosé that goes equally well with red meat or with fowl.

Fifty passenger
crash of the Pr

Pan Am Archives

Flying Boats when all flight attendants were male and had to do much of the shopping and catering themselves, an extremely creative group of guys. It was a very sad time for me.

On the flight from San Juan to Belem, Brazil, we were advised that a Pan Am Vice President, Mr. Humphrey Toomey, was aboard. Norm told him about Pat and after the meal service, he visited us in the galley, expressed condolences to me and advised us that a search party was being organized in Belem – as that was the closest location to the crash. Jungle and survival experts were being gathered from all over the United States and Brazil. There was to be a meeting the day after our arrival in Belem. We were scheduled to be there several days as the DC-4 did not make daily trips to South America. After Mr. Toomey went back to his seat, Norm told me he planned to "crash" the meeting and go on that trek with the group. As I gasped at how this could be accomplished he said: "I can camp, cook, and they need me!" The rest is history. He talked his way into joining the group, and I learned later from Bob Weeks, a pilot based in Rio (where all the cockpit crew on that flight were based), and who also joined the search, that he was really a great asset in every way. Six months later when another expedition was needed, Norm was called on again.

I was distraught but mustered enough strength to fly the next day. I worked that flight out of Belem by myself, but Mr. Toomey helped me serve the passengers as he was headed to Rio to acquire jungle search equipment. By then a purser was "deadheaded" to Rio to join me for the rest of the trip.

While the above was a devastating memory of that wonderful airplane which I will never forget, a short time later, one of the most memorable times in my flying career happened on the Stratocruiser when Louis Armstrong and his band were downstairs in the lounge longing to get to their instruments. As it happened, there was a door to the cargo compartment right next to the bar. In fact, the liquor kits were kept in the same compartment as the luggage with only a mesh rope curtain separating us from what they could spot as a few of the instruments. I can only say it was fortunate for the weight and balance of the airplane that the lounge was centrally located or we might have been in trouble. Almost all the passengers were in the lounge seats or on steps. Passengers were helping me serve drinks and neither they, nor I, will ever forget it.

Of course, I have many other memories over my more than thirty years of flying (purser, check purser and flight director on the 747) as I am sure every crew member and employee of this wonderful company has over their careers. But the loss of my friend still haunts me and will always remind me that although travel by air is safe (especially today, compared with the pre-jet era), an accident can cause life-long scars on those who lose loved ones.

Courtesy of the Author   *Courtesy of the Author*

Barbara started as a Flight Attendant (Stewardess) in July 1951 and served as a Purser, Check Purser and In-Flight Director for the Boeing 747 until February 1986 when she departed San Francisco for Narita and Manila in a Pan Am uniform and returned in a United uniform. She was with Pan Am for almost 35 years.

THE BOEING 707 INAUGURAL FLIGHT

By Jay Koren

America's First Jet Flight

Growing up mid-century in Los Angeles, it was movie stars and foreign cars, but my passion really took wing with airliners. I would hang out for hours each weekend at Lockheed Air Terminal in Burbank, observing the glamorous Hollywood crowd climbing aboard those objects of my obsession – back then usually "enormous" 21-passenger Douglas DC-3s. But by the late '40s, most scheduled airlines had moved to the new LAX, leaving Burbank to become hub of charter and the booming non-scheduled operations.

Pan Am Archives

Inside cover from the October 1958 Time Table

10

One Saturday morning in my senior year at Beverly Hills High, six-foot-two, well-groomed, looking more sophisticated than seventeen, I made a nostalgic pilgrimage out to Burbank. My friend Gary, formerly with United, now ticket counter manager of one of the "non-skeds," recognized me. "Hey, Jay, how'd ya like to take a trip up to San Fran for the day...specifically, Bay Meadows Race Track?"

I tried not to answer too quickly, "Sure, why not." Gary explained that the flights, about two hours each way and carrying just a dozen or so "track aficionados," did not really require a flight attendant. "But they're good, repeat customers and we like to keep them happy. All you have to do is offer coffee and Danish northbound and bar service on the flight back after the races. They'll have their own booze. My lead agent, Betty, normally does the trip...just for tips and to play the ponies...but she called in sick this morning."

Thus began my career.

Pan Am Archives

John McCoy Watercolor of the takeoff of Flight 114.

For the next couple of years, I bounced back and forth between college and the non-skeds. Hoping to make it with a "real airline," I applied to Pan American in San Francisco. Rejected as too tall and too young, I tried again at their tiny Seattle base—some two dozen flight attendants crewing flights just to Alaska and Hawaii. Harry LaPorte, the flight-service manager, liked me, "but we've no class planned for the time being. I understand that Northwest is interviewing..."

I was hired by NWA that same day and joined a class of thirty at their Minneapolis base the following Monday. Six months later I received a call from Mr. LaPorte. "I've gotten the green light on a class and a waiver on your height. Would you be interested in switching to Pan Am?"

Pan American World Airways — the crème de la crème. Indeed, I would and did. On a snowy Boxing Day morning at Seattle's Boeing Field, I became half of a student body of two, the smallest Pan Am class on record and my best Christmas present ever. Following two years at Seattle, I transferred to New York, the

Latin-American Division, then the Atlantic, each for a year, before returning to the West Coast for a stint at San Francisco. A brief vacation in beautiful Beirut, the only overseas flight service base at the time, convinced me it was worth the minimum two-year assignment. I transferred back to New York en route to Beirut just as hostilities broke out in the Middle East and, alas, the Beirut base became history. Not surprisingly, no one else seemed to notice. Much bigger business was at hand.

Pan Am had just taken delivery on its first Boeing 707. The United States was at last positioning for take-off into the Jet Age. Pan American flight 114 to Paris, slated to depart New York on October 26th, would not only mark America's entry into the Jet Age, it would mark the inauguration of the world's first daily trans-Atlantic jet service.

Crew rosters had been posted weeks earlier and the lucky chosen few notified of their assignment to the first flights. Four days before the inauguration, my supervisor called. "We've decided to add a seventh flight attendant to the inaugural, Jay, and you've been selected." I couldn't have been more excited if I were being sent to the moon. On the day before our departure, we were given an extensive briefing. Our pursers, Mickey deAngeles and Hank Gummasson, were veterans who regularly crewed the President Specials. First Class on the Boeing 707s, with seats and aisles wider than any pre-jet aircraft, was designated Deluxe Class and Pan Am's President Special dining service would be featured.

Purser Kay Landing would be flying as senior stewardess. The others were Betty Ganz, Hope Ryden, and a petite Parisienne, Claudette Vivet, whose French announcements were always delivered with great savoir-faire. I, baby of the crew, would be down-flying as steward. On the eve of participating in this historic event, although supercharged with anticipation, we all confessed to a sense of apprehension. We were about to zap across the Atlantic at more than eighty percent of the speed of sound—nearly twice as fast as any of us had ever flown before—at an altitude nearly twice as high, and in an aircraft capable of carrying double the load of our old, familiar, piston-engine airplanes.

Inauguration Day arrived. Departure formalities begin with a briefing by Captain Sam Miller, pilot in command. Also attending were Captain Waldo Lynch, who would be flying as first officer, Jim Etchison, the flight engineer and Captain A.O. Powell, functioning as navigator. As is the tradition in all pre-flight briefings, Captain Miller quizzed each of us on emergency equipment and procedures. "Where are the life rafts? How many are there? How many passengers should you direct to each?"

At six p.m., an hour before scheduled departure, the crew bus dropped us off at the foot of the forward loading stairs. It was drizzling lightly and members of a military band, assembled on the tarmac to lend the occasion appropriate pomp and circumstance, looked damp and uncomfortable. We climbed the stairs and stepped aboard jet *Clipper America*. Captain Miller and the other cockpit crew members were in their seats going over their checklists. A trio of *LIFE Magazine* photographers who were traveling with us were busy stowing their lights and cameras.

Kay, Hope, and I, assigned to the tourist section, proceeded through the lounge and forward cabin toward the rear of the airplane. Until boarding began we were busy checking out our new workplace: its closets and cabinets, galleys and equipment, food and bar provisioning. Outside on the ramp, the band played stirringly. New York's Mayor Wagner and Pan Am founder, Juan Trippe, lent their presence and words to the momentous event. The ribbon was cut and passengers eagerly ascended the steps. Last to board, actress Greer Garson, who was delivered ship-side in a Rolls Royce, stole the scene. She climbed to the doorway, turned, and displaying her Oscar-winning Mrs. Miniver smile, tossed an enormous bouquet of pink roses to the crowd below as photographers lit up the night with a frenzy of flash bulbs.

Everyone was seated and every seat was occupied. The stairs were pulled away and we swung closed the entry doors and engaged the emergency evacuation slide pouches. We listened to their muffled screams as, one by one, the four giant jet engines whirred to life. Appropriately, at 7:07, with the band now standing at attention and saluting, Captain Miller initiated our taxi-out. We checked seat belts. As the brakes released, the aircraft surged forward with such unexpected thrust that I grabbed for the nearest seat back to keep from falling in the aisle. Sam Miller, the last one to be accused of a bent for the theatrical, without doubt had not intended such a dramatic departure. We were all learning.

Mickey and Claudette completed the welcoming announcements in English and French while the rest of us took our positions to demonstrate the emergency instructions. Captain Miller came on. "Ladies and gentlemen, we have reached the runway. Flight Service, prepare for take-off." Kay and I quickly moved aft to our stations on the double jump seat just inside the rear entrance door.

As we began our roll down the runway and Captain Miller opened the throttles to full thrust, the powerful force of our rapid acceleration pressed our backs into the thinly-padded bulkhead behind us. Even more startling was the unexpected vibration and violent roar of the jet engines as we gathered speed for our leap up into the night. We grasped hands and stared wide-eyed at one another in disbelief. Where was that vibration-free, quiet-as-a-whisper ambiance the airline ads have been touting? We discovered why the first-class section is now located in the front. Just opposite to piston-engine aircraft—where the cabin becomes quieter toward the rear—we were seated in the noisiest spot in a jet.

Also unlike conventional airplanes that lift off the runway in a horizontal attitude, jets do it nose up. No one had given us prior warning of this characteristic either. As we attained take-off speed approaching 200 mph, Captain Miller rotated the nose of the *Clipper* sharply upward. This caused us, seated in the very tail of the jet, to drop sharply downward—a sensation I would never become totally comfortable with. We wee airborne!

In half the time required of the "pre-jets," we reached cruising altitude. The vibration disappeared completely and the engine roar subsided to little more than a gentle hum. The lights came up, seat belt signs went out, and it was time for champagne and canapés. An exhilarating aura of festive exuberance prevailed. The *LIFE* team began snapping photos as passengers crowded the aisle and clinked glasses. Most aboard this evening had booked seats on America's First Jet Flight months—some more than a year—before the actual date of departure had even been announced. Many came along simply to experience the historic event and would return to the States within a day or two.

Barely two hours after lift-off in New York, we touched down for refueling at Gander. Fast-fueling equipment especially designed for jets stood by. Passengers scarcely had time to stroll across the frost-covered tarmac to the terminal before the flight was called for reboarding. Airborne once again, it was past ten o'clock as we rushed to get dinner service underway. Hard to believe, Captain Miller advised we would be landing in Paris in just five hours—a total of seven hours flight time from New York. (Thirty-one years earlier, when Charles Lindbergh made history with the first solo, non-stop trans-Atlantic flight—carrying him over a very similar 3,600-mile route, Long Island to le Bourget—he was airborne for thirty-three-and-a-half hours.)

With the meal service completed, the party atmosphere continued in the tourist cabin while all but one of the forty passengers in first-class drifted off to sleep. Aft of the cockpit, opposite the forward galley, was the lounge with seating for six. It was unoccupied and we grabbed the chance to sit down for a moment and have our crew meals. I glanced at Ms. Garson in the front row, writing—a pile of sealed and addressed notes on the table before her. Her shoulder-length red tresses shined gloriously under the reading light as the first hint of dawn illuminated the sky outside her window.

We landed at le Bourget just before 4 a.m., New York time, breaking all commercial trans-Atlantic speed records. Local time was 10 a.m. in Paris, October 27th—one day shy of the thirty-first anniversary of Pan American's first inaugural flight, 90-miles, Key West to Havana. As in New York, there was a brass band, dignitaries, a brief ceremony, and an army of photographers to welcome America's first jet flight to the *City of Light*. Once again, Ms. Garson was propelled center stage. She posed in the doorway, posed surrounded by crew, posed under the wing, white-gloved hand resting on a tail-pipe of one of the jet engines. Withdrawing her hand, she discovers her glove now blackened with soot. The "shoot" is over and she disappears toward town—as eager, I suspect, to get to bed as I am.

13

Aboard our inaugural return flight the following afternoon were several passengers who had flown over from London that morning to be among the world's first to jet their way across the Atlantic. They included Danny Kaye and Frank Sinatra—Kaye, immaculately groomed and well dressed, Sinatra appearing to have slept in his clothes or, perhaps, not to have made it to bed at all. As we touched down in New York, I adjusted my watch for time-zone gains. It read just three hours later than it had when leaving Paris. Total elapsed time, Paris to New York, including one fuel stop in Keflavik, Iceland—nine hours versus twenty on my Stratocruiser crossing, the same flight number, the previous week.

The *LIFE* cover we had been encouraged to expect—of Pan Am's *Clipper America* soaring aloft from that rain-soaked runway at New York International—did not materialize, usurped by a portrait of newly-elected Pope John XXIII. Though the photo story featured inside the magazine did well in capturing the excitement of our historic crossing, I need no photographs to remember America's First Jet Flight.

Courtesy of the Author

Jay is shown at right with tumbler—this photo
was on the cover of his book *The Company We Kept*.

**Jay is enjoying retirement
in Southern California.**

DINNER WITH SIR WINSTON

By Bronwen Roberts

Serving Dinner to Sir Winston Churchill on Pan Am Flight 100

When I was hired by Pan Am in February 1958, one of 11 from 5,000 applicants, I could not in my wildest dreams have imagined the exciting life I would lead and the fascinating people I would encounter during my 31 year career.

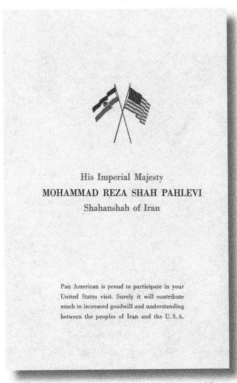

His Imperial Majesty
MOHAMMAD REZA SHAH PAHLEVI
Shahanshah of Iran

Pan American is proud to participate in your United States visit. Surely it will contribute much to increased goodwill and understanding between the peoples of Iran and the U.S.A.

Courtesy of Jamie Baldwin

Courtesy of Jamie Baldwin

In the 1960's Pan Am was the airline of choice for the rich and famous. Among the celebrities I had on board were the legendary Charles Lindbergh, films stars Robert Taylor, Warren Beatty, Susan Hayward, Sophia Loren and her husband Carlo Ponti, Audrey Hepburn and her husband Mel Ferrer.

One of my favorite British film stars at the time was Laurence Harvey and one Christmas Eve on a flight from New York to London he was the only passenger in the First Class cabin. He made my Christmas by asking me to sit and join him for dinner and, with the permission of the captain, I was delighted to do so! There were also singers from Lily Pons and Placido Domingo to Billy Joel and Bon Jovi and royalty, including Princess Alexandra of Kent, the Princess Caroline and Prince Albert of Monaco.

On one particularly memorable flight, we carried the Shah of Iran and his wife Farah Diba from Tehran to New York. For the occasion, Pan Am painted his name and title on the fuselage of the aircraft and constructed a special compartment in the rear of the first class cabin complete with a double bed. Only one flight attendant was allowed in this compartment, a German girl who was a friend of the royal family. In our briefing she was instructed to exit backwards so as never to turn her back to the Shah. Despite the fact that we had not served them, each flight attendant received a presentation box containing a 100 rial gold coin and Farah Diba graciously gave me one of the menus which she had signed--both of which I still have today. The cockpit crew received gold cigarette cases.

However my most memorable flight occurred early in my career. As a child I had been subjected to the terror of air raids over Britain during World War Two and I remember listening to the inspiring speeches given over the radio by our then Prime Minister, Winston Churchill. How could I possibly have known then that on April 14, 1961 I would be serving the great man on a Pan Am *Clipper* flight. To my everlasting gratitude and indeed to my amazement, I was selected to serve Sir Winston on flight 100 from New York, along with another British flight attendant, Valerie Wilton, and American purser, Mickey Deangelis.

Courtesy of the Author

The Crew – Bronwen is second from the right.

The First Class cabin of this regular scheduled flight was blocked for Sir Winston's party which consisted of his personal physician, Lord Moran and his wife, two nurses, his secretary, Anthony Montague-Brown and his wife, and his bodyguard, Sgt. Edmund Murray of Scotland Yard. To our delight Sgt. Murray was carrying a cage containing a young budgerigar (a parakeet), a gift from Aristotle Onassis to replace one Sir Winston had recently lost.

The reason Sir Winston was travelling on Pan Am, much to the dismay of the British Airline, B.O.A.C, was because he was the guest of Onassis, who always flew Pan Am at the time. He had been cruising in the Caribbean on Onassis' yacht, Christina, and had sailed to New York before departing for home. Onassis accompanied the party on board along with Bernard Baruch, another close friend of Sir Winston, in order to say goodbye before departure.

The flight was uneventful and very pleasant with cocktail service followed by a leisurely lunch. Along with the regular President Special menu consisting of Hors d'oeuvres, including caviar, Terrapin or cream of mushroom soup, entrees, including Lobster Thermidor, Filet of Sole, Himalayan Partridge, Sweetbread Financieres, stuffed Rock Cornish game hen, double lamb chops or Prime Rib of beef, choice of vegetables, salad, a selection of Continental cheeses, desserts and fresh fruit items. Colmans mustard and horseradish, Stilton cheese, imported teas and crumpets were added.

Catering had provisioned extra spirits to the bar --- Chateau Lafite Rothchild red wine and Bisquit and Remy Martin Extra cognac. The final, and very important, addition, was a box of Romeo and Juliet cigars.

Sir Winston partook all courses; indeed he had two entrees, the Lobster Thermidor and then the Prime Rib of beef, ending the meal with several cigars and cognac. On arrival in London I will never forget the rush of aircraft cleaners to empty the ashtray in seat 1A in order to have a souvenir-a Sir Winston's cigar butt!

After the excitement of the arrival I was taken to be interviewed by the British press and that is how my parents learned in the following morning newspapers that their daughter had had the privilege and honour of serving one of their heroes, something neither I nor they could have ever imagined so many years earlier. THANK YOU PAN AM!

Bronwen travels back and forth between her homes in Queens, NY and her native Wales.

Courtesy of the Author

The Charter for the Shah.
Bronwen is second from left.

OPERATION PEDRO PAN

By Yvonne Conde

Pan Am's Participation in the Program to Evacuate Children From Cuba

August 11, 1961: My first airplane ride filled me with so much anticipation as I sat alone waiting for my flight, passport and Pan Am ticket in hand, that I didn't notice other unaccompanied children also waiting for this flight to Miami. Leaving my homeland or my parents behind did not worry me; they assured me that we would see each other very shortly.

Thirty years later I discovered I was among twenty unaccompanied children who left Cuba on that hot August day, and that our flight made me part of an exodus of 14,048 Cuban children, now known as Operation Pedro Pan. The Pan Am/Cuba connection was making history again. In 1927 Pan Am's first flight crossed the *Tropic of Cancer* from Florida's Key West to Havana; this time we were reversing its route.

After Fidel Castro took power on January 1, 1959, he transformed every layer of the country. Promised elections never materialized and a dictatorship asserted itself. Repression intensified after the failed Bay of Pigs invasion in April of 1961. Throughout Cuba, youth as young as thirteen were armed for police and sentry work. All Catholic churches and schools were closed. In June, 1,000 students left Cuba bound for the USSR.

Courtesy of the Author

18

In the fall of 1960, James Baker, Director of Havana's *Ruston Academy*, received the first of many requests from worried parents for help in finding American schools for their children. Given the political climate, Baker knew the demand would increase and flew to Miami to meet with a group of American businessmen looking for the possibility of setting up a school. He was referred to Bryan Walsh, a Catholic priest, who was already caring for a handful of unaccompanied Cuban children. Father Walsh agreed to help and thus the exodus of Cuban children began on December 26, 1960.

By the summer of 1961, a Cuban child was faced with the following prospective: if he or she was seven to thirteen years old, membership in the *Union of Rebel Pioneers* was mandatory. Those twelve or older had to go to the mountains for weeks to alphabetize the "peasants" and, upon turning thirteen, join the *Association of Rebel Youths*. Refusal to participate equaled isolation, and worse, a counter-revolutionary label.

A rumor also spread that the government was going to issue a law, the *Patria Potestad*, that would take away all parental rights and transfer them to the government. Castro had sent his own son, who was my age, to the USSR. Terror set in among Cuban parents—they needed to send their children to the safety of Uncle Sam.

Courtesy of the Author

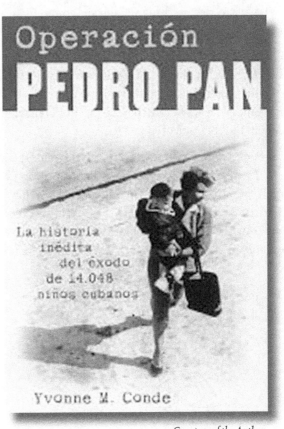

Courtesy of the Author

Unbeknownst to me, my mother was planning to send me away. Since my parents were divorced, she needed my father's approval. In the web of secrecy that was Cuba at the time, she did not know that my father, a Pan Am ticket agent coincidentally named Pedro, was involved in getting children out of Cuba.

To leave Cuba for the US, Cubans needed not only an exit permit from the Cuban Foreign Ministry, but also a United States visa. Also, per a revolutionary decree, seat reservations could not be made ahead of time; you had to make them with an exit permit in hand. This permit was good only for seven days.

The modern Pan American ticket office, located in Vedado's fashionable 23rd street, with its round glass front and ten-foot tall world globe in the center, had never been busier. Lines formed hours before the office opened, as visa-holding Cubans clamored for seats to leave the island on one of the airline's fourteen weekly flights, enduring the jeers and shouts of *"Worms"* and *"Traitors"* as they waited.

Children under eighteen however, were exempt from the visa requirements. The US State Department approved a visa waiver program for minors and issued an exception to Father Walsh authorizing him to distribute these permits, which were then smuggled into Cuba. This is where Pan Am got involved. Pan Am station manager Ignacio Martinez-Ibor made the decision to block seats for children on every flight. Pan Am's Havana staff was also involved in falsifying the Visa Waivers. The program was called *"Pedro Pan."*

Time Magazine, in its October 6, 1961 issue, reported, "At Havana's José Martí Airport last week, adults with airplane tickets were implored to give their seats to children....Some Pan American flights arriving in Miami have as many as sixty children on board."

Tony Comellas, a Pan Am manager, told me in an interview, "We would always give unaccompanied children seating priority, about ten or twenty per flight." Ticket agents made daily reservations with fake names and then gave those seats to *Pedro Pan* children. Comellas also told me, "I took a flight to Miami sitting on a toilet so a child could have my seat."

By the time 1962 arrived, Cuban parents felt that the year could not be worse than turmoil-ridden 1961 when Castro declared his revolution communist and a totalitarian regime was firmly entrenched. Yet, the worst was yet to come.

On October 23, 1962 the missile crisis stopped all flights between Cuba and the US and 150,000 Cubans who were ready to leave the island were deprived of their dreams of freedom. For many *Pedro Pan* children--half of whom lived in foster homes or orphanages scattered throughout the US, and the rest with family and friends --it would be years before they saw their parents again. These desperate parents left through third countries or freedom flights instituted in December 1965.

Luckily, I reunited with my parents almost a year later. Flying captured my imagination, and eleven years after that fateful August day, I received my Pan Am Stewardess' wings. I journeyed the globe for seventeen years, but there is one destination I've never travelled to again--my homeland.

Yvonne wrote a book about her experiences titled Operation Pedro Pan *available on Amazon.com. She lives in New York.*

Courtesy of the Author

AFRICAN ODYSSEY

By Lou Berman

Pan American and Africa

Since my early school days in France, Africa had always been somehow on my mind. Books about the adventures of Burke, Stanley, Livingstone, Speke and de Brazza stoked my teen imagination. But at that

African landscape from a Pan Am menu by Dong Kingman.

time it was just that, only fleeting fantasies of adventure and to forever remain out of my reach. Thanks to Pan Am, it eventually proved otherwise.

My first experience with Africa occurred while I was working in the Commissary, Food & Flight Service Department and was dispatched to represent it on a DC-8 proving flight to test Africa's readiness for the Jet Age. The flight, from New York to Johannesburg, made stops in Dakar, Sénégal, Roberts Field, Liberia, Accra, Ghana, and Léopoldville (LEO).

At each of the brief stopovers, we were met by the Pan Am director and staff, the local civil aviation authorities, and representatives of the local American mission. We were then briefed about the facilities which we then assessed. All were found to meet Pan Am's and the FAA's strict safety standards. The flight proved successful, and shortly thereafter, it was a "Go" for scheduled jet service.

My next experience, in 1963, was of a more dramatic nature. It involved the airlifting of Tunisian troops stationed in the former Belgian colony of the Congo back to Tunis. They had been assigned to the Congo as part of a UN peace keeping contingent. A crisis was looming in their home country of Tunisia involving a dispute about a former French naval base at Bizertand and they were needed home urgently. A Pan Am aircraft was chartered to move all these soldiers and their equipment, and our flights it seemed, shuttled endlessly until the contingent had left the Congo.

I had another experience in Africa, when then President Kwame Nkrumah, the "Father of Ghana" and advocate of African unity, had his own ideas on how post colonial Africa should be organized. He chartered a Pan Am DC-8 to carry him and his entourage to the United Nations General Assembly in New York. President Nkrumah was an impressive and affable figure. He had selected Pan Am as it was then the only carrier offering direct service between Accra and New York. Ghana Airways had not yet been formed and its predecessor, West African Airways, did not have the capability to operate trans-Atlantic flights.

I was in charge of organizing the President's menus and, with others in my department at JFK, we endeavored to ensure our Flight Service personnel would have everything required to provide a faultless on board service. To assist in coordinating matters en route, I accompanied the President on his round trip journey. Upon his return to Accra, we presented President Nkrumah with a Pan Am gift worthy of the President's position and popularity. To express his appreciation, President Nkrumah invited all Pan Am personnel to Flagstaff House, official residence of the President of Ghana in Accra, where we were all regally entertained.

I later spent five years in Douala (1965-1970) and afterward, was transferred to Abidjan, which had become our regional headquarters for Sub-Sahara Africa. Our Africa headquarters had been in Casablanca, Morocco when Pan Am operated flights from New York to Roberts Field via Boston, Santa Maria, Lisbon, Rabat/ Casablanca and Conakry in Guinée.

Pan Am also had a presence in Nigeria. Peter Legro, Trevor Lewis, Dick de Nazario, Mike Schumacher and Knox Devol and all their predecessors and successors, were Pan Am's backbone in Lagos. They were all involved or witness to more than one interesting experience. Once, in Lagos, evidence emerged that some aluminum airline cargo containers were being put to good use for housing, when not cut up in small pieces and fashioned into pots and pans. Fortunately these were not Pan Am containers, but we had to give credit to the Lagos people for their resourcefulness. Dodging bullets seemed a way of life in Lagos as well as in The Congo as Bob Heemskerk could no doubt recount.

We often lifted our hands toward the skies in desperation and felt we would never win the battle, no matter. But in the end, we somehow managed to keep the flights safe and basically on schedule. To describe the frustrations of our Africa team the acronym "WAWA" was coined by some unknown author, which meant "West Africa Wins Again." The Africans somehow always seemed to have the last word and it was not malicious on their part. Their ways of doing things were adapted to their conditions, their traditions, and were just simply different than ours. We never gave up. And neither did they.

We also maintained close personal contacts with the various American ambassadors, keeping them and their staff happy with the *New York Sunday Times* and turkeys offered courtesy of Pan Am for the celebrations of Thanksgiving and Christmas. We were the best friends of these embassies and that was well recognized and helpful.

I could go on, but the colleagues who were with Pan Am or with the Roberts Field International Airport crew or with the Technical Assistance Project (TAP) in Zaire, or with Inter-Continental Hotels-Africa, led by Alex Furrer in Nairobi; all have dozens of tales to write and talk about; one more frustrating than the other, or more tragic than the other, or more gruesome, or more hilarious, or finally more successful. One can laugh, cry, or both, about experiences shared in different ways by each one of our colleagues who served in Africa.

In spite of and because of experiences common in one way or another to each of us, a unique bond of *Esprit de Corps* was forged. It was a *Band of Brothers* type attitude of which we were rightly proud of and to this day still attached to in various degrees. I am certain I express the feelings of most of us who served in Africa in one capacity or another.

But not to be overlooked, credit is due to our African colleagues who assisted us to the best of their abilities. Things could have been tougher without them. And lest we forget, our thoughts go out to those whose lives were ruined or lost due to murderous savage raging civil wars.

In 1980 after some 18 years in Africa, I obtained a transfer to Brussels, a different scene, a different climate, a different set of challenges.

For those who served there, however, Africa left an indelible mark on the life of each of us.

Lou is now retired, living in the French Alps with his wife, Christel.

Courtesy of the Author

23

WITH PRESIDENT KENNEDY IN DALLAS, NOVEMBER 22, 1963

By Kari-Mette Pigmans

Working on the White House Press Charter to Dallas

My ticket to the United States was aboard Pan Am.

    I was not a regular passenger for I was hired in my native country of Norway and as I flew to New York to begin my career as a stewardess, I felt privileged to be in the United States and working for the airline that was the icon of America.

Courtesy of the Author

Captain Doug Moody and his ladies on a Pan Am charter.

24

During my first year of employment, I was chosen to fly the White House Press Charters. The year was 1963 and John F. Kennedy was the President. I was among the select few chosen to fly the press that tailed Air Force One wherever President Kennedy went. Then, Air Force One was a 707 and was used exclusively by the President and his staff. Today, Air Force One is a 747 and can accommodate some of the "pool" press.

I would not say that we were special, but we were the 11 chosen and led by Captain Doug Moody. There were four in the cockpit and seven in the cabin rounding out the crew for that year. On traveling days, we were picked up at 3 a.m. by car service and taken to the airport where we boarded a stocked plane filled with food and beverages and flew to Andrew's Air Force Base in Maryland. Now when I say stocked, I am talking about gourmet food, not what is today considered "airline food." Every seat in the 707 was a first class seat and the service might as well have been white gloved.

Courtesy of the Author

President Kennedy greeting the Pan Am Charter Crew on an earlier trip as Kari-Mette jumps rope.

I am writing about a particular day, however, and as I sit down to write this, tears fill my eyes and drip down my cheek to the notes I have scribbled down. The day was Friday, November 22, 1963. We flew from El Paso, Texas to Dallas (Love Field) where the President was fulfilling an invitation from Vice President Lyndon Johnson to visit his home state of Texas. I remember the day vividly; it was a beautiful fall Texas day probably in the 70s.

The press had left the plane in their normal quick fashion they normally would so that they could get positioned to cover the Presidential events. With our plane parked right next to Air Force One, the other six girls and I walked down to the tarmac to catch a glimpse of the President we had all become so fond of. Jackie Kennedy joined him for this day in Dallas. We saw the motorcade leave the airport with Gov. John Connally and his wife in the front of the open-air limo and JFK and Jackie in the back seats. Little did we all know this was the last time we would see the President and it was also the last time a President would ride in an open car without protective glass.

The crew was set to have a short layover in Dallas, so we headed to the terminal for a quick meal. It was not

Courtesy of the Author

President Kennedy's Motorcade leaving Love Field.

long before we were called back to our plane where the news we received hit us like a rock. After what seemed like an eternity, a very solemn row of cars appeared. Jackie Kennedy stepped out of the car. She was still wearing that iconic, beautiful pink and navy Chanel suit, but now stained with blood. Her body language told it all. She was in utter shock and grief was written all over her.

Vice President Lyndon Johnson and his wife Lady Bird arrived right behind Jackie and they all quickly entered Air Force One. We experienced the sorrow of seeing the coffin which was later lifted into Air Force One. There was not one dry eye around us and we stood there in complete silence as there was nothing really to say – conversation was just out of the question.

As we soon found out later, Lyndon Johnson was quickly sworn in as the 36th President on Air Force One. A few minutes later, the President's plane took off and we headed behind in tow for Andrews Air Force base. Everyone remembers where they were that tragic afternoon. We had truly witnessed history. American History. World History. Whether it was to celebrate like the Beatles coming to America, or just a young girl from Norway coming to America, or a tragic day like this... Pan American was there.

Kari-Mette and her Purser husband, Han, commute back and forth between Florida and Long Island, NY.

Courtesy of the Author

Kari-Mette in 1963

26

INDELIBLE IMPRESSIONS

By Carla Marshall

Rome's Homage to JFK; Brutality in the Congo

The world's collective heart seemed to stop on November 22, 1963, when the news broadcasters announced that the President of the United States, John F. Kennedy, had been assassinated. Americans were glued to their televisions and radios around the clock trying to absorb the shock, yet wanting to hear every detail. I tore myself away on Sunday, November 24th to report to New York's Idlewild Airport for Pan American Flight 110 to Rome. I didn't want to go, feeling as though it was some sort of treasonous act to leave my country during this terrible crisis.

Our 707 was filled to capacity with anxious passengers. It turned out most of them felt just as I did – they were leaving home and preferred to stay to support America. Throughout the long hushed night across the Atlantic, no one slept, whispering to us and to each other, communicating sadness, homesickness and despair, crying and comforting each other until we all arrived exhausted in the morning mist at Fumicino Airport in Rome.

As soon as we stepped into the terminal, members of our Pan Am ground staff came up to greet us, first to offer their sympathy, but also to show us an article in the local newspaper announcing a proxy memorial service for President Kennedy to be held that day, Monday, November 25th, at the *Basilica St. John Lateran*, the Pope's own Cathedral. Another Flight Attendant and I immediately decided that we should attend the service. It was the least we could do to show our respect.

Upon arrival at the Metropole Hotel, everyone, from the concierge to the porters to the housekeeping staff, expressed their condolences to us. President Kennedy's photo was on the wall in the lobby draped in black. We changed clothes as quickly as we could because there was little time and jumped into a taxi to take us to the Cathedral. We didn't realize thousands of Romans would obviously have the same idea. When our driver stopped the taxi, we told him to keep going because the Cathedral was nowhere in sight. He then pointed to a huge throng of people all dressed in black, which we suddenly recognized as the end of an impossibly long line of fellow mourners. We had no choice so we paid our driver and joined the many Italians who had come to pay their respects.

My friend and I were worried that we would not be able to see the church, let alone get inside to participate in the service, because the line was well over a mile long. Someone near us asked in heavily accented English, "Are you Americans?" We nodded, and then the miracle began to happen. In Italian, I heard them say to the people in front of them that we were Americans and, with that, a few people stood aside to let us move up in the line. This incredible courtesy repeated itself over and over, until we found ourselves being gently pushed inside the Cathedral. There was *San Giovanni in Laterano* in all of its palatial glory.

The courtesy extended to us did not stop there. Unbelievably, the Italians continued to open a path for us until we were actually standing directly in front of the High Altar encased in its brilliant gold. Television klieg lights were above us and shined down upon the most stunning scene: On the High Altar was a coffin draped in the flag of the United States. Stationed at each corner of the altar were Honor Guards in full dress uniforms from each of the United States armed services, and also from each of the Italian armed services. Behind the High Altar was the entire assemblage of the *College of Cardinals* and the *Ecumenical Council* dressed in their scarlet robes. Pope Paul VI, dressed in white robes, began the High Mass for President Kennedy, and we joined in the prayers with hearts filled with love for our President and gratitude for the wonderful people who had allowed us to witness this astonishing event. Tears were streaming down my cheeks when a very small elderly lady at my side reached up and began patting my arm, saying, "*Mi dispiace tanto*"—I'm so very sorry.

The following day, my crew and I flew on to Tehran. The sentiment, "I'm so very sorry," was repeated by almost every passenger during our flight, and by every Iranian with which we came into contact on the ground – the airport staff, our crew bus driver, the hotel staff, and even strangers on the street who saw us in our Pan Am uniforms. Again, President Kennedy's photograph was on the Hilton Hotel lobby wall, and there were other photos of him on the walls of our individual rooms, all draped in black.

This global outpouring of grief and sympathy took place early in my career, and it was the first time that I comprehended how completely the rest of the world identified Pan American Airways, and those of us who worked for the Pan Am family, as extensions of America, and extensions of what America stood for: Freedom and Hope of Freedom. The rest of the world had recognized that the death of young President Kennedy was a blow to those hopes of freedom. The expressions of sympathy were not really directed at me, but to the symbol I had the privilege to represent.

Pan American represented hope and freedom in every corner of the globe, and served this role in many capacities. In January, 1965, I boarded a flight in Roberts Field, Liberia, which had begun in Nairobi, Kenya with a stop in Lagos, Nigeria. I was informed by the incoming Purser there were a number of victims from the Congolese uprising on board, particularly the family of Dr. Paul Carlson. I suddenly remembered reading about the tragic death of Dr. Carlson, who had recently been featured on the covers of *Time* and *Life* magazines, describing his missionary efforts in the Congo. Africa was erupting and the Congo was its flashpoint. The Congo had been given independence suddenly and unexpectedly from Belgium in 1960 and was highly volatile. For five months, rebel insurgents (Simbas) had held the city of Stanleyville, deep in the country's interior, and had proclaimed a "People's Republic".

Inside Stanleyville's *Victoria Hotel* were 250 hostages, most of them Belgians, many families with children, several diplomats and one, kind, 36-year-old physician and missionary, Dr. Carlson. The brutal Simbas routinely killed and tortured their enemies, sometimes consuming the dead prisoners' organs in front of others. The Americans and the Belgians attempted to launch a rescue effort with paratroopers, which turned into a slaughter of the victims and Dr. Carlson was sprayed with machine gun fire just as he was about to be rescued, killing him as he tried to escape over a wall.

I went to the back of the 707 where I was told the Carlson family were sitting to introduce myself and to find out what, if anything, we could do for them that night during the long ten-hour trip home. Mrs. Carlson and her daughter were mercifully sleeping. Their son, Wayne, 10 years-old, was definitely not. He told me he wasn't able to sleep, was very restless, and seemed to want to talk. I told him that if he wanted to help us with the meal service right after takeoff, I would give him some things to do, and when it was completed, I'd be happy to sit and talk with him. I have never forgotten that conversation, and never will.

Looking at this child, I saw a picture of innocence – a cute clean-cut boy with a strawberry blonde crewcut, wide blue eyes and freckles. But the words that tumbled non-stop from his mouth while we shared a crew jump seat, were horrifying. This child with the unlined face told me that he knew people who were tortured to death; that they had had their eyes gouged out with broken *Coca-Cola* bottles; their spines broken with heavy objects, one vertebrae at a time; that his father had been murdered; that others who had been members of his father's medical staff had been murdered, and on and on. He was only TEN!

He could not stop talking; it seemed a type of therapy and I just sat and listened and tried to tell him that when he got back to the United States, his world would be all right again. I'm not sure even I believed it. In addition to the Carlson family, we had a number of nuns on board who had been badly beaten and tortured by the Simbas as well. My encounters that evening were with the ugliest side of humanity I had ever seen.

Shortly before landing in New York, the Captain informed me that he had been alerted that the media were preparing to meet our flight in hopes of an interview with the Carlsons. It immediately became our crew's goal to prevent that intrusion from happening. We let Mrs. Carlson make the decision, and they stayed on board with us until we heard that most of the media had left. We then walked with them through the international arrivals area, surrounding them with all of the crewmembers, in an attempt to hide them from unwanted eyes until they went through customs. We felt good about thwarting the media that morning.

Pan American helped enable their family to escape and return to freedom and to achieve productive lives, and I am hoping that the nuns have had equal success. Again, I felt very privileged to be a small part of that process.

In 1975 while serving standby duty, I was given 90 minutes notice that I was to be at the airport ready to spend an undetermined amount of time flying special evacuation flights from Saigon, just before it fell in the Vietnam War. It turned into an odyssey of six weeks of rescuing Vietnamese who wanted to flee to the freedom of the United States, and Pan Am was the answer to their prayers. Those between the ages of 16 – 45 came in droves. The very young, elderly and infirm were left behind. Every 747 was filled to its capacity of over 400 seats. They were exhausted, frightened, apprehensive, hungry, but most of all relieved that they were within the safe confines of an American jet. They escaped with the clothes on their backs and not much else. Several times men handed me pieces of their currency as a souvenir, since it was then basically worthless. Again, they would talk to us throughout the flight about their lives, their hopes and fears of starting over in the United States. We did everything we could to reassure them that they had made the difficult but right choice. Pan Am even changed their breakfast menu from the usual French toast to rice with fish!

Our goal was to fly them to Guam or Honolulu where they could begin the entry process. Once the aircraft was emptied, we would ferry it back to Saigon. This routine occurred non-stop over the next six weeks. Pan Am again had stepped up and saved thousands of lives, allowing the Vietnamese to achieve the freedom they longed for, and to spend productive lives in America. Most of the male passengers we met were highly educated professionals – doctors, lawyers, businessmen – people who truly could contribute to society if they were given a chance. Last year, I was in New York City at a beauty salon that employed several Vietnamese women. I told them about my experience with Pan Am and the Saigon airlift. One of the women left the room and brought back her mother whom she introduced to me. The three of them suddenly bowed, and said, "Thank you so much. Our mother was on one of those flights." We all had tears in our eyes. It was a very gratifying moment. So many owe so much to Pan Am.

Courtesy of the Author

Carla Marshall

Carla was a flight attendant and purser with Pan Am from March 1963 to August 1986 stationed in Los Angeles and New York. Upon retirement, she founded her own company in 1991, International Marketing Partners, Inc., specializing in fund raising and special events and lobbying and still operates today. She also entered the world of wireless telecommunications. As President of Great Western Cellular Partners LLC, she owned and operated a cellular system in southern Minnesota. She is married to another great Pan Am airman, John Marshall. The Marshalls live both in St. Louis and Sun Valley, ID.

THE BEATLES ARRIVE IN NEW YORK ON PAN AM

By Gillian Kellogg L'Eplattenier

On Board Pan American Flight 101

The Pan Am crew bus picked up 12 of us from our designated London "layover" hotel, the *Athenaeum Court*, to work the scheduled Flight 101 to New York on February 7, 1964. It was anticipated as a normal day and a normal flight. However, what was not normal was to have two extra stewardesses in our crew. But no one questioned the two extras, as this was often the luck of the draw – except for the Captain, who was briefed about our special flight.

Pan Am Archives

Beatles Press Conference

All of us were settled into our seats, the cockpit crew sitting forward in the bus (as they usually did), and ready for the fifty minute drive to Heathrow Airport. Just as our bus pulled out into traffic, the first officer stood up facing us with a clearly recognizable mask on his face. Was this a joke? As he sang a rather poor rendition of the song *I Want to Hold Your Hand*, he exclaimed, "Guess who we have on board with us today?"

"The Beatles!" we all cried out with excitement and disbelief.

The remainder of the bus ride was more than just exciting. Many of the stewardesses were not much older than the Beatles themselves and were reveling in the liveliness and unusualness of what was to ensue this day. Even the cockpit crew, in their dignified way, was animated. This prompted a contest as to who could remember the most songs and hits of Britain's Fabulous Four. I was not the winner!

FEB. 7, 1964   BEATLES ARR JFK

Jill Kellogg

Courtesy of the Author

The Beatles arriving at Kennedy Airport, New York.
Jill at the top of the steps, right.

I was the most junior – it was only my second trip. Having been a former boarding school teacher (German, English, and History), athletic coach, and one of three house-mothers for 53 girls at a co-ed boarding school in western Massachusetts, I was oblivious to all the "pop" entertainment happening around the world.

On the way to Heathrow, I recalled my training: Probably one-third of our classes were devoted to the meal service, especially First Class. We cooked the main entrees, such as prime rib, roasts and turkey in the aircraft ovens and heated some meals and vegetables prepared in the Pan Am kitchens by chefs trained by Maxim's in Paris. Each of the many courses, cocktails and hors d'oeuvres, soup and salad, entrée, dessert and coffee or tea, wine, cheese and cordials, were served on separate carts, always using linen napkins, silver tea and coffee pots, silver cutlery and crystal wine glasses. The meals were served with elegance and grace. It was a time in aviation history incomparable to any other.

As our crew bus approached Heathrow Airport and our departing terminal, all around there was a fevered atmosphere with hundreds of people all over the place. The air was electric.

The cockpit crew went in for their flight briefing and the rest of us went out to the aircraft to check the provisions. We also learned *en route* to the airport that our plane was configured differently. Usually there were only 12-18 seats in First Class with the balance in Economy. That day, however, we had (if memory serves me correctly) 36 seats. I had been assigned to work the First Class section and thought, "Oh, my God, what an enormous number of people for A-1 service." I felt a bit apprehensive.

After our purser viewed the passenger manifest, we learned some of our guests besides John, Paul, Ringo, and George, were John's wife, Cynthia, Brian Epstein, the group's manager, a few other Beatles girlfriends and the remainder, important persons from the media, journalists and photographers, all together thirty-six First Class passengers.

Before we knew it, passengers began to embark onto our 707 – the First Class passengers came up the stairs to the forward door while economy passengers were designated to embark only through the aft cabin door. Once our four notables and news media were seated, it seemed like the balance of the trip was a seven and one-half hour un-staged play of excitement, bustling around, picture taking, laughing, talking (no singing) and trying to keep our Fabulous Four in their seats for the meal and cart services. That was a major challenge.

One must remember that this was the Beatles first trans-Atlantic "voyage" and they were like young guys just having a grand old time! But this was just the prelude for their appearance on the *Ed Sullivan Show* the next day, and following that, many years of being one of history's most popular and successful singing groups and songwriters. Our four-some were not particular to any choices of entrees, just saying, "I'll take whatever." The elegance we provided only mildly impressed them, as it was something they were not yet used to.

Paul was the most active of the group, not only talking to others, but also photographing passengers and crew alike, myself included. I often wish I had some of those photos... what fun to cement a lifelong memory! John was the quietest of all while Ringo and George seemed to be enjoying themselves, moving around and talking with other passengers.

Courtesy of the Author

Gillian was a Flight Attendant and also worked in Pan Am's Marketing Department.

There was literally no time for us, as crew, to interact with our passengers, due to the amount of service and the large number of people to serve and the need to convince them to stay in their seats! Service carts and passengers in the aisle was an impossibility!

Meanwhile, passengers in the economy section were so excited to be on board this flight, they were continuously asking the stewardesses in that section to please take their menus forward for the Beatles to autograph. The hours just flew by and the atmosphere aboard did not lose its magnetism. We were just able to finish the service, clean up, and get all carts and gear secured when we were already halfway in our descent into Kennedy Airport. Cheers were heard throughout the airplane on landing.

Taxiing up to our gate produced another glimpse of their unprecedented popularity. We opened the cabin doors to about five thousand loud cheering fans, some screaming, sobbing, and waving signs, "We love you, Beatles." This was truly the beginning of the "Beatles Invasion." And it was the unbelievable beginning to my career with Pan Am.

In the short time I flew as a flight attendant, I was fortunate to meet and talk with many well-known and famous people; State Department staff and couriers, US Ambassador Ted Wahl and his wife Sarah. He was Ambassador to Lebanon in Beirut in the 60's and prior to that, in Istanbul, and lived with my family during World War II while he was attending law school in Boston. Sophia Loren and husband were on my flights on several occasions. I flew with Charles Lindbergh on two occasions between New York and Bermuda: on one flight, he was the only person in First Class, although he usually flew incognito in Economy. I had the opportunity to spend time discussing history and world politics with him. He was also on the Board of Pan Am and a personal friend of Pan Am's founder and Chairman, Juan Trippe. Also on flights were Ella Fitzgerald, going to London to give a concert, and who kindly invited the entire crew to attend; Kirk Douglas, Eddie Fisher, Gordon Parks, the famous photographer, to name just a few more.

Whenever news, events, or music of the Beatles are aired, I am constantly reminded of that incredible trip. Some sixteen years later, while I was in the kitchen preparing dinner, my husband exclaimed quite loudly from the living room, "Come quickly, you're on the news!" It was February 7, 1980 and there was a recap of the Beatles US arrival at JFK on the television. There I was, standing on the right hand side of the First Class cabin door, as the Beatles disembarked on the stairway.

Today, my husband claims this famous trip has been my own little "claim to fame" for the last 47 years!

PAN AM'S NISEIS/SANSEIS

By Eva R.M. Kama, nee Miyahara

On Being a Pan American "Nisei" Stewardess

In the 1960s, being a Pan American stewardess was every young woman's dream. To most people, it was a career that offered everything—glamour, excitement and travel.

Pan Am Archives

Pan American Poster 1960s

Courtesy of the Author

Eva R. M. Kama, née Miyahara

34

However, there were others who felt a stewardess was nothing more than "a waitress in the sky". My parents were in this latter group, so you can just imagine their reaction when I announced to them that I was resigning from my teaching position to become a Pan American stewardess. They were horrified! They thought I had gone crazy! They said I was bringing great shame upon the family. They said no daughter of a respectable Japanese family would ever be a stewardess. What would the relatives say?

Up to that point in time, I had never disobeyed my parents, but this one time, I held my ground. When they realized they could not convince me to change my mind, they called in the "Big Guns." Two of my uncles and their spouses came to our house and, together with my parents, interrogated me. First, they tried to reason with me by saying I was throwing away a good education and a highly esteemed teaching career. I just sat there and cried. Then they lectured me about my duties as a filial daughter. I continued to cry. Finally my parents threatened to disown me. I cried harder. After almost two hours of lecturing me, they reluctantly gave in.

Looking back, it was the best decision I ever made. Being a stewardess with Pan American helped me to be more understanding and tolerant of the peoples I met from around the world. I learned to appreciate my family and, living in Hawaii, I came to realize how fortunate I was to be an American and to represent the United States on Pan American World Airways.

Pan American was clearly looking for specific characteristics in their hiring of stewardesses. You had to be a minimum of 5' 2" tall, with weight in proportion to height. You had to be a high school graduate with at least two years of work experience or a college graduate. In addition to speaking proper English, you had to speak a foreign language. Most of these requirements were what differentiated Pan American from other US carriers.

Pan American wanted its "cabin attendants," the term referring to the entire cabin crew of pursers, stewards and stewardesses, to be able to converse with customers from around the world, helping them to feel welcome in what was often a stressful situation for them. To be based in Honolulu, that second language had to be an Asian one, preferably Japanese. The need for Asian languages was probably the main reason why Pan American recruited in Honolulu.

The first Japanese stewardesses hired by Pan American were Nisei, i.e., second generation young American women. Most of their parents spoke Japanese at home, so they were raised bi-lingual. Later, as Pan American hired more Japanese stewardesses, they turned to the young Sansei women, i.e., third generation Japanese Americans. Although their parents were bi-lingual, they spoke mostly English at home. After the attack on Pearl Harbor, speaking Japanese was discouraged. Therefore, we Sansei were hired with limited ability to speak Japanese. (Company officials and employees referred to all of us as Nisei though many of us were Sansei.) We Sansei had to attend classes every week for six months until we passed our probation.

During my first year of flying, my parents continued to show their displeasure at my choice of career. When friends inquired as to what I was doing, they would mumble that I was a stewardess and quickly change the subject.

In my second year of flying, I took my parents on a trip around the world. They got to see first-hand the kind of work the stewardesses did on the Boeing 707s. They also met some of my friends. The trip changed their opinion about stewardesses. From then on, whenever they met their friends, they would proudly say, "My daughter is a stewardess for Pan American."

I was hired in 1964 and left Pan Am in 1986, with the sale of the Pacific routes to United Airlines. I was always based in Honolulu and, in my later Pan Am years, I became a Flight Attendant Supervisor. I accepted employment with United when the Pacific routes were sold.

Courtesy of the Author

LINDBERGH AS MY CO-PILOT

By Ken McAdams

Pan Am Eagles

For those pilots fortunate enough to have been hired by Pan Am, their lives in the sky were broadened, in many ways actually defined, by their experiences as employees of the World's Most Experienced Airline.

With bases around the world, from Hong Kong to Berlin, and the major markets in either direction in between, the genius of Juan Trippe gave to each of the Pan Am family unique opportunities, introductions, and associations never considered in our early years in aviation.

Courtesy of the Author

Ken McAdams

Courtesy of the Author

Charles Lindbergh

A small group of us were offered positions in the Business Jet Division under the command of Chief Pilot, Les McDevitt. We had many tasks. We flew acceptance test flights on the Dassault Mystère Vingt or Falcon 20 as it was known in the American executive jet market. We demonstrated these aircraft for sale over all the Americas, even on down to Australia. We flew in air shows, chauffeured impressive assortments of world leaders, along with serving the busy days of top Pan Am executives.

Invariably the highest echelons of our company were gentlemen and gentlewomen who, even in their hectic business lives, were gracious and considerate of we who served them. Paramount amongst these was *The Lone Eagle* himself, Colonel Charles Lindbergh.

As a member of our board of directors, we often flew Colonel Lindbergh to Washington to meet with the President of the United States, as well as to and from the many nests of Chairman Trippe, from Westchester to Bermuda, or on down to Eleuthera in the Bahamas.

Charles Lindbergh was never a man to stand on ceremony. On the line, as our flight attendant staff will affirm, though he always had First Class authorization on the big jets, he would never presume to sit up front, but always in the bulkhead seat, first row of Economy Class. He said those seats forward were for important people who needed their rest *en route* ... as if he were not one of these himself.

Flying him as often as we did, usually at night to and from Washington, he liked to join us in the cockpit, to sit on the small Falcon jump seat between captain and first officer. Being a straight-wing propeller man, he was most interested in the different technique used to bring a jet gently onto the runway. Since our pilot team at Business Jets spent an awful lot of time demonstrating exactly that, we got to be pretty good at it.

I will never forget one night landing at Westchester, after our cat-paw touchdown, he said to me, "Captain, how did you do that.....so smoothly?"

I decided this was an incredible opportunity, so I called for a touch-and-go, allowing us to climb back into the pattern, of which we were the only plane, and invited him to take the co-pilot seat to get the feel of it.

Think about that. Colonel Lindbergh, first solo flier across the Atlantic, was asking, "How do you do that?" of a twenty seven year old, Pan Am "New Hire."

We went around. He followed on the controls, and after another smooth landing, we disembarked and walked together to his car. Along the way he turned to me and said, "Thank you, Captain, that was a wonderful experience."

I could hardly speak realizing this great man was thanking me for a tiny moment in his illustrious career in aviation.

Such a warm, decent, deeply talented and gracious man, Charles Lindbergh.

Ken is a graduate of Yale University and a former Marine Corps Naval Aviator who has broken four civilian world records and received a military decoration as a first civilian volunteer to fly Marines into Iraq. As Pan Am's youngest divisional Chief Pilot, he was later appointed a National Transportation Safety Board investigator. With the demise of Pan Am, he joined Korean Air then later moved on to KIWI International Airlines as Chief Operation Officer before retiring to write full time. Ken lives with his wife, artist Bing, in Greenwich, CT and France.

Courtesy of the Author

Ken McAdams with his wife Bing and
a cover of his book, *Bon Courage*.

SKYGODS

By Robert Gandt

In the Company of Skygods

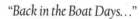

Sky-god \ski-god\: a being who reigns supreme while aloft in man-made flying contrivance 2: an aeronautical creature endowed with godlike attributes and worthy (in his or its own estimation) of human worship.

"Back in the Boat Days..."

Pan Am Archives

That was an expression we heard a lot during our pilot indoctrination at Pan Am. Whenever an old-timer spoke of an event that happened in the first half of Pan Am's existence, his voice would take on a reverential tone: "Things were different in the *Boat Days*, you know. Back then we used to. . ."

Never mind that this was 1965, that Pan Am possessed the largest fleet of commercial jets in the world, or that futuristic craft like the 747, the SST, and even spacecraft were on the drawing board. *The Boat Days*—the era of the great flying boats like the *China Clipper* and the majestic Boeing B-314—were the spiritual epicenter of Pan Am's history. And the high priests of *The Boat Days* were a generation of legendary airmen we called *Skygods*.

And they were still around. We caught glimpses of them in the big blue Pan Am hangar at the San Francisco airport where we attended classes. Like living artifacts from another age, the lordly airmen could be observed striding down the hallway to attend to their worldly business in the crew scheduling or personnel offices. Their heels clacked like hammers on the marble floor.

Even their uniforms were distinctive. The gold on their cap visors and the four stripes on their uniform sleeves had a weathered, salt sprayed dullness. The white caps rode atop their graying manes with a windward tilt. In their double-breasted, gold-encrusted Pan Am uniforms, they looked like ancient mariners.

Their trademark was *The Look*. *Skygods* squinted at the world over the tops of half-frame spectacles, down the lengths of their leathery noses. Wearing *The Look*, they would lock their imperious gaze on whatever subspecies happened to warrant their attention.

Not until a year-and-a-half later, when I was a freshly-qualified B-707 first officer, did I actually fly with one of these legendary captains. He was a *Skygod* of monumental reputation, a man whom I'll call Jim Howland, and we were scheduled to operate a Pan Am round-the-world flight. The experience would stay seared in my memory for the rest of my career.

It started off badly. When I introduced myself at check in, Captain Howland ignored my outstretched hand. After a perfunctory glance over his half-frames—the Look—he turned his back and busied himself with paperwork. In the cockpit his only utterances came in the form of terse commands: "Read the check list," "Get the clearance," "Gear up." My half of the exchange was limited to "Yes, sir."

So it went for the next few days —the Skygod issuing commands, the lowly first officer complying. It was impossible to tell whether Howland was pleased or disgusted with my performance. His expression never changed. Nor did the monosyllabic stream of orders. He made every take off and landing, sharing none of the flying duties with his first officer.

This condition lasted until we reached the Middle East. It was then, while we were in our descent toward Beirut airport, that history and geopolitics converged on us like a perfect storm. "Clipper One," called the air traffic controller, his voice an octave higher than before, "be advised that this region is in a state of war. Airports in every country are reporting air attacks. What are your intentions?"

Intentions? I looked at the captain. He appeared to be deep in thought, his eyes fixed on the hazy brown desertscape ahead of us. The controller sounded flustered, and so did the Pan Am operations agent on the ground in Beirut. No one knew what was going on or where we should go. The controller offered the opinion that since Beirut airport didn't seem to be under attack at the moment, it was probably safe to land. Probably.

At this the captain's eyeballs bulged, and he rose to full Skygodly stature. "To hell with that idiot," he thundered. "Tell him we're not landing in Beirut."

"Yes, sir, but where do you want to—"

"We're going to Tehran."

Tehran? Ooookay. The Skygod had spoken, and it didn't matter what air traffic control or our man in Beirut had to say. Clipper One was headed for Tehran. The problem was, getting a clearance to there—or anywhere else—wasn't possible. The en route frequency had become a bedlam of hysterical chatter about airports being bombed, fighters in the air, warning shots fired.

Off we went, eastward over the desert, while the relief pilot and I re-calculated our fuel and pored over the charts and tried to get clearance through the airspace. We encountered no fighters, no one tried to shoot us down, and somewhere along the way I actually obtained an airways clearance. When we landed in Tehran and deplaned our 120 passengers, we learned that we had just experienced Day One of what would be the Six Day Arab-Israeli War of 1967 .

That night the captain invited me to join him for a drink. For the first time I observed a softening of the fearsome Skygodly countenance. Peering over his half-frames, he raised his glass and spoke words that would stay with me for the next half century. "You know something, kid? You did good today."

I was speechless. You did good today. Coming from a Skygod, it was like an accolade from the Almighty.

Thereafter, for the remainder of our trip around the planet, Howland actually shared the take offs and landings. And he talked. In quiet moments high over the ocean, he recalled adventures from the Boat Days when ships like the China Clipper ruled the skies. They were exotic stories, and it didn't matter to me that they might be a bit embellished. I listened like a kid hearing fairy tales.

Over the next couple of years I flew with more of these ancient pelicans, and while the experience was seldom heartwarming, I always had the sense of being connected to a slice of history. The era of the Skygods spanned a time from fabric-and-wood mail planes, through the glamour-filled Boat Days, through WWII and the arrival of long-range landplanes, all the way to the jet age. They had seen it all.

But the long reign of the Skygods was coming to a close. Their numbers dwindled rapidly as they reached retirement age. They were being replaced by a new generation of airmen—and a new philosophy. It was called "crew concept," and it grew from the recognition that flying a jetliner across the ocean was a different task than commanding the China Clipper. No longer would a captain rule his aircraft by divine right or Skygodly decree. Henceforth crews would function as cohesive teams. It was a painful—but necessary—transition for Pan Am.

It was also the end of an era. The Skygods would become as extinct as dinosaurs. The Boat Days were officially over.

Robert, a former Pan Am captain, was based in San Francisco, Berlin, Hong Kong, and New York during his twenty-six-year career. He is a novelist, historian, and the author of thirteen books, including Skygods: The Fall of Pan Am *(Wm. Morrow, 1995). His most recent work is* The Twilight Warriors *(Broadway Books, 2010) for which he was awarded the prestigious 2011 Samuel Aliot Morison Award for Naval Literature by the New York Commandery of the Naval Order of the United States. Visit his website at www.Gandt.com.*

Courtesy of the author

Courtesy of the author

CITY TICKET OFFICE—VANDERBILT/NEW YORK CITY

By Florette Vassall

Working at the New York City Ticket Offices

Pan Am had several City Ticket Offices (CTOs) in the New York area. The two where I worked in Manhattan were Counter Fifth Avenue (CF) and Counter Vanderbilt (CV). While working those counters, I was fortunate to meet many celebrities and famous people. Saxophonist Stan Getz had his ticketing done at our busiest ticket counter — CF near St. Patrick's Cathedral as did TV and film stars such as Candice Bergen, Michael York, and the late Mel Ferrer.

My association with Pan Am started in 1967 while living in Acapulco, where I met many Eastern Airlines employees who used passes to commute between Mexico and the US. I then decided to return to New York and during the flight, I thought about which of my careers I would pursue—teaching or modeling. When the DC-8

Courtesy of the Author
Florette Vassall at Counter Vanderbilt, Pan Am Building.

made the last turn during its climb showing the beautiful view of Acapulco Bay, I knew I would have to find a way to return to this paradise. My friends from Eastern recommended I try for Pan Am because of my fluency in Spanish and French. I did and Ms. Joan Hagen interviewed me on the 48th floor of the Pan Am Building. I told her I wanted to be a ticket agent. She explained that new hires were not sent directly to ticket counters because there was so much to learn. Mr. Jim Reid of personnel was pleased to see that my job application showed I attended St. John's University College. He pulled a book from his desk drawer telling me he had written it when he was teaching at St. John's--I was hired!

I did not have to wait long. I was assigned to Counter Fifth Avenue. There I worked under the management of Mr. Aldo Ferraro and the supervision of Ms. Sharon Grasso and Ms. Dotty Sweet. CF was a very busy counter and its location at the corner of Fifth Avenue and West 48th Street gave passengers easy access. They came to get information, book trips, pick up tickets, and have their tickets validated, endorsed, or reissued. I became expert at this procedure because we received so many reissues at CF.

One day I received a notice I was being transferred to Counter Vanderbilt. What a surprise! My dream was to be able to work at that ticket counter because it was in the Pan Am Building. My good friend Lisa Chin also wanted me to work there.

Before moving to Acapulco, I worked a night job in the typing pool at First National City Bank headquarters. It was located at 399 Park Avenue at East 53rd Street. On my dinner breaks, I would walk down to the construction site of the soon to be new Pan Am Building. I was very fascinated by the promotional information that this was to be the building with the largest workspace area in the world. I never dreamed that several years later I would be working in this edifice, much less as an employee of the famous airline.

Of all of the ticket counters, the most popular and attractive was CV. It was located in the building of the company's headquarters. It was the largest ticket counter in the world at that time. It was beautifully designed, modern, bright and spacious, exuding much international atmosphere. The curved wall design was of white plaster featuring a sculpted relief of the world map. The Pan Am destinations on this relief were highlighted with small pink opaque lights. The work counters were laid out across the expansive area as "circular islands". We called them "doughnuts." The southeast doughnut opened from the building lobby off East 45th Street. The northeast doughnut opened from Vanderbilt Avenue. The center doughnut faced East 45th Street and was to the left of the circular information booth from which the passengers who entered through the East 45th Street revolving door were greeted.

The late Naomi Sims was the first super model of color making headlines when I began working at CV. I was one of the original door openers for models of color in New York and was able to chat with her about fashion and modeling, while ticketing her for our JFK to Paris flight 114 that evening. I greeted the comedian, the late Buddy Hackett at CV. I validated the ticket for the late famous German actor Horst Buchholz. He didn't have a photo that he could autograph for me, so I had him autograph one of my modeling head shot photos.

One very special incident affected my personal and professional life. It happened the day before my departure for Rio de Janiero in late November of 1969. Jose Silva was a Brazilian American supervisor in the reservations department of the Pan Am Building. He approached me with a passenger. We spoke in Spanish. I noticed that his ticket was punched with the "I for IDENT." At that time, this was the procedure to identify a passenger or regular flyer for VIP handling or special attention. The Frequent Flyer program had not yet been introduced. The OSI (other special information) field in his passenger reservation record (PRR) noted that he was a famous Brazilian movie star and politician. His name was Adhemar Ferriera da Silva. He was leaving that evening on flight 201 to Sao Paolo via Rio. While reviewing his ticket, I mentioned that my daughter and I were leaving for Rio the next evening. I told him I was very excited because this would be my first time visiting this fantastic city. He gave me his telephone number and asked me to call him when I reached Rio.

Adhemar met us in Rio the day after our arrival. He had driven there from Sao Paolo and he introduced my daughter and me to many dignitaries and places of interest. Having learned I was an international model, he presented me as "an international figure." I even met the dazzlingly beautiful, Miss Brasil. Many told me Adhemar was "a very important man".

In fact, he was the only Brazilian athlete to win gold medals in two consecutive Olympic Games. He won gold medals for the triple jump in the summer Olympics in Helsinki, Finland in 1952 and the summer Olympics in Melbourne Australia in 1956.

He also acted in the 1958/1959 French Italian film Orfeu Negro (Black Orpheus). It won the Oscar as Best foreign film and the Golden Palm in the Cannes Film Festival. The Olympic champion/actor continued to have me handle his ticketing each time he was in New York. He found me at CV and on occasions at CF. During his visits, he continued presenting me to more celebrities, one of whom was Donna de Varona, the Olympic swimmer and gold medal winner.

As a world-class carrier, Pan Am gave me the best of both possible worlds. I was able continue my life in Mexico and Acapulco and even represent Pan Am as a fashion model at times. I had a great feeling about working in the Pan Am building. Counter Vanderbilt let me meet and assist so many famous people, the "experience" leaves me with a lifetime of happy memories.

Courtesy of the Author

Florette worked in ticketing, sales and customer and passenger service in a career spanning from 1967 to 1991. She lives in New York, active in fashion modeling and beauty care consulting.

Courtesy of the Author

WELCOME TO VIETNAM

By Dr. Helen Davey

Working R&R Flights

I will never forget my first glimpse of Vietnam. It was the spring of 1968, after the disastrous Tet Offensive had resulted in an escalation of the war. I was flying my first volunteer flight as a Pan Am stewardess into Saigon to pick up American soldiers and deliver them to their "R & R" destinations. Glued to the window as we approached Tan Son Nhut airport, I was astonished to see bomb craters and smoke rising from scattered skirmishes on the ground. I had to give myself a reality check: was this really me, and was I really seeing this, and were American men really being killed right below me? I thought I had seen it all, on the nightly newscasts at home, but somehow I was shocked to see this vision of hell first hand.

Dr. Helen Davey's Stewardess Class

As briefed, the pilots made the steepest descent I had ever experienced in an airplane. I remember thinking of all the stories of bullets found in the fuselage of Pan Am airplanes, and the jokes about Pan Am pilots sitting on their manuals for a little extra protection while flying in and out of Vietnam. In my purse, I carried the paper that awarded Pan Am stewardesses Second Lieutenant in the US Air Force status, which meant that under the Geneva Convention, we would be treated as officers in the event of capture. Accustomed to providing elegant in-flight service to our passengers in a rather formal atmosphere, I was about to experience the most surreal flight I had encountered to date. We had been told that "almost nothing was by the book," but only the male purser on our flight and the pilots who had flown many flights to Vietnam knew what that meant.

As we taxied around the airport, I felt overwhelmed to see the sheer numbers of war machines of all types buzzing around seemingly everywhere. As we swung the door open, the noise was deafening, and the hot humid air enveloped me, taking my breath away. Our stewardess uniforms were made of fabric that was supposed to be "all weather," which really meant it was too thick in summer and too thin in winter. Add to that the fact we were still required to wear stockings and girdles, and I think you can imagine our discomfort. As I stared out of the open door, I became aware of the pallets of aluminum coffins lined up on the tarmac – each one containing somebody's precious husband or son or father or boyfriend or uncle or friend.

I don't think anything could have prepared me for the sight of the soldiers who boarded our airplane. I was expecting to see excited young men ready for a new adventure, laughing and joking with each other, and relieved to get away from the war. But as the men quietly filed aboard the airplane, I clearly saw the faces of trauma. Many were strangely quiet, with expressionless "masks," and most of them stared at our "round eyes," as if trying to take in a bit of home. I had no idea how young these men would be, but I wasn't expecting them to look like they should be in high school! Twenty-five at the time, I wasn't used to being called "Ma'am," and I felt strangely old. I'm convinced my experiences with these traumatized men helped fuel my later professional interest in the study of trauma.

The Pan Am pilots, mostly ex-military men, felt deep empathy for these soldiers, and their announcements reflected it. And here's where our very talented male purser came in. As funny as any stand-up comedian, he knew exactly how to handle these traumatized men. Totally throwing aside our traditional announcements, he used colorful language I had never heard uttered on a Pan Am intercom. He spoke right to the men, as if he were waking them up from their nightmare. And he loved to tease the stewardesses! As we were doing our regular emergency demonstrations, we were supposed to point overhead to the forward, center, and aft life rafts in the ceiling. During the part where he was supposed to say "forward, center, and aft life rafts," he mixed it up and said, "aft, center, and forward." By rote, all of us stewardesses pointed out the rafts in their normal sequence. He said, "So you see, guys, our young ladies don't seem to know their 'forward' from their 'aft!'" The soldiers exploded in laughter, and the tone was set for helping to relieve these young men's burdens for a short time. By the end of the flight, some of the soldiers seemed less robotic, and their eyes were coming alive.

Nothing about this flight felt familiar. Several of the men got up and helped with the serving of meals, leaving us stewardesses with more time to talk to the homesick men. Some of them wanted to ask about what was happening at home, especially about the escalation of protests. One of them asked me to call his mother when I got home, which I did. They showed us pictures of family, children, girlfriends, and wives. They wanted to know all about our crew, where everybody was from "in the world." One Vietnam vet wrote about Pan Am stewardesses--that we were "some of the sweetest, caring women I've ever known and need to be recognized for their contribution. Nurse, psychiatrist, mother, sister, daughter, girlfriend, confessor, sex object--they wore all the hats."

So hungry for a touch of home, their eyes pleaded for just a little conversation. I learned on that first flight that if anybody had gone to sleep due to exhaustion, we had to be very careful waking them up; they would awaken in an extremely startled state, arms flailing, reaching for their imaginary guns. I didn't realize at the time I was witnessing Post Traumatic Stress Disorder, which might stay with them for the rest of their lives. I picked out one particularly vulnerable looking soldier who was very shy, and as we talked, I decided to become his pen pal. I knew that having a Pan Am stewardess as a pen pal would qualify any soldier to be regarded as a "rock star."

This was the first of four soldiers who I eventually agreed to have as pen pals. When I began to receive notices, one by one, that each one had been killed, I started to regard myself as a jinx and stopped writing letters. Now I regret this, but at the time, it became too painful for me to be able to put a face to the names of dying men.

Music is where my memory of Vietnam lives, and this time of my life comes with its own special sound track: Creedence Clearwater Revival, The Doors, Buffalo Springfield, Jimi Hendrix, Jefferson Airplane, Marvin Gaye, Ike and Tina Turner, Bob Dylan, Crosby Stills & Nash, Otis Redding, the Animals, Aretha Franklin, and Edwin Star, who sang *"War"* (*"War! Huh! Good God, y'all! What's it good for? Absolutely nothing!"*) The music describes wartime--especially the ambivalence about this particular war--better than words can convey. When I hear it, I feel as if I am back there. I think any of us Pan Am employees who flew into Vietnam feel that we, too, were a part of that war. At the time, many of our regular destination cities in Asia were teeming with American soldiers, and wherever there were American soldiers, there was the music, blaring and insistent.

In a bizarre conclusion to my first flight to Vietnam, I asked the Captain if I could sit in the cockpit for landing. He said, "Of course." Again, since all rules were mostly suspended, the Captain decided to generously allow the engineer, who never really got to fly the airplane, to help with the landing. On final approach, just before touchdown, the left wing of the airplane dipped way too close to the runway. At the last moment, the Captain grabbed the controls back, and I think every person in the airplane knew we probably narrowly escaped disaster. Nobody in the cockpit spoke. I could tell the blood had drained from the pilots' faces, and the engineer was shaking.

Trembling from what had just happened, I stumbled out of the cockpit. The purser was up to his old tricks, and was just waiting for me to step through the door. He had signaled to the men, and when I appeared, a soldier yelled, "Nice landing, Ma'am!" Again, everyone exploded in laughter. After all, what was a little "near crash" to them? These brave men were facing death every day anyway. I sat down by the purser on the jumpseat and said, "We were just in the middle of a battle and we almost crashed!" He replied with a phrase that I was to hear often:

"Well, welcome to the world of Vietnam!"

Dr. Helen Davey is a psychoanalyst and psychotherapist in private practice in West Los Angeles and a former Pan Am Stewardess. Her doctoral dissertation, A Psychoanalytic Exploration of the Fall of Pan American World Airways, *is a study of the trauma experienced by Pan Am employees when the airline collapsed. She published an article entitled "The Effects of the Trauma of 9/11" for airline employees following the terrorist attack. She is a regular contributor to the Huffington Post.*

Courtesy of the Author

PAN AM OPENS MOSCOW

By George Hambleton

Negotiating Scheduled Service with the USSR

At the end of the fight is the tombstone white,
with the name of the late deceased–and the epitaph drear,
'A fool lies here who tried to hustle the East.'

Mr. Kipling's quotation, under the glass on my desk in Pan Am's office on the second floor of the musty old Metropol Hotel, was helpful in coping with the frustrations of starting Pan Am's New York-Moscow scheduled service at the peak of the Cold War.

Juan Trippe sent me to Moscow from Helsinki in the mid 1960s to develop good relations with Marshal Loginov, Minister of Civil Aviation, in an effort to persuade Aeroflot to join Pan Am in developing an InterContinental Hotel in Russia. Contracts for an Inter-Ccontinental Hotel in Helsinki had recently been signed while I was Director for Finland. Mr. Trippe told me not to tell anyone about the Russian hotel proposal–not even my own boss in Pan Am. Relations with the Ministry and Aeroflot developed favorably, but a hotel agreement was never concluded. The favorable relations helped set the stage for eventual introduction of scheduled services between New York and Moscow. The close cooperation that followed made possible CEO Najeeb Halaby's visit to see the TU-144 "Concordski" long before American Embassy officials had been permitted to see the relatively secret supersonic aircraft.

During the early airline negotiations, I remember, with some amusement, our US technical team telling Aeroflot the FAA required two American-made instruments, DME and transponders, on all aircraft entering New York airspace. This was long before GPS. The Pan Am team said with these two instruments, pilots could know their exact location. The answer from Aeroflot was, "Soviet pilots always know their exact location!" After service began, if one had looked closely at the belly antenna of the Russian IL-62 one would have seen the insignia, "RCA" (Radio Corporation of America).

In the Cold War decade of the 1960s, after Sputnik, the Cuban missile confrontation, and the Kennedy assassination, life in Moscow was grim. The city was bleak, drab and grey. There was no lighting or advertising signs on the sides of buildings–no color printing–only some faded reds and blue. The terror of the years of Stalinist purges had diminished, but fear was still pervasive–particularly among older people. The attitude of many was, "We have always been at war: with the Germans; before that with the French–the Swedes–and the Tartars. Our memories are all of sadness."

On one hand, there was an ingrained belief in the all healing, all educative power of socialism–a faith in their system–a pride in "Russianism," and an obsession with being a "Great Power." On the other hand, there was a yearning for material things–and an admiration of cleverness in manipulating the system.

There was hyper-sensitivity to criticism, extreme suspicion of foreigners (you're either "one of us" or you're "against us.") They had the cautiousness of a nation of chess players (if I had known where I would fall down, I would have put straw there) a great emphasis on reciprocity, and, above all else, a pervasive system of bribery and corruption.

Into this world I walked as a relatively young man, with a young English wife, two young children, and a Labrador puppy. How to cope with this system, and to launch an efficient Pan Am operation successfully, start was the question. Given Pan Am's strict worldwide policy against bribes and corruption, it seemed almost impossible, until we remembered a clause in the bilateral air agreement. Aeroflot was permitted to distribute advertising material in the United States and Pan Am was permitted to distribute advertising material in the Soviet Union.

Here was our incredible secret weapon. There was nothing in Russia like the Pan Am calendar, with its large, beautiful color pictures of worldwide destinations. People who had no other color pictures would frame the calendar pictures to hang in their otherwise drab and crowded apartments. I was told that Pan Am calendars would sell for the equivalent of some twenty or thirty dollars on the black market. During communist days, the Soviet poet and playwright Vladimir Mayakovsky wrote "Without a piece of paper you're an insect–with a piece of paper you're a man!" We had a piece of paper that made it legal for us to distribute these valuable items–a box of a hundred calendars was a pretty handsome gift, it was advertising material.

Eventually service began.

On July 14, 1968 Richard Witkin wrote in the New York Times:

> At Pan American World Airways' second floor sales office in the Hotel Metropol, 15 sons and daughters of American Embassy officials spent much of the rainy Moscow Sunday putting 16 kopek's worth of stamps on 22,000 envelopes marking the inaugural flight.... The letter will be flown to New York on the... Pan American flight, and delivered to stamp collectors and others with special interest in the start of the route.
>
> The (Pan Am/Aeroflot inaugural) flights will culminate a diplomatic effort that had its fragile beginning in the first Soviet-American cultural exchange agreement in 1958. It also will be another in a series of recent signs that relations between the two countries are being selectively improved, despite strains imposed by the Vietnam War."

Shortly before Pan Am's first scheduled flight, another Pan American 707 "protocol" flight, with Government officials and VIP guests took off. I remember suggesting to New York that the person with the most impact possible to be invited as an inaugural guest would be Jacqueline Onassis. Secretly, the Russians loved John F. Kennedy. He had stood up to Khrushchev and made him back down. Jackie Onassis would have been a sensation!

Aeroflot's inaugural "protocol" flight was led by the Deputy Minister of Civil Aviation. The Russians had taken our inaugural guests to the Bolshoi Ballet in Moscow, so we felt obligated to reciprocate. Finding forty seats to the ballet in New York was not easy. We arranged for dinner at a very nice restaurant near the Lincoln Center. The restaurant had made a major effort to look old fashioned–bare brick walls, with gas lights protruding from the walls. When the Russian Deputy Minister saw the gas lights, he said, "In Moscow we have electricity!"

The first New York-Moscow flights made one stop on the way–Montreal for Aeroflot and Copenhagen for Pan Am. Our initial weekly flights were 10 hours 50 minutes eastbound; 11 hours 45 minutes westbound. First class fares were $584 one way, and $1,109 round trip. Economy fares were $384 one way off season; $429 during the summer peak.

Pan Am's operation, very efficiently led by Airport Manager Walter Nelson, at Sheremetyevo, had a much greater impact than its relatively low initial schedules would have indicated. An analysis of the flights to Moscow by themselves could show a money losing "National Interest" route, but if incremental trans-Atlantic traffic, connecting over other gateways, was added, the Moscow operation was quite successful. Most connecting passengers would not have called Pan Am if we had not been serving Moscow.

In spite of constant "stealing" of our passengers by rank and file Aeroflot employees, we managed to generate more Moscow originating trans-Atlantic traffic than other western airlines. Aeroflot would not help pending passengers until the long exit and entry visa processes were completed. The wife of the US Consul came to work for Pan Am, giving us access to visa applications. We were able to help Russian passengers early in the visa process. Many of them had prepaid tickets, paid for by relatives in the US

All tickets had to be issued by Aeroflot's Moscow reservations office. It was called the Central International Agency–until I pointed out that was "CIA." They changed the name!

Cargo was also frequently diverted to Aeroflot. A US embassy diplomat, for example, was transferred back to Washington. His household goods were to be shipped by Pan Am to his home in Alexandria, Virginia. The shipment disappeared, much to the chagrin of the embassy, the diplomat, and our Pan Am staff. Weeks later, the household goods were discovered in Alexandria, Egypt–diverted and misdirected by Aeroflot.

No advertising signs were permitted on the outside of buildings in Moscow in those days. Our corner office on the second floor of the turn of the century Metropol Hotel had two huge bay windows. We ordered two large signs (white squares, with huge Pan Am blue balls, some seven or eight feet across), and mounted them on the inside of the large bay windows, directly across a square from the Bolshoi Ballet, in the center of Moscow. With no other advertising signs, and, particularly, no other American signs in the center of the city, this caused quite a stir.

Moscow city officials were bemused, but chagrined. We were not advertising on the outside of the building in violation of their regulations, and they empathized with this "manipulation of the system." "We see what you're doing!" Moscow bureaucrats did not know much about New York. We assured them, if they let us keep our signs, we would make sure that Vladimir Samaroukov, Aeroflot's manager in New York, would be permitted to put up Aeroflot signs there! We waited a month or so before turning on the lighted Pan Am signs. By then it was clear to all that an American Company was firmly ensconced in the heart of Moscow–unheard of until that time. To help cement the arrangement, we may have asked the bureaucrats to help us distribute a few boxes of Pan Am calendars.

We managed to negotiate a dacha (vacation home) at Zavidovo, a hunting base two hours northwest of Moscow, where the Shosha River meets the Volga, in the Kalinin Oblast. It was necessary to obtain permits each time to leave Moscow in order to pass through police check points, but it was very helpful to be able to invite others to use our dacha.

One extremely cold winter night, we were returning from Zavidovo in our unmarked Dodge Polara station wagon (the Russians thought it must have been made by the company that made Polaris missiles!) We were driving through blizzard conditions, with my wife, three children and our dog onboard. Suddenly, we had a flat tire. There was no other traffic on the road. We were in the boondocks. I managed to unload the spare, and was trying to change the tire in the zero weather. After a while, two headlights appeared through the thick snow. A militsia truck pulled up behind us. Two burly policemen, in heavy black coats, with black fur hats, approached. One of them said, "American aviation company!" Surprised, I said, "Yes–how did you know?" The policeman said, "Last year in my checkpoint, you gave me a Pan Am calendar!" They helped me change the tire.

As a symbol of confidence, Pan Am had a custom of bringing the entire Board of Directors, with the wives or husbands, on the same airplane for board meetings at different locations around the world. The Board decided to come to Moscow. Preparations were exhaustive. We even had my good wife, Janet, do a survey of ladies' rooms in areas we planned to take the Board. Intourist was helpful, but, as the Russians say, the reason Napoleon failed in Russia was because his plans were made by Intourist!

We arranged a private meeting between Minister Loginov and Juan Trippe. I was privileged to attend. Although nothing had yet leaked to the press, Mr. Trippe confided to Marshal Loginov that Pan Am had decided not to go forward with supersonic operations, but instead to develop widebody aircraft. Loginov was stunned. Aeroflot and the Russians had clearly put all their emphasis into developing their version of the supersonic Concord. Suddenly, they feared being left behind by the airlines of the world following Pan Am with widebodies.

In spite of continuing tight controls of the Brezhnev era–small cracks in the Kremlin walls, (hardly noticeable at the time), were beginning to appear. Alya Andersen, wife of New York Times bureau chief, Ray Andersen, worked in the Pan Am office. She said quietly one day that her father, who lived in Ryazan, a closed area south of Moscow, had devoted his life to this great cause, communism, which he thought was the answer to everything. In his late forties, he began to realize it was not working–it was all a big mistake. Alya said he was totally frustrated–he was afraid to discuss it with anybody–but felt he had wasted his life.

Painting Reproduced Courtesy of the artist Lesley Giles

Odessa Fliers

There must have been millions of others like him, waiting for glasnost and perestroika, which did not come until Gorbachev's era, a couple of decades later.

In the early 1960s, Mr. Khrushchev had been saying the Soviet Union would soon "overtake and surpass" the United States. Speaking at a ceremony celebrating Pan Am/Aeroflot service in the late 60's, Ambassador Llewellyn Thompson said there was one field in which he would welcome the Soviet Union overtaking and surpassing the United States–that was in the number of visitors from Russia to the United States overtaking the number of visitors from the United States to Russia.

George commutes between New Jersey and Maine. He is an active member of the board at the College of the Atlantic in Bar Harbor, the Pan Am Historical Foundation in New York, and the American-Russia Culture Cooperation Foundation in Washington, DC.

Courtesy of the Author

MOSCOW ADVENTURES

By Ilona Duncan

Learning Russian in Moscow

The afternoon of January 12, 1971, as the Pan Am Clipper flight 44 makes its final approach to Moscow's Sheremetievo Airport, I glance down at snow-covered fields framed by dark lifeless bushes and trees. Here and there I can make out a house forlorn in the vast wintry Russian landscape exuding the melancholic mood of the Russian soul so often described in the works of Tolstoy and Pushkin.

Tired from an all-night flight starting in New York via Copenhagen, a sense of excitement drives away my feeling of drowsiness. I am one of 31 Pan American stewardesses, who signed up for a Russian language course in Moscow. To alleviate the shortage of Russian speaking

Courttesy of the Author

Ilona at Aeroflot Flight Academy.

cabin personnel since Pan Am started operating flights to the Soviet Union in 1968, Pan American arranged this 4-week program at minimal cost of hotel and meal expenses to us, while we agreed to an unpaid leave-of-absence. Within our group of 11 nationalities, (French, German, Swedish, Norwegian, Israeli, Yugoslavian, Argentinean, Honduran, Uruguayan, Dutch and American,) I am one of the few with a background of studying Russian at Hunter College, in the hope of eventually adding it to the other four languages (French, Italian, Dutch and German) I am qualified to speak on board. Federal Air Regulations required at least one person to be able to communicate in the language spoken at the destination country of every flight.

We arrive at the *Hotel National* in time for dinner, served from 6:30-7:30 p.m. A *babushka* (Grandmother) who occupies a desk on every floor hands me the room key and, as we observe from then on, notes down every one of our movements, an outcome of the ongoing Cold War. My room, which I share with my Swedish friend, consists of two single beds separated by a table. Heavy curtains hide the view from the window. A single light bulb dangles from the high ceiling and gives off enough light to reveal the cracks in the lime green walls. When I go to take a long bath, I discover no stop in the tub, and a shower head is non-existent.

"Let's go for a walk," my roommate suggests.

"Great idea!"

Dressed in fur hats and winter coats, we are among a small number of pedestrians walking along the poorly lit streets half a mile from Red Square. Snow is starting to fall. Awe-struck by the immensity of the square, we watch snow flakes dancing under the shimmering lights that illuminate the Kremlin Wall and St. Basil's Cathedral.

"Oh, this is so beautiful," says my roommate.

"I agree, we are so privileged to be here," I answer.

Our daily schedule allows for little idle time, starting with breakfast between 9 a.m. and 9:45 a.m., lessons at the department for foreign students at Moscow State University from 10 a.m. to 1 p.m., followed by lunch from 1:30-2:30 p.m., and excursions on most afternoons. Bus transportation is provided by Moscow's Intourist Office. Every second day drivers are exchanged for fear we might become too friendly with them.

We attend a fashion show where we get an authentic taste of life in the Soviet Union where Russian models present lackluster and unappealing outfits. We visit Moscow's Wedding Palace to witness a line-up of grooms in dark suits and brides in frilly white dresses ready to take their vows. We sleep in bunk beds on a night train for a weekend in Leningrad (now St. Petersburg) and wonder what is so important to hide from our view, that the windows had been boarded shut. During an outing to Lenin's house and Museum on the outskirts of Moscow, I am reminded of the intimidation prevalent during this era. When the guide explains how the original owners of this mansion that Lenin came to occupy, simply abandoned it, I pose the question: "Why would they suddenly leave their home?"

"Do you want to create trouble?" The guide shouts, while she moves in my direction and stares at me viciously. I want to say something, but her demeanor strongly hints, that I better keep my opinion to myself.

Although interchange with Russians is strongly discouraged, we attract the curiosity of young people. Among the drab colors worn by everyone in Moscow we stand out in our fashionable attire .

"Your capitalist Government provided you with this coat to show off," someone yells.

"No, I work hard and pay for my clothes," I reply.

Others want to practice their foreign languages with us. After meeting students at a café, I suggest: "Why don't we all go to my hotel and sit in the lobby?"

The minute we climb the stairs to the main hall, two men emerge, grab the young students by their arms, shouting in Russian: "Rusky nyet." (No Russian)

"All we want to do is talk," I plead.

"No Russians allowed in this hotel."

One afternoon, my roommate and I walk up to the roof-top terrace on the 23rd floor of the Russia Hotel for a postcard view of Saint Basil's Cathedral and Red Square. Raising my camera for a photo, a male voice screams from behind: "Stop, or you will be arrested." In a frenzy, we make a run for a lady's room where I quickly remove the film before a uniformed man enters. Terrified we endure a tirade of reprimands. Finding my camera empty he lets us go. I had forgotten that we are never to take photos from high places.

The scarcity of food is reflected in our daily ration of unrecognizable fish or chicken pieces and cabbage. Only breakfast is adequate with heaps of dark bread, butter, and various delicious jams. A long line of Muscovites around a street block is an indication of some special offering. One day we come across a vendor selling oranges, two per person, from a cart.

"I would love one" my roommate says.

"Yes, let's wait."

But, we wait in vain. He runs out. Disappointed, we stop at a small-goods store to buy a bottle of sweet Crimean wine and a hunk of blue cheese, the only product not in short supply.

"Slovensky Bazaar," the most fashionable restaurant for Muscovites, admits only select customers as we find out one evening.

"You have to wait outside."

"How long?" we ask.

"Three hours."

With the help of Pan American personnel, my friend and I get a reservation for a later date and join the table of privileged Russian couples offering to share a bottle of vodka with us. The Russian airline, *Aeroflot*, welcomes us to visit their Training Academy where we are proudly introduced to many aspects of their operation by the *Honorable Pilot of the Soviet Union*, as his title is displayed on his desk. We learn that stewardesses train for over a year, which includes language instruction. A select number of them are eager to practice their foreign language skills with us.

"How much money do you make?" I ask in German.

"Sufficient," she answers.

"How do you like visiting other countries?" I ask.

"I prefer the Soviet Union," she answers in flawless German.

Despite some anxious moments, the highlights of our stay are the cultural events. Every evening we occupy the best seats at one of the theaters or concert halls. During intermission at the Bolshoi or Kremlin Theatre, we savor dishes of mushrooms in cream sauce or ice-cream topped with loganberries. Never again will I see a performance rising to the level of perfection and beauty as at the *Bolshoi Theater*.

On our last day of school, we receive a certificate of attendance. Our teacher has tried her utmost to drill some basic Russian into our brains. But without prior knowledge, most of the students have trouble understanding her and reading the alphabet. Back in New York, a few months later, I become qualified as Russian speaker on Pan Am flights thrilled to return to Moscow.

My enthusiasm ended one year later when Pan American re-scheduled me during a lay-over in Amsterdam to operate a flight to Moscow against my wishes, after my visa had expired. No sooner was the front door of the Boeing 707 opened, that two armed, uniformed men grabbed me and hauled me off the plane to an unspecified location where I was taken down a long corridor and escorted to a cell. My pleas to call the American Embassy fell on deaf ears. I tried to get information from the woman who unlocked the cell door to accompany me to a toilet. She shrugged her shoulders. The following morning a guard opened the door shouting in Russian: "Time to go."

Once the airplane lifted off the runway, I knew I had left Moscow for the last time.

Ilona is married to Pan Am Captain Jim Duncan.

Courtesy of the Author

ARIANA AFGHAN AIRLINES

By John Bigelow

Giving Technical Assistance in Afghanistan

It all started during the Hajj, the annual Muslim pilgrimage to Mecca, for the faithful, a mandatory rite of passage and a passport to heaven and eternity. For years, Afghan pilgrims had made their way across the deserts and mountains of Afghanistan, Iran, and Saudi Arabia by bus, truck . . . and even camel caravan. But a visionary King, Mohammed Zahir Shah, with the dream of leading his people into the twentieth century, blessed the conception of the country's first airline. In 1957, Ariana Afghan Airlines was born. At last, pilgrims could fly to Jeddah–the staging point for the pilgrimage to Mecca–in hours rather than days or weeks.

Courtesy of the Author

Ariana 727 over Hindu Kush.

54

Years later, in early May, 1968, Pan American's Captain Richard Vinal, Chief Pilot of Latin America, summoned me to his office in Miami. My reaction was predictable. Chief Pilots were not in the habit of asking you in to inquire about your health. I began to formulate complex denials and thought about calling my union representative. I drove over to the office and sat under the suspicious eye of the Chief Pilot's secretary who, I was convinced, knew of my misdemeanor, whatever it was. At last, I was invited in and asked to sit down. The heavy oak door closed behind me, and I noted with some alarm that Captain Vinal and I were alone.

"Bigelow, how would you like to go to Afghanistan?"

I had a vague idea where Afghanistan was–somewhere in Africa, I thought. Whatever I'd done was about to condemn me to the other side of the world. So I asked my Chief Pilot for some background to his startling question. A little more kindly now, he explained why we were having this conversation.

"Sam Miller, our Vice-President of Flight Operations, called me this morning, wanting to know if I had any young, eager pilots interested in a foreign flight training assignment. He thinks you might be ready for something like this.

"Pan Am owns 49 percent of Ariana Afghan Airlines and we run a Technical Assistance Program (TAP) with the airline. Ariana has just acquired a new Boeing 727. Our Project Director out there thinks they need some help training the Afghan pilots. If you're interested, I'd like you to go up to New York to talk to Sam Miller. They need someone out there right away."

At the time, I'd been with Pan Am for two years and still felt like a new boy. My wife, Mary Lou, and I talked it over. We discovered Afghanistan was not in Africa but a land-locked kingdom in Southwest Asia. To us, it sounded exciting and different, full of adventure and opportunity.

I bought a paperback copy of James Michener's Caravans and began reading it on the way to New York. I was captivated by what I read, spellbound by descriptions of Kandahar, Kabul, and the Hindu Kush. Suddenly, I was very keen to go there.

My interview with the legendary Sam Miller went well. He had been the commander of the first scheduled commercial flight of a Boeing 707 across the Atlantic in 1958–a major milestone in Pan Am's history. Captain Miller was a gracious, quiet-spoken man and, despite his aura, made me feel at ease. He was interested in my pre-Pan Am flying experiences in the Canadian Arctic and Middle East. He had read my personal file and seemed pleased and handed me off to Erskine Rice who headed TAP field operations.

Rice noted, "Were you to accept this assignment, you would be assigned as 'Advisor' to the Chief Pilot, Rahim Nowroz. You would be responsible to him for assessing pilot standards and recommending steps to improve pilot performance. The Afghan pilots have been trained and released by Boeing instructors, but Charlie Bennett, our project director in Kabul, feels there is a need for ongoing monitoring.

"The assignment would be for a year. We need someone out there right away. If you're interested, I need a decision by the end of the day."

I was their man, and I immediately told him so. He got up smiling, walked around his desk, and we shook hands. Erskine Rice became more guarded when the discussion turned to Rahim Nowroz–the man I would be advising in Afghanistan. He said that Nowroz had a reputation for being difficult at times, adding that he was also the King's personal pilot, and–oh yes–rumored to have a fondness for drink.

"John, I'm sure you'll get along just fine out there. Go out there and do the best job you know how. I'm sure we'll all be proud of you."

Now I knew I was being conned. No, he wasn't smiling. He was smirking.

"What am I getting into?" I thought.

I was in Kabul when, early in the morning of January 5, 1969, Ariana's Boeing 727, YA-FAR, crashed three-quarters of a mile short of Runway 27 at London's Gatwick airport during an instrument approach in a thick, freezing fog. Our chief of maintenance, Ed Mix, had put his daughter, Karen, on the flight at Kabul. With landing gear and flaps extended, the aircraft briefly touched down in a muddy field before becoming airborne again. The pilot, none other than Captain Nowroz, aware at last that something was wrong, had jammed open the throttles but, seconds before, ten feet of the Boeing's right wing had been torn away by a large tree. The aircraft began an uncontrolled, climbing roll to the right, and would have become inverted had not a large two-story house stood in its way. The house and most of the aircraft then exploded in a large ball of burning kerosene. The cockpit passed inches above the roof and detached itself at the moment of impact, remaining airborne briefly before skidding to a halt in the mud.

Sixty-nine of the ninety-eight passengers and cabin crew burned to death. Of those few who survived, most were difficult to recognize as human, even after months of restorative surgery. One of the survivors, a baby girl lying in her bassinette, a toy clutched in her hands, was unharmed in the smoking rubble. Her parents were not so lucky.

The accident could have been prevented. But because of a perverse and persistent aspect of human nature, people had to die before anything would change.

Ed Mix and I travelled to London on Iran Air, a flight that duplicated Pan Am's flight 115, stopping at Tehran, Beirut, Istanbul, Frankfurt, and London. Word of the accident had spread to all of Pan Am's European stations and also that Ed and I were en route to London. Ed was well known in Pan Am's world and well-regarded. At each stop along our way, I deplaned to get an update, leaving Ed in his seat in the cabin, distraught and alone, but grateful for what I was doing. Pan Am station personnel, waiting for our flight, met me with the latest news: few survivors, still no news of Karen. At each stop, as we continued up the line to London, I returned to my seat next to Ed: "Nothing yet, no news. But don't give up. Don't give up! You hear me?"

This hard-bitten, cigar-smoking, maintenance manager was now crying. He reached over to hold my hand. "I'm sorry John. I can't help it. I can't stop thinking about Karen. Our beautiful daughter I love so very much . . ."

On the last leg, from Frankfurt to London, Ed wrote me a note in pencil on an airsick bag. It said: "I can't express myself properly with words at the moment. But I will never forget how important it is that you are here with me, or how grateful I am. Your friend, Ed."

I still have the bag.

We were the first off the airplane at Heathrow. Pete Dunstan, Pan Am's maintenance manager in London, and a close friend of Ed's, waited at the head of the jetway. He was tight-lipped, a look of infinite sadness on his face. Ed looked up at him, unable to speak. Pete shook his head and said: "I'm sorry, Ed. Karen didn't make it."

Two days later, he and his wife, Libby, boarded Pan Am's round-the world flight, Clipper One to New York, with their daughter's remains in the belly of the 707.

Ed Mix would never return to Afghanistan.

"You will be leaving us soon, won't you?" asked my administrative aide, Captain Gran.

I answered, "It's time. We both know it. What can be worse than a guest who overstays his welcome? My job is done here. Ariana and its pilots now rank with the best in the world. You don't need me anymore."

He answered, "I disagree with you. We—and I speak for all the pilots—want you to stay. We will always need you. You are no longer *ferangi*. You are part of us; you belong with us."

I said, "Look, Gran. I will always be available, but I must leave Afghanistan. It's the essence of the program. From the beginning, I came here to work my way out of this job and train my Afghan replacement—my replacement, not surprisingly, with whom I'm now having lunch." Maybe I derailed him with that remark. When he regained his composure, he said: "It is strange how events sometimes unfold, isn't it? When I look back four years ago, how different things seemed then . . .

He answered, "We were suspicious of you from the start. I agreed with Rahim–we didn't need you. Boeing had trained us, and we knew what we needed to know. You were yet another example of an unwanted foreign presence. One way or another, the sooner we could get rid of you, the better. At first we assumed you would just give up and leave like so many others who, for whatever reason, had come to Afghanistan. But, to Rahim's frustration and, to a lesser extent, mine, you didn't. You were behaving like . . . like an Afghan! You didn't give up. You had the testicles of a goat, and it was driving Rahim crazy!"

He paused, took a deep breath, and continued.

"This is the part I find most difficult to admit: I began to see what you were trying to do. But because of my loyalty to Rahim, and because, honestly, I was afraid of him, I did nothing. If I had cooperated with you then, and you had left, Rahim would have made my life unbearable. We are a small country. Never forget: Rahim and I are Pashtun, and blood, as they say, runs thicker than water. . . .

"The accident changed everything. Captain Rahim Nowroz, my Chief Pilot, I discovered, had committed a dreadful and unforgivable error. He had killed many people, not the least, the daughter of your friend, Ed Mix. And of course, I knew about his drinking. I was being split down the middle, in an impossible position. I will never forget my first meeting with you in London after the crash. I saw myself on a buzkashi field–the calf fought over and pulled apart by opposing chapandaz. You, Pan Am, and the British on one side, Afghanistan and everything it stands for on the other. I must tell you, John, it was the worst moment of my life."

He continued, "What you did–and this is perhaps the most important aspect of your time with us–was to take our natural inclination to compete and to win at any cost, and to turn this inclination into something positive. No longer could we buy our way into the seat of an airplane. No longer was it a question of who we knew or how we were related. Only through training, only through passing through the necessary gates could we expect to succeed. We were all now competing with each other to be the best. . . .

"We could not figure this out for ourselves; it took a pale-skinned, blue-eyed ferangi to do it for us."

I thought about what Gran had said. I was flattered by his words, but it went beyond the apparent success of this Afghan endeavor. For me, from its outset, it had been born out of failure. In that moment, I saw what I was really doing here:

John Bigelow, Chief Pilot (Berlin)

JOHN G. BIGELOW

CHIEF PILOT
ARIANA AFGHAN AIRLINES
COMPANY LIMITED

POST OFFICE BOX 76
KABUL, AFGHANISTAN
25541, EXT 328
RES. 32286

Courtesy of the Author

John is still at it, training pilots on the A-320 family at CAE in Dubai.

proving to myself I wasn't quite the hopeless screw-up I'd always seemed to be. After so many false starts in my life, I'd needed a win. Maybe, at last, I had one.

I went on, ignoring him.

I said to him, "You, my friend, belong in an airplane, not behind a desk. You know it. No one ever was killed by paperwork, only inconvenienced. We'll find someone to fill those administrative duties. I'm recommending that you be appointed Chief Pilot, Training and Check. It's the only reason I can leave Afghanistan and sleep at night".

I still sleep at night; now I am doing the sleeping in Dubai, training pilots at my ripe age of 75. Never will I forget my Afghan Journey, the frustrations and accomplishments. The turbulence and mistrust today, however, cause me to question whether Afghanistan can ever return to the era of serenity and enlightenment which I experienced in the sixties.

May peace overcome.

.

WAITING LIST FOR THE FIRST COMMERCIAL FLIGHT TO THE MOON

By Bill Dreslin

Making Reservations for the Moon

I worked in the Public Relations Department of Pan Am from 1968 until 1974, first as Manager of Marketing Publicity and then as Director of Public Relations, Programs and Services, reporting to Tony Lutz who was Staff Vice President for Public Relations. There were many interesting and exciting assignments during this time period, as well as grim ones, as we were the folks who were charged with publicizing the good times and doing damage control during bad times. But perhaps the most fun project I was personally involved with was "The Waiting List for the Moon."

The 1960s were the times when the space race was on, and commercial flights to the moon and other planets were thought to be something that would come to pass within the next twenty years or so. I don't personally know how the reservation list for Pan Am's first flight to the moon got started, but I've read that an Austrian journalist named Gerhard Pistor was the first to walk into a travel agency in Vienna and ask to reserve a seat on Pan Am's first scheduled lunar flight. Since Pan Am had always thought of itself as a "pioneer" – first across the Pacific, many firsts across the Atlantic, and first to fly the Boeing 747 – it was a logical assumption, and hope, that it

Courtesy of Artist Lesley Giles

The Painting, "Moon"

Courtesy of the Author

Membership Card, First Moon Flights Club

would be first to pioneer commercial moon travel as well. So when requests to get on the stand-by list for a trip to the moon came trickling in, the official Waiting List for the Moon began. After the Apollo 8 mission in December of 1968—and who can forget Pan Am's exposure in the film" *Space Odyssey 2001*—the requests increased to a deluge! By then the airline was mentioning the list in their radio and television commercials. Often they began with, "Who ever heard of an airline with a waiting list for the moon?"

The official list had more than 200 names when I pitched the story to the New York Times in January of 1969. The resulting piece pointed out that Pan Am had no space ship and definitely no authority to make the voyage to the moon, but all the people from the list that they contacted, including scientists, engineers and students, were very serious about the idea and had definite reasons for wanting to be among the first to blast off. I conceded, and they published, that there were many problems that had to be resolved before this first flight took off for the moon, including the high cost of rocket fuel, passenger comfort, and oh yes, accommodations once they got there. Still, the article resulted in even more requests to be added to the list. With the first lunar landing on July 20, 1969, travel to the moon became even more of a reality, and the mail requests increased dramatically.

We heard from an entire fourth grade class from the Hawthorne Avenue School in Newark, NJ, with individual letters, including drawings of what they thought Pan Am's first moonship would look like. All the children's letters and questions were answered, telling them that a commercial flight wouldn't be possible "for at least another 20 years," when they would no longer be in school, and that their pets probably couldn't live in the moon's atmosphere, and that the food would be different from anything they had ever tasted on earth. We then invited them to send in their names and addresses if they wanted to be on the list and also so "we can keep in touch with you."

Since most all the fourth graders were concerned about the cost of the trip, we added that the price hadn't been determined yet, but it would probably be expensive because of the distance and cost of fuel. All but two members of the class sent in their home addresses. Their teacher, Mrs. Roslyn Bernstein, signed up too because she thought it would be an opportunity to get a good rest, and "I'm sure in 20 years I will really need one!"

We never got to the point where we accepted any money or gave out any firm reservations, but we did distribute membership cards in the "First Moon Flights Club," each numbered according to the date the request was received. Had we asked for a deposit, I'm sure the list would have deflated in a hurry, but I understand that when it was officially "closed," there were over 93,000 names, representing residents in all fifty states and citizens of 90 other countries, including Ghana, Nicaragua, Iceland, New Zealand, Pakistan and Ecuador.

It is interesting to look back from my position of retirement on the living room couch and see all that has and hasn't happened. High-profile names from the list, such as Ronald Reagan and John Wayne, are no longer with us, and neither, sadly, is the airline. Twenty years plus more have been added to the original twenty-year timeframe when commercial moon travel was envisioned. Those fourth graders are now in their fifties and have probably been airborne at least a few times, but alas, they'll probably never get to the moon. After all, these days not even astronauts are going there!

Joyce and Bill, now in retirement, are big tennis fans and live in Dallas and Westhampton Beach, Long Island, New York.

Courtesy of the Author

Bill and his wife Joyce landing on their honeymoon in Honolulu.

BLACK SEPTEMBER

By Nellie Beckhans

The Cairo Hijacking

I was very content with my life. After working for Pan Am for three years as a Special Services Representative, I had finally become a Flight Attendant. Things were going well, and after I completed training, I was based in New York where I knew a lot of Pan Am people. Most of my flying had been to South America and Central America. Now I was going to Brussels.

The flight to Brussels with a very nice crew was uneventful. I remember sightseeing and visiting beautiful stores where we bought delicious Belgian chocolates. After dinner with the crew, we retired for the night to

Pan Am Archives

Arabs Blow Up Hijacked Jet

This is the wreckage of the hijacked Pan American 747 jumbo jet after it was blown up by Palestinian commandos at the Cairo airport Sept. 7, 1970. A spokesman for the airline said all 188 persons aboard had disembarked safely before the jet was blown up.

sleep and wait for the wake-up call in the morning for the flight back to New York. I was anxious to get home as I was going to a show with friends.

It was September 6, 1970. Flight 93 departed Brussels headed to New York, with a stop in Amsterdam. The short flight from Brussels to Amsterdam went smoothly. We picked up passengers in Amsterdam. Now it was time to go home. On taxiing to the runway, the plane stopped. A few minutes later I heard a commotion in the First Class section. From my assigned position at R3 door, facing the aft of the airplane, I turned around to see Captain John Pritty talking to the purser and some passengers. The aisle curtain closed and I could see nothing further.

After a short period of time the Captain made an announcement stating that he had to check some passengers and we were now ready for departure. We would later find out that these two passengers were denied boarding on an EL AL aircraft. Evidently whatever caused EL AL to deny the boarding was not found by Pan Am. The checking of the passengers was a search for weapons. The Captain, trained to fly aircraft, not trained to search potential hijackers who are trained to conceal weapons, did not find any guns or grenades.

The airplane took off, headed for New York. About 20 minutes later when we thought we were going to start our service, the In-flight Director made an announcement that we were to remain seated. We were going to a different destination. He told everyone to remain calm as we were going to a friendly country. There appeared to be a lot of activity in First Class. Curious, I went to the front of the plane. The flight attendant working First Class told me that there were two hijackers and they had a gun and grenades. They did not want anybody in First Class. She said that the Purser was taken to the cockpit with a gun to her head. Now I was very concerned. I went back to my area and informed other crew members.

Thankfully, the passenger load was light and everyone remained calm. We were told to mingle with the passengers. One hijacker moved about the cabin. He talked to passengers explaining the objectives of the Palestine Movement. He asked me where I was from. I told him Cuba, and then he asked what the handles on the door were for. I didn't know if he had a gun or grenade. I didn't expect hijackers to be so young and polite.

It seemed as if we were flying forever. We finally served non-alcoholic drinks and later something to eat. We continued flying and I was getting anxious because I knew eventually we would run out of fuel and maybe that's what they wanted to do.

Much later I heard we were going to Beirut. I was relieved; we were finally going to land somewhere and probably get off the plane. My thoughts were positive. I was finally going to visit Beirut, which I had always wanted to do. I would go to the gold market, go to dinner and forget about the hijacking.

The happiness did not last long. When we landed in Beirut we did not get off the plane. More hijackers got on with dynamite. I began to feel really sad—and terribly worried. We were going to be flying with a plane full of dynamite. We departed Beirut with the two original hijackers and an explosives man. What was going to happen to us?

The hijackers wanted to go to Amman to blow up the plane. I remember flying and flying. Meanwhile, a hijacker was stringing the dynamite fuses between the seats. I wanted to go to the lavatory in the aft end of the plane. The hijacker told me not to go in there, it was full of explosives. He told me to use one in the front. It was a very uncomfortable time.

When the hijackers finally agreed to land in Cairo, the In-flight Director called the crew together and informed us of the plan. After touchdown we would have eight minutes before the plane would blow up. We were to gather the passengers in groups near the doors and start the evacuation as soon as the plane stopped. I thought it was strange that we were so calm in such a dangerous situation. We gathered our group of passengers and notified them of the plan. They were to remove their shoes and go down the slides as soon as the doors opened. I took my passport and my little medal out of my purse and put them in my uniform pocket. We were ready for the evacuation.

As soon as the plane stopped, I opened R4 door and the passengers evacuated. When I was going down the chute, the airplane moved and I went off the slide. I had trouble getting up. The flight attendant who evacuated in front of me came back to help me. She said, "Nellie we have to run, the plane will explode any second." It was pitch black and we ran. After running a short distance the sky lit up. I turned around and saw this massive flame shooting straight up. Buses came and took us to the terminal. That's when I realized my hands, knees and feet were scraped and my uniform was torn. It was a happy moment when we heard that everyone had got off the airplane. We lost our possessions and our shoes but we were alive and safe.

While we waited for the plane that would take us back to New York, I was asked to go to a First Aid area that had been set up to examine the injured. I wasn't about to separate from my crew, so the purser went with me. I had some bumps and bruises but nothing that would keep me from going home!

The special airplane, designated Cobus 07, arrived in Cairo. Two and half hours later, it departed for Rome with the crew and passengers of Flight 93 (minus the 4 passengers that remained hospitalized in Cairo.) In Rome, some passengers disembarked to take connecting flights to their points of origin. At 3 p.m. (EST), Cobus 07 left Rome. We were going home.

The crew of the doomed Boeing 747 aircraft, N752PA, *Clipper Fortune*, was Captain John Priddy, First Officer Pat Levix, Flight Engineer Julis Dzeuba, In-flight Director John Ferruigo, Pursers Augusta Schneider and Jan Schreiber, Stewardesses: Jan Williams, Eileen Lonergan, Gabriella Remy, Nelida Perez, Sharon Fletcher, Carlene Pokora, Ruth List, Mary Auram, Bonnie Trustin, and Stewardess Trainees Sybille Frein Von Fricks and Lisa Hansen. The deadheading operating crew that assisted with the evacuation was Paul Lacchapelle, Donald McKay, Geraldo Fitzgerald and Charles Simpson.

Nelida was based in New York from 1967 to 1970 as a Special Services Representative and from 1970 to 1982 as a Flight Attendant, then transferred to Miami in 1982 to 1991. Her length of service with Pan Am was 24 years and eight months. She lives in Miami with her husband, Joe, a retired Pan Am avionics manager.

Courtesy of the Author

RIO REMEMBRANCES

By Joseph Sims

Pan Am's Man in Rio

In the early 1960s I moved from Washington, DC to Rio de Janeiro, Brazil, to become a foreign correspondent—a dream I had held since working as a reporter on two daily newspapers in my native Illinois.

My first real gig was with the Rio Bureau of United Press International, where I covered the military coup/revolution that overthrew leftist president João Goulart. I later became managing editor of the English language daily, the Brazil Herald. About a year into that job, another foreign correspondent and a close friend told me he had been offered two good-paying PR jobs: one with IT&T, the other with Pan American World Airways. He had decided to take the IT&T job in Santiago, Chile, and he said he would recommend me to Pan Am Vice President Roger Wolin for the airline job, which would be based in Rio. He told me the pay would be much more than I was receiving as a journalist, so I said, "Yeah, go ahead and give them my name!"

A few days later, I had a long-distance phone call from Miami. It was Roger Wolin, and he said he was really interested in hiring me, mainly because I had wire service experience, which he felt was extremely important for a PR professional. But then he gave me the bad news: Roger was a close, personal friend of John Montgomery, the owner of the Brazil Herald and also a daily newspaper in Junction City, Kansas.

"There is no way I can hire you away from my friend, John. The only way we can make this happen is for you to quit your job. Then we wait a week or so, and I'll fly you up to Miami and hire you here."

Gulp. What if I quit and this guy changes his mind, I asked myself? Where does that leave me? The most obvious answer to that question was, "up the creek without a paddle!" At this point, though, my Brazilian wife and I had four sons, and we could sure use a big pay boost.

"Okay, I told him, I'll resign tomorrow then wait to hear from you."

Sure enough, Roger flew me up to Miami a few days later, and we met in his office. Thank heavens he still wanted to hire me.

"I don't have a big budget," he said. "What kind of salary are you seeking?" I thought about that and decided to ask for $8,500, which was $1,000 more than I was making at the Herald. I hoped it was in his ballpark. "Well, tell you what. I'll hire you at $10,000, but don't come in here every year asking for a pay raise!"

Pan Am Poster circa 1938.

Wow! I said to myself. I've hit pay dirt! I'm going to work for Juan Trippe and the most prominent airline in the world and they're going to pay me more than I asked for!

When I joined Pan Am, the airline was the biggest in Latin America. Braniff and state-owned Varig were our chief competitors in Brazil, but Pan Am was head and shoulders above them. I was there when Pan Am became the first customer for the Boeing 747 wide body jet, and I helped do the advance PR work when they introduced the Boeing 727 to the Caribbean.

In the airline PR business, one has many opportunities to meet and help lots of interesting people, including many celebrities. The folks I met included Danny Kaye, Janet Leigh, Claudia Cardinale, and Maria Cole (Nat King Cole's wife). But the celebrity who most marked my Pan Am career was Grammy-award winner Roberto Carlos.

The Brazilian rock star was shooting a film, entitled "Ritmo de Aventura," about a singer in Rio de Janeiro who is kidnapped by an international gang and taken to New York. The producer approached me with a deal: Pan Am would fly Roberto Carlos, his crew and some props to New York and, in return, Pan Am's new 747 jet would be featured in scenes taking off from Rio's Galeão International Airport and landing at JFK. I decided to accompany the crew to New York to make sure all went well. We landed safely at JFK, but soon discovered the props were not on the plane! I panicked. The producer and some of the crew members were stomping around and shaking their fists at me and the Pan Am cargo guy. I was learning some Portuguese swear words I had never heard before. There was talk about suing the airline for any expenses incurred by the delay. Roberto Carlos was completely calm, though.

"Don't worry, guys, Joe will take care of it, won't you Joe?"

"Sure," I reassured them.

It was late at night so we all checked in at our hotel. I was awake most of the night asking myself, "What am I going to do?" Early the next morning, I got a call from the producer telling me they were going to shoot some scenes in Manhattan where the props were not needed. "But," he said menacingly, "Pan Am had better find those props by Tuesday or you're going to be in real trouble!" I rushed over to the Pan Am building and caught the next helicopter to JFK to see if the props had been found. No such luck. I got on the phone to Rio. They weren't there either. Now I was really starting to sweat. Maybe the easiest thing would be to resign my job, hitchhike back to Illinois and return to journalism. Reporters and editors just don't have these kinds of problems, I told myself.

Later that afternoon, the miracle I had been praying for happened. I got a call from Pan Am's PR chief in Caracas, Venezuela. "Hey, we found this huge container of stuff with your name on it. Shall we ship it back to Rio for you or to JFK?" The container with the props arrived safe and sound the next day, and I helped clear them through customs.

That night, Roberto Carlos playfully slapped me on my back and told his crew, "See, I told you Joe would take care of this!"

The film became a big hit in Latin America, but I made a mental note: never offer to help make another movie.

Joe does free-lance writing assignments from his San Diego home.

ESCAPE FROM SAIGON – WITH TWINS

By Clark (Scottie) Scott

A Manila Diversion and 'Escape from Saigon'

Following a vacation safari in Kenya in 1970, my wife Judith and I continued to Sydney for a scheduled meeting with my regional boss Hank Auerbach to discuss a transfer out of Saigon, where I had been working as assistant to the Airport Manager since 1968.

On arrival, we learned that Hank had been called back to New York City and I thought we might as well make the most of the trip and see the sights in Sydney until Judith unexpectedly became sick with a serious stomach illness. We called the hotel doctor who prescribed some 'relaxant' medication with advice to decrease the dosage should any reactions develop. The next day, Judith was not much better so we decided to take the next non-stop Pan Am flight from Sydney to Hong Kong and connect with an R&R flight back to Saigon. En route, Judith seemed to get worse and developed breathing problems. An onboard announcement calling for a doctor produced a response from a passenger who was a doctor in Hong Kong. He advised giving her oxygen which seemed to help, but she was still in some distress.

A diversion to Manila International Airport was requested and initially denied since MNL was closed following a severe typhoon which had just blown through a few hours earlier, leaving the airport damaged, without power and partially flooded. The captain insisted there was an en-route medical emergency which required landing, so the runway was lit with smudge pots and bonfires, since there was no electrical power. We landed. On the ground, there were extended discussions and negotiation whether Judith could be offloaded. In the end, permission was denied and the aircraft was told to refuel and continue to Hong Kong. By this time, Judith seemed to be recovering and calmed, so no longer as worried about her health, we were able to continue the journey.

Courtesy of the Author

Clark and Judith Scott and their twins.

66

We arrived in Hong Kong, and made the transfer to Tan Son Nhut Airport in Saigon (SGN). I took Judith to the US Army 3rd Field Hospital, and there learned the source of all her stomach ailments which she was continuing to experience. She was expecting a baby, actually turned out to be two babies, with twins Candice and Sean to be born in June!

This story sets up the scene for the following: fast forward eight months later. The twins were born in Saigon; that wasn't planned, as we had arranged for Judith to go to Bangkok and for 'the baby' to be delivered at the large well equipped Seventh Adventist Hospital. However, we decided the trip would be too risky. When Judith was ready to deliver, the ambulance made it to the Army hospital accompanied by the three jeeps of MP escorts! Hence the twins were safely delivered in Saigon the following morning on 21 June 1971, and caused some attention of becoming known as the only American twins ever born in the military hospital. Judith and the twins were placed in the VIP ward and their first visitor was a famous patient from the adjoining room who was in-country with a USO group entertaining the troops. Mae West came in to see who was getting so much attention and, as she said, "upstaging her appearance in the hospital." I remember asking her why she was in the hospital and she replied... "Honey, they say I have dysentery, but I tell you it's just the plain ole sh...!"

In accordance with US law, I quickly registered the births with the US Embassy and applied for US passports, but learned I had to also apply for Vietnamese papers, which would be required for the twins to exit from Vietnam. The processing for an exit visa for a Vietnamese national took several months, together with some liberal application of money to ensure the process was completed. At last we obtained the exit visas and planned to depart SGN for Los Angeles to my next assignment.

On the day of our planned departure, upon arrival at the terminal, we quickly began to encounter many problems and obstacles in departure immigration and customs, which were designed to delay and obstruct our departure. I quickly recognized these tactics which were observed daily being applied to local Vietnamese nationals when leaving the country. Money changed hands, but was insufficient to permit us to make our planned flight that day on PA 842. The consequences of missing that flight were catastrophic as the exit visas for the twins were valid only for that flight and for that date, meaning we would have to start all over again with new applications. While trying to comprehend all this, a Pan Am colleague and friend came to our aid and advised they had discussed the situation with another airline colleague in the terminal, the manager of China Air, and that passage had been arranged for us to 'all' depart on China Air's last flight of the day from SGN to HKG. We were told not to worry about the 'expired exit visas for the twins but to re-enter the airport complex late in the day through the military gate using a Pan Am vehicle with the twins hidden in two Pan Am flexible 'pet packs' which were common usage for carrying pets in the cabin.

We returned to Saigon and went to the Grall (French) Hospital where the pediatrician who had been caring for the twins provided some medication drops to put in their bottles to ensure they would sleep through this ordeal. At 3 pm, the time came to return to the airport and we re-entered the airbase through the military gate as arranged, passing through first Vietnamese and then US military check points; the twins in the pet packs on the floor of the Ops Van, and went direct to the office of the China Air manager. At the prescribed time after all passengers had boarded the bus to be driven to the aircraft parked in a remote location, a female China Air employee came and took both pet packs and we followed in a rush a short time afterwards accompanied by the manager.

We saw the pet packs placed in the back of an open Daihatsu tri-mobile vehicle which was commonly used on the ramp and as the female China Air employee drove down the ramp to the aircraft, my thought was, *My God, they could bounce out of the back.* In the meantime, we were rushed through (as if late passengers) and taken by the manager's sedan down the ramp to the aircraft. By time of our arrival at the aircraft, it was past departure time and with engines running, the flight was ready for immediate departure. The female employee was already going up the stairs carrying the pet packs ahead of us, while our departure papers were again checked by VN authorities at the bottom of the aircraft stairs. We were quickly cleared and being the last passengers, boarded the aircraft. The door was immediately closed behind us and before we could be seated, the aircraft began to taxi. My wife was frantic to open the pet packs and take out the babies, and although I was saying we should wait until after takeoff, she proceeded to do so. We were seated in the front row of first class with the flight attendant seated facing us.

As Judith took the first baby out of the pet pack, the stewardesses' eyes became as large as saucers in surprise, which caught the attention of other passengers in the cabin, some of whom stood up to see what was going on! There was some commotion and with nerves and emotions strained to the limit, Judith was crying as we held and began to kiss each baby as the aircraft lifted off and Vietnam became merely a memory.

Courtesy of the Author

Clark (Scottie) Scott at time of the story, was Assistant to Director Airport Services, Saigon for the years 1968-71. His Pan Am career spanned 1966 (LAX) to Dec 1991 (FRA). His last posting was Financial Controller for Eastern Europe, Africa and Middle East in the Atlantic Division Headquarters in Frankfurt. He and Judith live in suburban Washington, DC. Scottie works for the TSA today.

Judith and Scottie today.

NYET TO THE CONCORDSKI

By Tony Lutz

Meeting Andrei Tupolev at the Paris Air Show

In June 1973, I was Staff Vice President of Public Relations and had the honor to travel to the Paris Air Show at Le Bourget with our Chairman Bill Seawell, our Chief Financial Officer, Jim Maloon, and the legendary Charles Lindbergh, a member of the Board of Directors of both Pan Am and Dassault. We travelled to Paris to attend a Dassault board meeting as Pan Am was a partner with them in our business jet subsidiary division.

The Paris Air Show was—and still is—the queen of the aviation industry's shows. Industry leaders attend every two years to see the latest products and to boost the order books of the aircraft and engine manufacturers. On a Friday evening in June of 1973, Dassault threw a gala party in Paris where many dignitaries were on hand to socialize and talk business among the industry's elite. During the event, we were approached by a representative of the famous Russian aircraft engineer, Andrei Nikolayevich Tupolev, who invited us to tour the Russian version of the supersonic transport the next day. We gladly accepted.

The next day we visited the SST. It was quite a festive environment with Aeroflot stewardesses serving kilos and kilos of caviar and cases of vodka. I noted that General Lindbergh did not partake of the alcohol, but was very fascinated with the tour. We spent over half an hour getting a technical briefing from none other than Mr. Tupolev himself. The Great Russian aviator invited us to go on a demonstration flight the next day—Sunday—the beginning of the air show and its dramatic flight demonstrations. General Lindbergh somehow felt ill at ease about the invitation and on behalf of our entire group very gracefully declined. The next day, the day we had

Courtesy of Jamie Baldwin

Memorial to the Russian Crew,
who perished aboard the Tu-144.

69

been invited to go aloft on the "Concordski," it tragically crashed while making a turn in front of the world's media and horrified guests at the show.

I remember so well General Lindbergh, a kind, soft spoken man who seemed to measure every word that he spoke. He was truly saddened by the accident and showed real compassion for the Russians by repeatedly saying how truly sorry he was for this horrible disaster which ended the Soviet's pursuit of commercial supersonic flight.

Looking back, I have often thought about the internal radar Colonel Lindbergh must have had to decline the invitation. Although it is true that we would not have been on the demonstration flight which crashed, it did give me great pause to think that had it gone down with our small Pan Am group aboard, it truly would have been a dark day in American history to lose the great American Aviator in a senseless accident.

Photo from the Collection of George Hambleton

CEO Jeeb Halaby and George Hambleton with the Tu-144 in Moscow.

Courtesy of the Author

Tony volunteers at Miami's AWARE store....come and visit him.

ROME ATTACK

By Lari Hamel

Bikinis and Blankets and an Incident in Rome

When I was seven years old, my father, who worked for a large international company, was transferred from Rhode Island to Puerto Rico. We flew on Pan American for the first time and my love affair with the "World's Most Experienced Airline" officially began. The pilots invited us into the cockpit and the flight attendants gave us little medal wings and Chiclets (chewing gum). Throughout the years flying to and from Puerto Rico and becoming fluent in Spanish, the flight attendants would allow me to make the announcements. Several years later, we moved to Italy with much longer flights, thus more time to spend with the crew and I knew my goal in life, after college, was to work for Pan Am.

Bikinis and Blankets

There were so many smiles and tears throughout my career with Pan Am. At one briefing before going to Rock Sound, Eleuthera, we were told that in addition to bringing Juan Trippe, Pan Am's founder, we would be returning with a few men who were guests of Mr. Trippe. Upon landing at Rock Sound, the Station Manager came onboard and told us Mr. Trippe's guests would be staying for lunch and it would be several hours before our departure. He offered to bring the entire crew to the beach and bring us box lunches. He told us they would pick us up before boarding the passengers. Flight attendants always carry bathing suits in their tote bags even if going to Moscow in winter. We all changed into our bathing suits and wrapped ourselves with Pan Am's blankets as sarongs.

Several hours later, the Station Manager returned to pick us up and told us the passengers had already boarded. We were mortified! We tried to be upbeat boarding the airplane in our bikinis and blankets, knowing all of the passengers were Mr. Trippe's friends. As I was walking to the back of the airplane, I saw one man sitting alone in Coach in seat 15A. He stopped me and asked for a glass of water. I read the name tag on his seat and it said, "Charles Lindbergh." Astonished, I asked if he was *the* Charles Lindbergh and he replied yes, he was. Embarrassed, I explained the situation and I told him we don't normally wear bikinis and blankets. He laughed and I told him Mr. Trippe had reserved the First Class section for his friends and Mr. Lindbergh told me he doesn't fly in First Class and prefers seat 15A. He was charming and shy.

Incident in Rome

Rome, December 17, 1973: Our crew had been together all month and we had become great friends and worked well together. The night before, we had gone to the ballet to see *Giselle* with Natalie Makarova. The next day, we boarded the *Celestial Clipper* destined for Beirut and Tehran, but were delayed due to a late inbound flight from JFK. Purser Diana Perez and I were working First Class when suddenly Captain Erbeck made an announcement telling us there was trouble in the terminal and ordered us to get on the floor and stay away from the windows. I was the language-qualified flight attendant for the flight. I grabbed the p.a., threw myself on the floor translating his announcement. Diana was perched on a seat looking out a window and started screaming, "Oh my God, Lari, they're coming on the airplane!" I didn't know who they were, but I knew from her tone it wasn't good. I ran into the galley and tried to hook up the emergency slide but my hands were shaking so badly I couldn't slip the hook into the floor D-ring. There was a huge explosion as the two terrorists threw the first hand grenade. We were in a 707, a large aluminum tube and the blast was so great that I flew through the air, landing by the first row of seats in First Class. First Officer Bob Davison later told me that as I flew through the air I was shouting, "I've been hit!" Several passengers fell on top of me when the terrorists threw another grenade and then threw a white phosphorous bomb and then began shooting everyone who moved.

I was on the bottom of the pile and passed out. When I came to, it was deadly silent except for the sound of fire burning. I began screaming at the passengers on top of me to "Move, Move!" but everyone was dead. I began reaching up to dislodge them and I would grab pieces of bodies, a foot in a shoe or someone's hand. I finally managed to get out from under them, but everything in the airplane was on fire and the air was black. My contacts had burned in my eyes. I tried to get to the forward door but it was blocked by several objects on fire. I continued to cough and black out. I decided to go to the wing exits but still could not see. At one point I stood up to feel for the bump on the hat rack that would indicate the wing exit, but an oxygen bottle exploded and when I fell to the floor, I ended up back in First Class.

Despondent, I turned around and crawled toward the wing exits again. I saw a gray light through the blackness, crawled toward it and escaped. Diana died with the first explosion; we buried only her gold wings. We were later told the bombing had been done by Palestinian terrorists.

After exiting the airplane, I stood on the wing and began vomiting black material. The surviving crew was standing near the wing and was shouting, "Jump, jump! The airplane's going to explode." They had been told that plastique, an explosive, had been attached to our full fuel tanks. I jumped off the wing into the air. Dominic, the aft Purser, caught me in midair and commented, "Why, Lari, what beautiful Pucci underwear you have." "Why, thank you, Dominic," I said, to which he responded, "Let's get the hell out of here."

We began running and went to hide behind a large barrel, but there was a Carbinieri (Italy's premier police) hiding there. I started screaming at him to go after the terrorists who I had just seen boarding a Lufthansa aircraft and he replied, "They're crazy, I'm not going to get killed!"

There was a little girl around four years-old running and screaming, "Mommy, Mommy!" I ran over, hugged her, grabbed her hand, and told Dominic I was taking her to safety and I would meet up with him later. As I tried to get into the terminal, it was blocked by another Carbinieri policeman with a machine gun. He asked for my passport and I told him I didn't have one, that I had been on Pan Am 110 which was still on fire. He was adamant. No passport, no entry. Irate, I stormed past him yelling, "So shoot me, everyone else is." We found the Alitalia V.I.P. lounge, and they agreed to take the little girl. She begged me not to leave her and then I began crying. When I started to leave the lounge to return to help our passengers, everyone surrounded me, crying, hugging me in true Italian fashion, telling me that it was not safe. I returned to the area near our airplane where there were ambulances. Dominic and I started translating who needed to get in the first ambulances and began loading them. Most passengers died of burns at the hospital. We then went to Pan Am Operations and started compiling lists of where passengers were sitting, who was with whom, and who was missing. I finally found the parents of the little girl, who were hysterical with happiness knowing she was safe. We stayed at Operations until dusk. We were exhausted and finally boarded taxis to our hotel. We were all crying telling and retelling our horrific experiences. Even the taxi driver was crying. This incident in Rome proved to be my most life-changing event.

The Company told me I had been on the airplane, not for hours as I had thought, but only 22 minutes, a true miracle.

Lari was a Flight Attendant for Pan Am for 13 years, based in New York, Miami and Honolulu, and now lives in Boxford, MA.

PAN AM'S COMMUNITY ACTION PROGRAM

By Marilyn Weber Marsden

Escorting Orphans

"You'll need a Geneva convention card," I was told. "It will identify you as a 2nd Lieutenant in the Air Force. You're going into a war zone. It's required."

Marilyn (center) with Thu at Honolulu Airport.

It was 1974. America's involvement in the Vietnam War was winding down and there was fear the children of servicemen left behind would be harmed, or at best, discriminated against. A representative from The Pearl S. Buck Foundation contacted me. They needed help transporting Amerasian children from Vietnam to their adoptive parents in America. I was at the time a grounded flight attendant working as the New York Coordinator of Pan Am's Community Action Program (CAP), which was designed to help Pan Am flight attendants get involved in volunteer activities in their spare time. I was in a unique position to organize the escort program, be the first escort, and write specs for the flight attendants who would follow me. After a meeting with the Foundation, I knew how I was going to spend my next vacation.

I boarded a plane at New York with my passport, Geneva Convention Card, Immunization Card, and a carry-on bag filled with antibiotics. The antibiotics had been given to me by my brother, a doctor, to be hand-delivered to an orphanage called "Friends of the Children." It hadn't crossed my mind to be concerned about clearing customs in Saigon until I landed at Ton Son Nhat International Airport and realized the antibiotics I carried were as valuable as gold. My passage through Saigon Customs was uneventful and I was giddy with relief and anticipation knowing my first call, when I reached the hotel, would be to Rosemary Taylor, the Founder and Director of *Friends of the Children*. The hotel was modest, but clean. Bicycles by the hundreds sped by on the streets just below my open window. I made my first call.

Rosemary was waiting for me at the entrance to the nursery. I wove my way through the courtyard, which was strewn with mats covered with infants and their caregivers. Rosemary barely said hello, announced she had a sick child upstairs who was dying, and took my bag without another word and headed upstairs to save a life. My next call was to the former Army radio operator who was the Buck Foundation representative. I had expected to spend a day or two in Saigon and head back, orphan in hand. "Paperwork was delayed," he said, as though this was to be expected. Thu, the orphan, would not be ready to go for an indefinite period of time. I offered to help by walking paperwork through the bureaucracy. "No," he said, "it won't work." He was estimating a three-day delay and recommended I go sightseeing. "Go north to Nha Trang. It's beautiful up there, and there is still fighting south of Saigon. "

I then spent a few days in Saigon visiting orphanages and a hospital where a friend of my brother's was volunteering. I checked in with Al Topping, who was Pan Am's Station Director, and a great supporter of humanitarian causes.

After learning of possible further paperwork delays, I boarded a plane for Nha Trang, naïvely thinking I could hail a cab and check into a hotel and go sightseeing. I soon realized that, to the former radio operator, "a tourist spot" meant a place where soldiers weren't shooting at each other. Fortunately, I was warned by my seat mate en route that there would be no cabs and no hotels. The airport was surrounded only by sandbags. He recommended I go to the military compound and say I'm TDY (on temporary duty), which was true I guess. I did have my Geneva Convention card. I spent a day there at a nearby beautiful beach listening to what I was told by a military officer was the sound of land mines exploding.

Finally, the day came when I was to meet Thu. I went to her home, the place where she had been cared for by foster parents. Her foster father greeted me at the door and invited me in. We talked over tea as he spoke some English. He was kind and thoughtful. It was clear by the way he treated Thu, looked at her, and cared for her that parting with three year old Thu would be difficult. Soon, she would be leaving her foster parents and her little brother behind. The next day, it was time to go. Her foster father handed her over to me for the last time. The tears in his eyes seemed to say it all. "I love you and I will never see you again. I hope you are going to a loving family and that you will have a better life."

We were going on a journey from Ton Son Nhut Airport in Saigon, spending a night in Honolulu, and on to Philadelphia to her life as the child of a policeman and a stay-at-home-mom. Thu and I didn't understand each others' words, but we spoke with our eyes, and gestures, hugs and kisses and we had gotten pretty talkative by the end of our journey together.

She was tugging at the white band around her wrist which had her full name on it, Thu Nguyen Ngoc. With her eyes, and words I didn't understand, she asked me to remove it. I clipped it off and put it in my pocket. Right about then, a new world opened up to her as she gazed out the window, spellbound by the sights and sounds of take-off. I wanted to reassure her, tell her she would see her brother soon. (Another Pan Am Flight Attendant volunteer would escort him as soon as his paperwork was processed.) But we couldn't wait for him. No one knew how soon Saigon might fall. He was being adopted by the sister of Thu's mother-to-be. So they would be brother and sister by blood and first cousins by adoption. This information was out of the range of sign language. I prayed for the swift release of his paperwork and kept smiling and hugging, letting her teach me about what she liked and what scared her.

At our hotel in Honolulu I found she was frightened of running water in a bathtub. It seemed to be a brand new experience for her. She began to cry. I wrapped her in a towel and turned on cartoons on the TV, which turned unhappy Thu into smiling Thu in an instant. I had so much to learn and tried to remember everything Thu taught me on our journey so I could communicate it to her new mom. There was a knock at our hotel room door. Again my Pan Am family came through for us. A Pan Am Vietnamese flight attendant named Tu (another CAP volunteer using personal time to help) greeted us warmly and spoke to Thu in her own language. Soon after, there was another knock at the door. It was time to go.

It is a long trip from Honolulu to Philadelphia, especially with a change of aircraft. I knew I'd be tired, so I kept notes on all I learned about Thu and wanted to tell her new mother. Her adoptive parents met us at the Philadelphia Airport and took us to their home. Her new mom was blonde and bubbly and thrilled to finally have Thu home. Thu was smiling at me when I hugged her goodbye, her nametag still tucked in my pocket. She had been mine for a few days, and I have wondered many times over the last thirty-eight years, what happened to her, how she is, and did her mother tell her there was a man with tears in his eyes when she left Vietnam?

Her little brother arrived in America a month later, escorted by another Pan Am flight attendant volunteer.

Marilyn and her husband, former Pan Am Finance VP Charlie Marsden, live in New York City and Minnesota.

Courtesy of the Author

Marilyn Marsden holding Thu in Honolulu.

THE PERSIAN ODYSSEY

By David K. Redpath

The Unpublished Inside Story of A Deal That Didn't Happen

Odyssey – a long wandering voyage usually marked by many changes of fortune

My role in this Odyssey began in 1974 in the Berkshire Hills of Western Massachusetts. From there I was dispatched to Persia—the present day Iran. I was visiting family on the Columbus Day weekend when I received a call from Jim Maloon, Pan Am's Executive Vice President—Finance. At the time I was Senior Director—Investor Relations and worked directly for Jim. The message: go to Tehran

The next day, October 12th, the journey began – from Massachusetts to my home in Westchester County, to the Pan Am Building in New York City for a 3:15 pm briefing by Pan Am Chairman Bill Seawell, and then to John F. Kennedy International Airport to board Pan Am flight 110 for Tehran. Accompanying me was Willis Player, Pan Am's Senior Vice President – External Affairs and Ned Stiles, representing Pan Am's outside law firm, Cleary, Gottlieb, Steen & Hamilton.

At the time Pan Am was faced with serious financial problems including a lack of liquidity. The Company was running out of cash. In early September of 1974, Mr. Seawall was in Tehran and visited Lieutenant General Ali M. Khademi, the Managing Director of the Iran National Airlines Corporation (Iran Air). Later that month, the Chairman delivered a proposal to Gen. Khademi designed to ease Pan Am's cash crunch. The proposal said, in part, "...Pan Am

Courtesy of the Author

The Shah of Iran

would be willing to enter into an arrangement whereby the Terminal Building (at JFK) would be sold for $125 million. Pan Am would immediately lease back the Terminal for a long term, such as 21 years.....it would (also) be willing....to arrange the sale of ....(its interest in) the Pan Am Building." In addition, the proposal said, "Pan Am also would be willing to make available for purchase an equity interest (stock) in Pan Am...." The final agreement bore little resemblance to this initial proposal.

On my first trip to Tehran my colleagues and I, working out of the Inter-Continental Hotel with the help of Frank Gurney, Pan Am's Managing Director—Iran, put together a twenty page document outlining Pan Am's current situation and its outlook for the future. The document was presented to General Khademi on October 15th. A lot of activity was compressed into a very short period of time!

As the odyssey unfolded a steady stream of Pan Am Pilgrims made the journey between New York and the Iranian Capital. I made a second trip to Iran with Jim Maloon, Pan Am board member William J. Hogan and representatives from Cleary, Gottlieb, and the Company's investment banker, Lehman Brothers. Volumes of data about the Company, its regulatory environment, and the United States airline industry were provided to the Iranian side during the course of our negotiations. The primary contact on the Iranian side turned out to be Dr. Mehdi Samii, President of the Agricultural Development Bank of Iran and advisor to the Iranians.

By late 1974, memoranda were circulating within Pan Am detailing the possibility of the Iranian side purchasing some Company debt and "$100 million, with warrants to purchase Inter-Continental Hotels Corporation for $90 million.....". By year-end, the Iranian side was suggesting they might be willing to provide Pan Am with up to $300 million.

Negotiations with Iran were a closely guarded secret within the Company. Work on a memorandum of understanding for a financial transaction, whereby Iran would provide Pan Am with $300 million, was carried out in a Company suite at the Pierre Hotel in New York City. I was present at the hotel on a number of occasions, together with Dr. Samii, Jim Maloon, and my secretary. By January of 1975, however, the press was starting to report on some aspects of the transaction, although it was apparent they did not know the full story.

In mid-January of 1975, Jim Maloon received a call from General Khademi who was in Switzerland. Jim wrote, in an unpublished manuscript, that the General "....was very excited and insisted that it was urgent and of the utmost importance that I come to Switzerland immediately. He said it was at 'His Majesty's request'". Khademi met Jim at the Zurich airport and drove him to St. Moritz where the Shah was in residence for his annual skiing vacation. Jim also wrote "....the Shah wanted the President of the United States (Gerald Ford) to state publically that the US invited and appreciated his assistance to Pan Am." Jim further wrote, "I tried to explain to both Khademi and to the Shah that I had no idea as to how or whether they could expect the President to make a statement ....I did work for a full day on various drafts of a short statement intended for the Iranians to somehow get to the President with a request that he issue it or something like it". No such statement was ever made by the President.

Nevertheless, the memorandum of understanding was eventually signed by Jim Maloon and Dr. Samii. At this point I wrote a press release. It was to go to the investor and financial community as "Investors Report, Number 75-18, May 11, 1975." An identical copy was set to be released by Public Relations to the media. Copies of the "Investors Report" and the companion Public Relations release went to press but were "locked-up" pending the expected signing of the financing document by the Iranian Government. The first paragraph of the release said, "Pan American World Airways and the Imperial Government of Iran today signed a memorandum of agreement which will provide Pan Am with $300 million." The Investors Report and the Public Relations release were never issued. At the last minute, the Iranian Government declined to sign. The story, however, was leaked to the press. The banner headline of the May 13, 1975 edition of the Wall Street Journal proclaimed, "$300 million rescue of Pan Am by Iran is about to be effected." The New York Times echoed the same story. All of this occurred only a few days before Pan American's annual shareholder meeting in San Francisco. The scene in the Board Room at the Pan Am building when it was established that Iran would not sign the agreement wasn't very pretty. I know. I was there. Bill Seawell was there.

So, what was to be the final form of the agreement? It was based on the memorandum signed by Jim Maloon and Medi Samii at the Pierre. It said (1) Iran will buy 55 percent of the stock of Inter-Continental Hotels for $55 million, (2) Iran will loan $245 million to Pan Am to purchase a portion of its debt held by institutional lenders [insurance companies], (3) Pan Am will issue warrants to purchase 6 million shares of Pan Am stock and finally, (4) so long as the loan is outstanding, or Iran holds stock, Pan Am will include on management's slate of board of director nominees one person designated by Iran.

Here is the core of the drama: the institutional investors held senior Pan Am debt. They imposed very restrictive terms on what Pan Am could do financially. Because of the Company's precarious financial position, they were seeking to impose even greater restrictions. They were fearful the Company would fail and they would lose their investment therein or have it significantly devalued. With an infusion of Iranian capital Pan Am would propose to buy back this debt, but at a discount. The insurance companies would take a loss but rid themselves of a risky investment. (Insurance companies holding about seventy percent of the outstanding debt were agreeable to being bought out at a discount.) Some of the insurance debt was scheduled to be retired within a few years and it appeared unlikely the Company would have the cash to retire it.

Through at least the end of 1975 efforts were made to put the deal back together. It didn't happen. But why did the Iranian side decide not to sign the agreement? Jim Maloon's explanation: ".....in addition to the reluctance of an important institutional lender......there was also a beginning perception in Iran and with people around the Shah.....that (despite) the immense increase in oil revenues.....(they were) going to be inadequate for the commitments which had been made (by Iran)....perhaps accompanied by a fair amount of corruption, the Shah (was placed)....in the position where he was going to have to cut back on some of his plans for development."

The real reason may have been captured in a little remembered article in the April 28, 1975 issue of *Time Magazine*. It said, "The Iranians demanded that General Ali Khademi, chief executive of Iran Air, also be added to Pan Am's Board." Jim told me he delivered the message to the General that this was not possible. The head of a foreign carrier could not be on the board of a US carrier. Jim's description of that encounter was also not very pretty.

Courtesy of the Author

David K. Redpath today
at Lake George, NY.

David was with Pan Am for seven years. His last position was Assistant Treasurer, International. He and his wife, Kathy, live in Lake George, NY.

OPERATION BABYLIFT

By John McGhee

Airlifting Orphans from Vietnam

It was April 1975. We were pulling our troops out of Vietnam. I was in my 12th year with Pan American World Airways and I lived in Tokyo, Japan.

In Tokyo, we lived in a Pan Am compound with fellow employees and carpooled to work. As was the tradition in many overseas posts, we worked a half day on Saturday. Because of the International Date Line, we needed Saturday to see what went on at the Pan Am Building Headquarters in New York the day before and if necessary, respond to them when they opened for business on Monday morning.

One Saturday, Malcolm MacDonald, Regional Managing Director, James P. O'Hagan, Director of Maintenance and I, Director of Marketing, all arrived at the Pan Am office. We learned the Guam flight, a Boeing 747 had been canceled and was going to be operated as a charter flight to Tan Son Nhat airport in Saigon to pick up orphaned babies (American fathers, Vietnamese mothers). It was going to be a voluntary mission operating in a war zone, so the company could not assign a cabin crew; they all would have to volunteer, and several did. Jim and I said we would go as did two sales staff from Honolulu who happened to be in Japan for orientation and training. I asked our Japanese reservations staff if anyone wanted to volunteer and five of these agreed to help as well. Keep in mind the Vietnam conflict was not Japan's war and the sympathy that one might have as a US citizen was not in evidence locally.

We drove to Haneda airport. Once there, we had the insight to take a supply of boxes normally held in the check-in area to accommodate passengers who arrived with too many bits and pieces. We departed on our seven-hour flight to Saigon shortly thereafter. While en route, we placed the check-in boxes on the

Courtesy of the Author

Almost 750 babies and tots crammed into two Pan Am 747s.

80

floor between the seat back and seat, and put a pillow and a blanket in each box. This was where we were going to place the babies on the return flight.

As we flew we talked about a US Air Force C-5A Galaxy that crashed the day before with babies on board. We also had read an article in the US military newspaper, *Stars & Stripes*, where World Airways President Ed Daly was aboard a Boeing 727 in Da Nang that had started its takeoff roll under heavy fire with the back airstairs still down. A picture was snapped of Daly using a 45 caliber pistol to fend off additional people trying to board the aircraft. This led to concern that our aircraft could be rushed by people trying to depart Saigon before the North captured the city. As a safety measure, Jim O'Hagan climbed down from the First Class compartment to lock the belly doors from inside. Once on the ground, Jim and I had no weapons so we positioned ourselves with fire extinguishers at L-1 thinking we could deny entrance by spraying them.

Anxiously we waited; the door opened and we were pleased to see an orderly assembly of people including Bill Cowden the Regional Managing Director and Al Topping, Director of Vietnam. Buses drove to the aircraft and we all ran down the stairs. A baby or two with his or her ditty bag of possessions were put into our arms and we ran up the stairs and placed a baby in a box. After what seemed little more than an hour, we had 350 souls on board but none were visible. Against policy, we also took the Vietnamese wife and two children of the Saigon Maintenance Manager onboard. The Vietnamese had confiscated their US Passports, but it seemed like the right thing to do.

Official White House photo

President Gerald Ford meets the Clipper – and babies – in San Francisco.

Once airborne we began to feed the babies starting at the front of the aircraft working our way back. By the time we got them all fed, diarrhea had broken out either from the boarding excitement or the unfamiliar formula, so our next job was to change 350 diapers starting from the front to the back. After several hours of this the only place to get a breath of good air was in the toilets. We touched down at 3:00 a.m. at Yokota, a US Air Force Base near Tokyo. Japanese Public Health Inspectors came aboard and ascertained that measles were on board and requested that all personnel deplaning in Japan go into a two week quarantine period. Fortunately my title and the prestige of Pan Am provided enough pressure to convince the Public Health staff to appoint me responsible for letting them know of any illness. Wrapping the maintenance manager's wife and children in blankets, we slipped them off the aircraft and into a PAA station wagon that had come up from Haneda to meet the flight. We knew we were bringing them into the country illegally, but after all, this was war.

A crew of Air Force nurses took over the responsibility of caring for the babies as the aircraft flight departed with a fresh Pan Am operating crew. On April 5, 1975, President Ford met the flight, which was designated Clipper 1742, in San Francisco, and welcomed these young souls into the United States.

Once back at the Pan Am compound we reported to the Managing Director that we had sneaked the family of the Saigon employee into the country, but felt that no one had seen us. He advised us to report it to

Japanese Immigration authorities the next day, which we did. The next day *Stars & Stripes* had a photo on the front page with the headline "Mystery Woman Enters Japan." It seems we had caused an international incident and as a consequence, had to formally apologize with cap in hand to the Japanese Government. A simple enough punishment for what we still think was the right thing to do.

Over the years, I often wondered if we did the proper thing by removing the babies from the country of their birth, but the prevailing thought at the time was that they would be killed or severely ostracized as social misfits being children of American fathers and Vietnamese mothers.

I felt fully exonerated when in April 2005 I attended the 30th reunion of the Last Flight Out held in Washington, DC. Former Pan Am staff mingled with the babies, now young adults. Several were medical doctors, one was a CNN broadcaster, and there were other bright and accomplished young Americans who just happened to have been born in Vietnam.

John McGhee spent 19 of his 26 years with Pan Am living and working in Liberia, Germany, Japan, Australia and Great Britain. His last posting was Divisional Director, UK, Benelux and Northern Europe. He is now retired in Arizona after ending his long airline career with Japan Airlines.

Courtesy of the Author

A PLANELOAD OF BABIES

By Karen Walker Ryan

Working an Operation Babylift Flight for Pan Am

Our crew climbed onto the crew bus in Hong Kong that fourth day of April, after a particularly long day of flying from Delhi via Bangkok, long because we had to avoid the war raging in Vietnam. We had all seen the news reports of Da Nang falling that spring of '75; desperate Vietnamese clinging to the wheels of ascending (and retreating) US jets, only to fall to their deaths. But Vietnam was not on my radar that day, only a long, hot bath at the hotel and the pleasure of heading towards home next day. Then, a telegram from head office was handed aboard. We all sunk into the bus seats in shock and exhaustion as it was read:

Courtesy of the Author

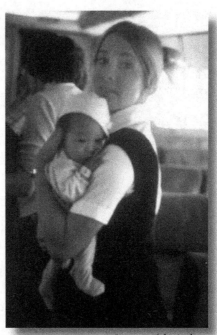

Courtesy of the Author

Karen Walker Ryan at the door on the left and with a baby in the cabin on the right.

"Scheduled pattern cancelled. Depart April 5 for Saigon to pick up orphan charter. Two-hundred-ninety five infants, 100 children between two and 12 years, 60 escorts—five doctors—10 nurses. Place infants two per bassinet under middle seats. Use only Zones C-D to insure constant surveillance..."

At the Hong Kong Hyatt we watched television footage of the smoking wreckage of a US Air Force C-5A which crashed that very day on takeoff from Saigon with 328 babies aboard, almost half of whom perished. We went to bed that night not knowing if that plane had been shot down, but we knew "high sources" had given South Vietnam only days until they would be engulfed by the army from the North.

The next morning we boarded an empty, spotless 747, a crew of nine stewardesses (three had declined), three pilots and 10 volunteers from Hong Kong. The 90 minute flight was crazyily busy as we put together cardboard bassinets, filled cartons of baby bottles with formula (oh, if we had only known about lactose intolerance!), positioned barrels of clothing and bags of diapers for the mind-boggling number of infants we would soon deal with. Upstairs, where the wealthy dine on lobster and cherries jubilee, our team of doctors and nurses were uncoiling IV tubing, syringes and setting up a serious ER.

Preparing dinner for 350 special passengers

Like a Boeing test pilot, our captain dive-bombed the runway at Saigon's Tan Son Nhut airport and taxied past the smoking wreckage of the giant C-5A. No other US jets were on the ground. We parked far from the terminal and watched as several battered buses pulled up to our ramp. Little faces looked up at us in our six story, climate controlled majesty of a jet. Then we opened the door. The torrent of heat was intense and quickly overwhelmed our air conditioning. And the onslaught of little bodies being carried up the ramp and thrust into our arms brought tears to our eyes. All we could do was lay them on seats or in bassinets under the seats and turn around and take the next bundle of hot and crying child. I have never seen so many very ill and malnourished babies; some looked to be at death's door. Then came the older children, many of them also emaciated or somehow injured, most of them extremely upset. The roar of outrage at their situation reached a high crescendo as we frantically tried to sort out who needed to go to the front for immediate medical attention, while also trying to secure the cabin for takeoff. After less than an hour of ground time, we roared straight up and out of there, spreading our arms over as many babies as we could; FAA rules be damned.

As the cabin cooled down, babies were fed and exhausted calm overtook many of them. We had hot meals for the older children whom we served while dodging midget bodies crawling in the aisles and took innumerable tackles from small torsos wanting a hug not a hamburger. Babies found their thumbs and grew quiet as the vibration of the engines lulled them to sleep now that their tummies were full of warm milk. (It would be the next leg of this historic flight where it would become clear that milk did not agree with many of them.) We constantly peeked into bassinets to make sure each baby was still breathing. I froze as I flashed my light on each little back, waiting for what seemed like hours to see a ribcage move with the breath of life.

Five hours later, I heard the familiar whine of the engines as we descended to Guam. I couldn't imagine how we would cope if anything went wrong with this landing, but the pilots set us down as lightly as a feather. It was 3 a.m. and 18 hours since we first boarded that spotless 747 in Hong Kong. A grim, fresh crew came aboard and observed the littered plane with sleeping little bodies everywhere. Then, a child whimpered, a tiny hand reached for manicured fingers and the grim faces flushed with tenderness. And then we departed, changed forever by our experiences.

After reaching our home bases of either Los Angeles or San Francisco a few days later, we were all ordered to quarantine ourselves for a month because of the various diseases to which we had been exposed. It was during this enforced indoor stay that I wrote about my experience with Operation Babylift. In May of 1976 Reader's Digest published it. I received letters from all over the world thanking me, and many were from adoptive parents telling me about the progress their children were making. I treasured them. I quit flying in 1978 when the commute from Missoula, MT, where I was then living, was getting to be tough, plus our planes were getting blown up in the Middle East with alarming regularity. It seemed time to move on.

In 1999, out of the blue, Reader's Digest found me—no easy task, as I had dropped my maiden name for my husband's name. We were raising a son and ranching in Montana. I was asked: *Did I know what happened to those babies?* I had not a clue, although I had certainly thought of them often over the years—and my box of letters after the '76 article had disappeared in one of my moves. "Well, find out," said the editor, "and let's do an article for the 25th anniversary of the fall of Saigon and end of the Vietnam War."

I had not known there was a group of former Pan Am flight attendants who called themselves World Wings International and had chapters around the world that met regularly. I thought all my memories and experiences of the most glamorous job in the world were meant to be my memories only. But find them I did, and these amazing former Pan Amers guided me to Holt Adoption Agency in Eugene, OR who orchestrated much of Operation Babylift and the adoptions of the children. World Wings welcomed me into their fold and also put me in touch with other flight attendants who shared that historic flight with me. I was also honored to meet Al Topping, who was Pan Am's station manager in Saigon in '75. He was largely responsible for cutting through South Vietnam government red tape to fill our big birds with these littlest of chicks. He also managed to smuggle aboard quite a few of our local Pan Am employees and their families, at much risk to himself.

I am now very close to many of these very sharp, witty and wonderful young Americans who made up Operation Babylift. It led to some very emotional reunions and my picture on the cover of the May 2000 issue of Reader's Digest (oh, if my folks had been alive to see that!). A tearful reunion on Good Morning America with three of the adoptees, a long piece on CNN's Paula Zahn show and several newspaper and magazine articles about our flight from Saigon followed. I truly had my fifteen minutes of fame.

The families who adopted these children in need? I call them The Quiet Moral Sea. In the midst of this controversial war that tore at the social fabric of the US, at a time when Americans were largely segregated, they took in children of unknown origin and the children became theirs, completely. As they grew up, these children certainly suffered hurtful racism from the most ignorant among us. Most of them had no close relationships with anyone of Asian descent until the first adoptee reunion held in 2000. At that time, the youngest of them were turning 25. They now meet regularly and have formed several groups that offer mentoring to young adoptees of different racial backgrounds and they offer support to each other. Many of them have been back to Vietnam, if not to trace roots long eradicated by lack of paperwork, to at least get a feel for their country of birth. Some have found family members. These kids have contributed much to the melting of racial lines in our western societies.

Although that day of flying for the world's greatest airline was probably the most unglamorous of my nine year career with Pan Am, it will always stand out as the most rewarding.

Operation Babylift is generally defined as occurring from April 3-26, 1975, and brought approximately 3,300 infants and children out of Saigon to the US, Australia, France and Canada. A combination of commercial airlines and the US Air Force participated in this historic airlift.

Karen flew as a Pan Am flight attendant from 1969-1978. Now retired, she is the founder and CEO of Heartland Caregivers Inc. (www.estatestaffing.com), a worldwide estate and home staffing service and is now raising sheep with her husband in Ronan, MT.

THE DARKEST DAY

By Dorothy Kelly

On Board Clipper Victor *at Tenerife*

On the morning of March 26, 1977, I started a five-hour drive to Kennedy airport in New York to report for a 747 charter flight to Las Palmas in the Canary Islands. At the crew briefing, I met my friend Francoise who was to be the senior purser—I was the junior purser. She approached me and asked, "Would you mind working up front tonight and making the announcements? I'm so self conscious about my French accent."

"Of course I will."

She didn't survive.

The flight originated in California, stopped in Chicago, then New York. We carried 380 vacationers going on a Mediterranean cruise. *Clipper Victor* left New York early in the evening and the flight was uneventful until the captain called me to the cockpit in the morning. "We're diverting to Tenerife because of a terrorist bomb attack at Las Palmas." We landed at Los Rodeos airport and parked next to a KLM 747, named *The Rhine*.

For several hours, while we were busy caring for our passengers, a heavy fog rolled in. Another delay. Finally, we received our takeoff clearance to go to Las Palmas. While we were getting the cabin ready for departure, fellow crewmember Miguel Torrech said, "Dorothy, you haven't had anything since last night. I have fresh coffee."

"Yes, I'd love a cup of black."

He handed me a cup then slyly splashed in a dollop of milk. "You need the nourishment." He disappeared upstairs to talk with another crewmember, Mari Asai. That was the last time I saw both of them.

The one runway at the airport was also the taxiway. KLM taxied ahead of us and turned around waiting for takeoff clearance. *Clipper Victor* slowly followed the same course. Before we were off the runway, the Dutch pilot, misinterpreting a radio transmission, started his takeoff roll, speeding straight at us. Our pilots tried desperately to turn off the runway, but a 747 doesn't turn very quickly. The KLM pilot had only one option. He rotated his aircraft early, ahead of V-2, hoping he had enough speed to lift off. The 747 rose only enough to peel off the top of our plane, just like opening a sardine can. *The Rhine* crashed and burned behind us.

At the time, I was standing at the right forward door talking to a stewardess, Carla Johnson. I remember everything suddenly flying around in slow motion. I was struck on the head and fell unconscious into the cargo compartment. When I regained consciousness, I couldn't figure out where I was. It was dark and everything was distorted. Crawling around, I saw light above and slowly climbed towards it, losing my shoes. I felt as though I had just awakened in the middle of a Fellini film—confused, disturbed—and frightened.

At the top, I squeezed out onto what was left of the upper deck. A few people were wandering about so I quickly searched for other openings. There were none, as I think the aircraft was constantly readjusting to its new configuration.

"We've got to jump," I ordered. It was a daunting proposition not only because of the height (I guessed about 25 feet—the NTSB agreed), but also because of all the debris scattered below us. We jumped and survived!

People were milling around close to the airplane. "Get away, run, far away," I shouted as I also moved away to assess conditions. My vision was blurred with blood when I noticed the three other surviving flight attendants and ran towards them.

"How bad is my head?"

"It's not that bad."

Wiping the blood away, I ran back to where people were escaping from an opening in the fuselage, also over the left wing. There was fire all around now and explosions.

Something white caught my attention under the front of the airplane. While running towards it, I also noticed the left inboard engine was starting to spin out of control. What I saw was Captain Victor Grubbs.

"Can you walk?"

"No, the grass is so cool." Above us, the airplane was making ominous crunching sounds.

"We've got to get out of here, now!" Turning him over, I grabbed him under his arms and dragged him backwards. About halfway, the engine blew up, sending white hot metal flying. We were able to dodge it and I left him safely on the grass. Shortly after, the front part of the plane that we had been under moaned, turned on its side and collapsed like a great, beached whale, finally succumbing to the exhaustion of battle.

Occasionally I saw First Officer Bob Bragg going back and forth. We met up when there were no more people escaping and did a walk around the plane. People were screaming and banging on the windows, but there was no way we could get to them. The memory still haunts me. A woman was trying to crawl on her back away from the wing area where someone had moved her. She said people had been jumping on her and she was badly hurt. With only a few people left, I waved down a van and had two men carefully lift the injured woman and place her across the middle row of seats. She later became a lifelong friend.

Then I approached a man, whose clothes had been almost completely blown off, leaving only remnants of his former garments; I guided him to the front seat.

We left the airport at breakneck speed, the van driver maneuvering through the crowded streets waving a white handkerchief and blowing the horn. I knelt on the floor between the seats securing the woman with my body and left arm while holding onto the man in front with my right arm. The first hospital was full so we were sent to another. As the injured woman was carried inside on a stretcher, she begged me not to leave her. When I saw all the bodies and confusion inside, I felt compelled to help. But how? I wondered.

I kept saying, "I'm a stewardess, I can help!" repeatedly, until a doctor said, "Come with me." We entered a room with burn victims. "Get their clothes off," he said, handing me scissors. "We have to remove the burned skin."

I was working on a woman when blood started spurting out of her head. The doctor tossed me rolls of gauze telling me to press down hard, but the blood kept gushing. Grabbing a small pair of scissors, he punctured the wound then directed me to keep it twisted. With that situation under control, I continued removing skin until I got to the nails.

"Cut it off." That's when I almost lost it!

Next, I was put to work with a pen, scissors and a roll of tape. "We need as much information as possible-name, health, allergies and medications." I also thought my American accent might be welcoming to them, and I could help with their questions and concerns. A while into the process, my left hand began to weaken and my arm ached. "I must have sprained my wrist jumping off the plane," I thought and ended up tearing the tape with my teeth.

A nurse asked me to follow her to a room to be treated. The wound on my head was obvious. Dried blood made my hair stiff. I was afraid they might have to cut my hair, however they managed to clean and treat the affected areas with no damage to my vanity.

"My arm hurts," and rolled up my sleeve exposing a large bump protruding below the elbow. After radiology, the arm was set in plaster and tied up over my right shoulder with a sling.

Arriving back downstairs, the non-injured crewmembers were leaving for a hotel so I joined them. A doctor appeared and said, "You have to stay here for observation."

Feeling totally defeated, Carla sensed my mood. "I'll stay with you," she offered. An idea came to me. "I'll stay if you let me make a phone call." The doctor smiled and said "Dorothy, you drive a hard bargain." Later that evening I was able to talk to my husband and explained what happened, that I was ok, and gave him the names of the surviving crew.

So, hospital life began. Carla and I had adjoining rooms. We were talking when a nurse came in and said, "You shouldn't be alone," and wheeled Carla's bed into my room. Not long after she appeared with a tray of fruit, biscuits and cocoa. I was beginning to feel the physical effects of my injuries. My face and eyes were swollen and bruised, my scalp was tightening, my arm throbbing, not to mention the discomfort of dozens of briars in my feet!

"We have to find Captain Grubbs, he must be blaming himself for this mess." He was awake and when he saw me said, "How could I ever forget that sweet face." I noticed that even though he was bandaged like a mummy, his lips were peeling. Fortunately, I still had my Chapstick. Carla, Bob (with broken ankle), and I began our version of hospital rounds. The job seemed to carry on, they were still our passengers. A chaplain arrived, offering help and arranged for the Red Cross to deliver soap, toothbrushes and toothpaste.

Then the media arrived. They tried every trick in the book including posing as doctors. The staff finally put quarantine signs on our rooms.

On the third day, the Pan Am people arrived. Jeff Kriendler, from Public Relations and Dr. Joe Constantino, Medical Director. The question of departure arose, preferably a MEDEVAC flight, but the local authorities required passports for departure. Jeff worked some magic and soon the evacuation was ready. Carla and I watched from the window. The Captain was surrounded by media. Dr. Constantino insisted I stay at the hospital. The fourth floor was empty and the wind made an eerie sound. And once again, Carla looked at me. "Don't worry, Dorothy, I won't leave you."

Courtesy of the Author

Dorothy is now living in New York City and flies for United Airlines from its Washington-Dulles Base.

89

LAST FLIGHT OUT OF SAIGON 1975

By Al Topping

Closing SGN

During the fall of 1972 I learned that one of my goals as a member of the Pan Am management team was about to be realized. Pan Am was in the process of a worldwide reorganization resulting in significant changes in its international and domestic operations.

All of Pan Am's international destinations would now be managed by a country director. This was my aim, to be in charge of the day to day operation at a Pan Am destination as well as being the official company representative interacting with the local government officials, members of the travel industry and the commercial community at large. What I didn't know was that the opening in the Pacific Division was not going to be an island paradise.

I was the manager of Telephone Sales in San Francisco when I was offered the position as Director-Vietnam and Cambodia and would be based in Saigon, South Vietnam. My immediate response was thanks but no thanks! After all, there was a war going on. Why would anyone leave the beautiful San Francisco Bay Area and move to a third world country that was at war?

My future boss, Bill Cowden, suggested I sleep on it and, in fact, thought that I should fly to Saigon, spend a few days and then make a decision. So I did. The flight from San Francisco to Saigon took about 18 hours. When the ground time is included at the intermediate stops in Honolulu, Guam and Manila it's approximately a 22-hour trip—a long time to think about how my life would change should I decide to take the offer. After my visit and on the long flight back to San Francisco, I decided to take the position. I felt this opportunity may not come again and it was the job I really wanted.

So in November of 1972, I was in charge of the Pan Am operation in South Vietnam. Today, after all those many years I have not forgotten my first impressions. Saigon was very hot, very humid, very noisy, and due to the tens of thousands of motor bikes (the primary means of transportation), the air was polluted. The international arrivals area at the airport had dirt floors and no air conditioning. Downtown was a bustling crowded city with a variety of shops, restaurants, an open / active black market, street money changers, prostitutes and beggars roaming the streets holding babies---many of them scarred and crippled by napalm.

As for the war, there were signs of it everywhere. A tank guarded the entrance to the airport, and heavily armed troops guarded every government building. The most telling of all were the sounds of war. Every night one could hear muffled booms of shelling off in the distance. Nevertheless the war was supposedly winding down and peace talks were on-going in Paris. A peace agreement was finally reached and by June of 1973 the last American combat troops departed Vietnam. The 10,000 day war was finally over. So we thought. Optimism was in the air. The government began promoting tourism and encouraging foreign investments. Back in Washington, DC the United States Congress voted to virtually terminate all military aid to Vietnam. The South Vietnamese were now on their own.

Approximately 18 months passed and the political landscape of South Vietnam began to dramatically change. Huge chunks of South Vietnam were taken over by advancing North Vietnamese troops. Cities, provinces and villages were falling with hardly a shot being fired. It was becoming obvious to me that North Vietnam had Saigon in its cross-hairs. In early April 1975, panic was in the air.

Various American companies began sending some of their employees to places like Hong Kong and Singapore. As the situation deteriorated I convinced Pan Am to commit to evacuating all of our local staff and their immediate families. But it was up to me to come up with a plan for the actual evacuation, a workable plan that would not endanger lives. It was only later that I realized I was embarking on a decision-making process I would never forget.

Tension and suspense engulfed us as evacuation plans were being made. There were some surprises. When I asked our personnel manager for a listing of all 61 employees and their immediate family members, I was presented with a list of over 700 names. In the Asian culture, the immediate family is the extended family. Now what, I wondered? For the first time, I saw the enormity of the situation. Lives were at stake. I held some emotional, gut-wrenching meetings with our department heads. It was necessary to review again and again the company commitment of evacuating our employees and their "immediate families". It was extremely difficult to convince them of the differences in interpretations of an immediate family. In the end they would have to make the final decision as to who would go and who would stay. So it was now a matter of freedom for some and unknown consequences for others. Once the decisions were made I had a list of 315 employees and their family members. One more major challenge was lurking.

Although the government of South Vietnam was rapidly disintegrating, they were still in charge. A Vietnamese citizen could not leave the country without proper documentation. Under normal circumstances it could take two to three months for Vietnamese to obtain a passport and visa. However, we had little time left. We needed those documents in a matter of days. In the past, I had witnessed hundreds of orphans being expeditiously evacuated to the US for adoption. I soon realized evacuation was our only way out.

Our personnel manager spent countless hours at the Office of the Ministry of Interior to obtain the required documentation for adoption. My staff prepared stacks of legal documents for my signature that would also permit our Vietnamese employees to leave the country. In effect, the documents I signed said I was adopting more than 300 people, that I would be responsible for their well-being in the United States. It worked!

The situation in Saigon was now in panic mode. In order to avoid further chaos the final date and time of Pan Am's LAST FLIGHT OUT was kept secret until the night before. It was to be Thursday April 24, 1975. Most of our employees and their families spent the night in the back rooms of our downtown ticket office. Three buses brought them to the airport that morning. At the airport checkpoint armed troops boarded the buses to check the documentation. The tension in the air on those buses defied description.

The aircraft was Clipper Unity N653PA, a Boeing 747. After cramming 463 souls on board into a cabin configured with 375 seats, the LAST FLIGHT OUT lifted off the runway on the designated date. Many of the passengers doubled up in one seat. Others stood in the aisles, sat on the floor or found space in the lavatories.

The flight's departure, however, had not been assured. Shortly beforehand, the Federal Aviation Administration had banned US commercial flights into Saigon. It was not until high-level US officials had designated our flight as a US government charter that the jumbo jet could fly into Saigon to take us out. When Captain Bob Berg finally received take-off clearance and we began our take-off roll, my heart was pounding like a bass drum. The tension was overwhelming until we cleared the coastline and I could see the fleet of American warships in the South China Sea below us. At that point I said to myself, thank God we made it.

Six days later the North Vietnamese tanks rolled into Saigon. The War was finally over.

I can't commend enough our pilots and flight attendants who volunteered to operate a civilian aircraft in an active war zone, risking their own safety. They were tremendous.

Al served Pan Am in many capacities over a career spanning over 22 years. His heroics in the evacuation of Saigon were dramatized in the film "The Last Flight Out" a TV movie starring James Earl Jones as Al Topping. He and his wife, Jan, live in Miami where he enjoys as much golfing as time allows.

Courtesy of the author
Al Topping today.

TALES OF THE SOUTH PACIFIC

By Mike Merlini

An Attempted Hijacking in Sydney

This is the story of a Pan Am plane, an explosion in the outback, and a very cool customer, and it all happened in Australia, my home now for over 30 years.

But it was not just another Pan Am plane; it was a Boeing 747 SP. This "Special Performance" passenger jet had a range far greater than any of its predecessors and could fly non-stop across the Pacific. But because of this unique feature there was one unexpected disadvantage; the long range capability made it a prime target for at least one would-be hijacker. But let's start at the beginning.....

Pan Am Archives

Sydney Harbor – Dong Kingman menu cover

Chalking up another milestone in a history of many firsts, Pan Am pioneered commercial aviation to the South Pacific in 1937, slashing travel time between the US and Australasia from the number of weeks it took by ocean liner down to as many days. When Captain Edwin Musick lifted a Pan Am Clipper off the waters of San Francisco Bay he took with him the hopes of three countries joined by a common language but separated by over 7,000 miles of water and situated on opposite sides of the world. Setting down six days later on the harbor of Auckland, New Zealand, the flight was heralded as a landmark achievement in the history of commercial aviation and a huge step forward in cementing economic and cultural ties between the Americas and the South Pacific. Hard on the heels of the *China Clipper* to the Orient, Pan Am now had a route network covering the entire Pacific.

My life with Pan American World Airways started a short thirteen years later at the dizzying height of 12,500 feet. I was not, as it might seem, a crew member; I was, in fact, part of the team at the general sales agency of Pan Am and its subsidiary, Panagra in La Paz, Bolivia, a city nestled in the rarefied atmosphere of the Andes mountains . Together Pan Am and Panagra provided service around South America and, in a throwback to the earlier days of aviation, Panagra also operated a domestic network in Bolivia, serving nine towns and villages throughout the Andes and the Amazon basin with DC-3 and DC-4 aircraft. Even the airstrips were built by the two carriers themselves.

While comfort on those small Douglas aircraft in South America was not great, passengers on the trans-ocean flying boat Clippers enjoyed a level of luxury in air travel seldom seen since. However, the speed was slow, the cost was high and the passenger load was limited. So, as landing strips were built on islands across the Pacific, the Clippers were phased out and faster propeller aircraft, which were more fuel efficient and carried more passengers, were introduced. Subsequently Pan Am slashed the flying time yet again with the introduction of the 707s and, later, the 747-100s. But even these jet aircraft required refuelling en route.

For me, as it was for many of my co-workers, flexibility and mobility were important qualifications for life with the world's leading international airline, and many years after leaving La Paz, I arrived in Sydney as Pan Am's regional director of the South Pacific. I had lived and worked on five continents. I had met many dignitaries, most memorable of all being our chairman, Mr. Juan Trippe, who invited me to play golf with him at the Lima Country Club during a visit to Peru.

The introduction of the 747SPs to the South Pacific in 1976 was a record-breaking event. Although the planes were shorter in length than the 747-100s and carried fewer passengers, the ability to fly non-stop between California and Australia in roughly thirteen hours gave Pan Am a major advantage over its competitors.

And so it was that a Pan Am SP was routinely parked at a gate at Sydney airport awaiting takeoff for the afternoon flight to San Francisco. It was well before departure time, the cleaners had left and the plane was empty but was soon to be boarded. Meanwhile, back in the departure area a young lady was checking-in for an Air New Zealand flight to Auckland when a man armed with a knife burst through the main doors

Courtesy of Jamie Baldwin

Boeing 747 SP

and made a beeline for the girl. He grabbed her and, with his arm around her waist and the knife pointed at her neck, he marched her through the customs and immigration area and onto the concourse. Immigration officers did not challenge the kidnapper, fearing it would endanger the girl. The man and his hostage made their way past departure gates where several other airline flights were parked, and headed straight for the Pan Am SP. They lurched down the jetway and onto the aircraft.

Police were summoned immediately. First on the scene was Inspector John Sommers. He was soon followed by four other officers, all well trained in hostage negotiations. The man spoke only Italian so the team included an interpreter. They cautiously entered the now fully-loaded aircraft and confronted the kidnapper, but he stood firm. Still holding the girl at knifepoint with his legs tightly wrapped around her waist, he produced a beer can device with a fuse and demanded to be flown to Rome for a meeting with the Pope. He knew full well that the long range Pan Am SP was his best chance of getting there without a refuelling stop en route. But in an instant, while his attention was distracted, Inspector Sommers made a grab for the girl and dragged her from the cabin.

With the girl now free, it was decided to attack with a fire hose in order to douse any attempt to ignite the fuse from the can, but as the team rushed into the cabin the man attempted to strike a match. Instantly a shot was fired, hitting him in the shoulder and knocking him down. Even as he continued to try to strike the match, a second shot was fired at close range. He was rushed to hospital but died shortly after from a bullet wound in the head..

Ted Porter, Pan Am's Director of Public Relations in the South Pacific, attended the coroner's inquest. It concluded that the man, who had immigrated to Australia from Italy in 1973, was obviously deranged, and found that his grievance was prompted by dissatisfaction over an insurance compensation settlement following an accident. As for the policemen involved, Pan Am, in a gesture of appreciation for their actions, hosted Inspector Sommers and the other four officers, together with their wives, to a First Class all-expense paid trip around the world. Ironically, a highlight of the trip was a stopover in Rome.

The entire episode lasted a gruelling five hours. The cost was a man's life, but the plane and all others on board were saved. Two bloodstained seats were hurriedly removed by our maintenance team in order to expedite a delayed departure. The hostage, who had remained alert during her ordeal, made her way back to the departure area and calmly checked in for the evening Air New Zealand flight to Auckland. Days later a team of police took the beer can to a remote spot out of town, placed it under an old car and lit the fuse. The explosion blew the car sky high – not to 12,500 feet but well on the way.

Mr. Trippe, my golf partner, retired in 1968. I saw him for the last time in the early '70s. He was having lunch at the Bull and Bear restaurant in the Waldorf Astoria with a friend, the great American aviator and folk hero, Charles Lindbergh.

What a company!

Mike is enjoying retirement in his adopted home of Sydney.

Courtesy of the author

TRAGEDY AT TENERIFE

By Jeff Kriendler

Reacting to the Tenerife Tragedy

Although it has been exactly 34 years—to the day—as I write this, recollections of the tragic afternoon in late March 1977 are still vivid. It was a cold, rainy day, a Sunday, just like today, and I had gone to the squash courts near Wall Street in Manhattan to get some exercise. After a vigorous few games, I headed to the upper westside of Manhattan to attend my nephew's seventh birthday, a joyous event.

Courtesy of the Author

Tenerife Memorial, dedicated March 27, 2007

My sister greeted me at the door in a stunned state—she had just gotten off the phone with Pan Am's System Control (OX)—the operational nerve center of our airline—who had given her the devastating news that Pan Am had been involved in an accident with KLM Royal Dutch Airlines in the Canary Islands. I was in the public relations department at Pan Am and was the duty officer that week and would be the first person to be called in the event of an unusual occurrence which might generate media attention. This was in an era before the cell phone and my beeper was inoperative in Manhattan's subway system and therefore OX tracked me down at the party.

I immediately called OX and learned the shocking details that a Pan Am 747 had been struck by a KLM 747 while the Dutch aircraft was attempting to take off at Tenerife. I must have been like President George Bush when he got the news of 9/11 in a Florida school room while he was speaking to children. The world saw his stunned reaction but he continued on for a few moments and then took his leave. Much the same way, I gave my nephew a hug, said "hi" to his friends, and quickly swept off to return home to grab a bag of clothes and head out to New York's JFK airport.

Pan Am had immediately set up a company 707 to fly the "go-team" to Las Palmas, the main island in the Canaries and the closest operational airport. After several live television interviews, I joined the Pan Am team for the sad, seven-hour, non-stop journey to Las Palmas.

Our team consisted of various disciplines within the company. In addition to media relations, we had representatives from flight operations, in-flight services, finance, security, union representatives, insurance, and medical. The team was headed by Executive Vice President Operations Bill Waltrip. During the emotional journey, Bill briefed us on what our duties would be and reminded us of the importance to use me as the only spokesperson to the media and remain united as a group. Most importantly, he stressed the need to support the surviving crew members and passengers and protect them and show respect for local Spanish authorities under whose jurisdiction the investigation would fall.

When we arrived in Las Palmas, members of Pan Am's Madrid staff who had flown in to coordinate ground logistics met us. A bus was waiting for us to transfer the group to the port where we had a four-hour boat ride to Tenerife, where the airport was in shambles and completely shut down.

I had spent several years in the Public Relations Department but nothing could prepare me for the carnage that I saw when we arrived at the airport after being shuttled from the port in Tenerife. The charred remains of the two giant 747s littered the runway and the scene was still smoldering. There was a horrible stench of burnt human remains, although by this time, 583 bodies—or what was left of them—had been moved to an airport hangar.

Virtually all of the tarmac space at the small airport was occupied by aircraft of all types from all airlines in Europe. All of the aircraft had been diverted to Tenerife earlier that Sunday afternoon because of a bombing at Las Palmas airport in a flower shop. Fearing more explosions from Basque separatists, Las Palmas was closed and all aircraft diverted to Tenerife. The first to land had been the KLM aircraft followed closely by Pan Am's *Clipper Victor*. Eventually, some 20 aircraft would be on the ground waiting for word as to when Las Palmas would reopen.

After about three hours on the ground, KLM had obtained permission to taxi onto the runway to continue its journey to Las Palmas, followed by the Pan Am Clipper. The runway sat in a small valley adjacent to a mountain and, much like San Francisco, experienced afternoon fog around 5:30 p.m. The KLM 747 had taxied to the end of the runway and had been told to wait for takeoff clearance while the Pan Am 747 was to taxi up the runway and then exit on a taxiway and loop around to wait for KLM to take off. Without receiving take off notification, the KLM 747 began roaring down the runway, not knowing that Pan Am was headed in its direction. Although the able Pan Am crew realized too late the tragedy that was about to unfold, they tried to exit the active runway but the aircraft was clipped in the upper deck by the well carriage of KLM's massive 747 and an inferno erupted. All 283 KLM passengers and crew perished while some 300 Pan Am crew members and passengers met their fate on the Tenerife runway. Most fortunately, all three Pan Am pilots and four flight attendants survived this horrendous conflagration, although they were severely injured.

Despite life threatening injuries, Purser Dorothy Kelly managed to pull Captain Grubbs and several passengers away from the burning scene and is credited with saving their lives. The surviving crew members and passengers were taken to local hospitals and the most severely burned were evacuated two days later by a US Air Force medical evacuation transport aircraft.

To this day, the Pan Am/KLM accident is the worst in recorded history and at the time, created one of the largest media scrums ever for an individual event. What set this accident apart was the very early admission by the Dutch investigators that the KLM captain took off without permission because of a tragic mistake, much the same as running a red light in a car and having an accident at an intersection. Ironically, the captain in command of the Dutch aircraft was their chief pilot, the voice and the face of KLM to the public in a widespread advertising campaign. It was determined that he was trying to get out of Tenerife as quickly as possible to avoid having to cancel due to duty time limitations which would have stranded the return charter load from Las Palmas back to Amsterdam.

During those sad days in Tenerife, I was uplifted by the thoughts of the Pan Am crewmembers and their actions after the horrible event, particularly Dorothy, who put her life at risk to save the captain and so many others. I saw the three pilots off on the evacuation flight and visited the flight attendants at their hospital beds. After five days, we were all cleared to leave the island and once again took a boat back to Las Palmas where a 707 was waiting to take us home.

Four years ago, Dorothy and I returned to Tenerife to attend the dedication of a memorial funded and organized by the Dutch family members. On the morning of the dedication services, I fell on the steps in front of the Sheraton hotel and crushed my hip. I was rushed to a local clinic where a few days later, I was forced to have a total hip replacement—yet another personal tragedy for me in Tenerife. Dorothy was flying for United Airlines based in London and had taken the time off to come to Tenerife for the first time since the nightmare in 1977.

Like a true Pan Am family member, she called United and changed her schedule and remained in Tenerife with me until I had successfully made it through surgery, such was the dedication and friendship she had shown to her Pan Am co-worker. I have been asked many times to write a book about this series of events, but have never put these thoughts on paper until now. I would like to use this space to thank Dorothy and the other Pan Am employees who were so compassionate and professional in their handling of this tragedy. To all of us, it made us realize that life is short and one should get all one can out of each and every day.

Jeff resides in Miami Beach where he writes about aviation and tourism.

Courtesy of the Author

INTER-CONTINENTAL HOTELS

By Ruth Maron

Assignment to Africa for IHC

In May 1977, I joined Inter-Continental Hotels Corp. (IHC) as Director of Public Relations, based in the Pan Am Building in New York. Since my job would involve considerable travel and coordination with the Pan Am corporate communications staff, I was hired as a Pan Am employee with all the attendant rights and privileges – including space available travel. It was a dream job and I eagerly awaited my first trip for the company. The call came within a few short weeks. "We're sending you to Libreville," the vice president for marketing said. "Where?" I asked. "Gabon ... West Africa," he answered. Of course, my next question was "Why?"

Crew door hangers from the 1970's

Courtesy of the Author   *Courtesy of the Author*

The Libreville Inter-Continental Hotel and Conference Center was to be the site for the Organization of African Unity Conference in June. With heads of state from all over Africa – and a big contingent of press from all over the world at the event, it was decided that the new director of PR should be there to coordinate with the media.

Courtesy of the Author

Inter-Continental Hotels

I was soon advised that the Gabon consulate in New York could not issue me a visa in time for my departure. "No problem," I was told. "Someone from the hotel will meet you at arrivals with an airport visa."

After taking all my shots and inoculations, anti-malaria medication and a quick shopping trip to Bloomingdales, I was ready to go. I stood anxiously at the gate waiting for my name to be called from the stand-by list. Eventually, I was handed a boarding pass and settled in a middle seat somewhere near the rear of the crowded Boeing 707 that regularly plied the African routes. The night was long and restless. By morning we reached our first stop in Dakar. The crowds thinned. Then on to Monrovia before heading to our final destination in Libreville. By this point, the flight was nearly empty. I stretched out and the flight attendants stopped by to chat, curious about my solo trip to Libreville. I proudly told them that I was a Pan Am employee and explained the reason for my travels. I mentioned that I didn't have a visa but I would be met at the airport by someone from the hotel. The flight attendant looked worried.

A few minutes later, the Captain walked back and stopped at my seat. "I hear you don't have a visa," he said in his most nonchalant captain's voice. He calmly explained that security was tight with dignitaries like Idi Amin and Muammar Qaddafi arriving on presidential flights. He said that people arriving without the right visas were being detained at the airport and sent out on the next flight. Gulp! "Not to worry," he said. "You will deplane with the crew and we won't leave you until we are sure you are in safe hands with someone from IHC."

100

The line at the airport seemed to take forever. I stayed close to the captain and the crew as officials scoured our documents. And finally, I saw someone with a sign from IHC step forward to greet me. After a terse conversation with the Gabonese official, it was finally agreed that I could enter the country ... but they would hold my passport till an unspecified date. I said good-bye to my guardians from Pan Am and left the airport with my new guardian from IHC – somewhat reluctantly leaving my passport behind. Bleary-eyed from lack of sleep, I was soon escorted to a welcome dinner in my honor at the hotel.

The next day, the Pan Am flight departed, heading back to JFK. Later that same day, the airport was closed to commercial traffic, open only to official flights. Without a passport, I was advised that someone from the hotel would accompany me anytime I left the hotel. I was in good hands – traveling back and forth to the Conference Center and staffing the press room in the hotel. Eventually, my passport was returned and I was allowed out for some sightseeing – still under the watchful eye of IHC. My visit to Libreville was extended to ten days, until the airport reopened and I flew out on the first flight on Air Gabon, heading to the Inter-Continental Hotel in Abidjan, Ivory Coast.

My first trip for the company was a good introduction into the very special culture and values of Pan Am and IHC. Formed by Pan Am in 1947, the hotel group partnered with Pan Am as the airline opened routes throughout the world. Both could be counted on to provide a 'safe haven' for international travelers to world capitals and to developing nations. Both companies shared a strong sense of responsibility—to passengers, to guests, and to their employees. No matter where my travels took me over the next eight years, there was always a feeling of safety—a feeling of coming home—when I saw the Pan Am jets lined up at the airport or when I checked in to the Inter-Continental Hotel. I still hear that captain's voice saying, "Not to worry!"

Ruth was Director of Public Relations for IHC from 1977-1983 and resides in New Hampshire where she actively writes and consults.

Courtesy of the Author

PAN AM TURNS 50

By Pamela Hanlon

A Spectacular Flight and a Special Interview

At the time of Pan Am's fiftieth anniversary in October 1977, my job was editor of the company's monthly employee newspaper, the *Pan Am Clipper*.

Official Pan Am photo from Collection of Jamie Baldwin

Captain Mullikin, Miss Universe (left) and Miss USA (right)

Our special anniversary issue of the *Clipper* was chock-full of stories of how Pan Amers around the world were celebrating the historic day—Friday, October 28. From Key West to Hong Kong, Honolulu to Paris, banners were hung, birthday cakes were cut, and plaques were unveiled. In Sydney, the city's central Martin Place was taken over with lunch-time Pan Am-sponsored music and entertainment. London held a dinner dance for employees. In Boston, passengers were feted with champagne and corsages or boutonnieres as they boarded their flights. New York City Mayor Abraham Beame hosted Pan Am's top officials and guests, including Chairman William Seawell and his wife, Judy, at a reception in the mayor's official Gracie Mansion residence.

But the most spectacular of all the Pan Am celebrations was a record-setting round-the-world anniversary flight that hurdled both the North and South Poles. *Clipper 50*, a Boeing 747SP, carried 172 passengers, including aviation enthusiasts and Pan Am loyalists who paid $3,333 for First Class service and $2,222 for Economy; five employees selected by lottery; official guests, among them Miss Universe and Miss USA; a guitarist; caricaturist; hairdresser; members of the press; and a crew headed by Pan Am's Chief Pilot, Captain Walt Mullikin, and Astrid Seemueller on the flight service side. *Clipper 50* (in regular service, the aircraft was *Clipper New Horizons*, or N533PA) took off from San Francisco, flew over the North Pole to London, then to Capetown, South Africa, and over the South Pole to Auckland, New Zealand, before returning to San Francisco. The 26,706-mile flight was clocked in at 54 hours, 7 minutes and 12 seconds, slashing eight hours off the previous record set by a 707 in 1965. Reservations for the flight were on a first-come, first-serve basis, and the flight was sold out in less than a week after it was announced, due in large part to extensive media coverage of the dazzling plans. No one was disappointed with the experience. As *Clipper 50* taxied to the gate in San Francisco at journey's end, Captain Mullikin asked over the public address system, "Would you do it again?" His question was met with a resounding cheer of enthusiastic fliers. "Just say where and when," one passenger shouted above the rest.

In addition to stories about the company's celebratory events, the special anniversary issue of the *Clipper* included extensive coverage of Pan Am's storied past. A center spread of photos ran with the headline, "Picture Album Peek at Pan Am's Proud Past," and the *Clipper's* front page featured a reprint of the original newspaper story that had appeared in the *Key West Citizen* on October 28, 1927. The *Citizen's* headline read "Big Mail Plane Hits Hard Rain Near Havana" and it told the story of the hundreds of Key West residents who were on hand for the early morning take-off from Meacham Airport, and how, less than ninety minutes later, Cuba's President Gerardo Machado greeted the flight in rain-swept Havana. The tri-motor, carrying some 13,000 letters in seven mail bags, would have arrived earlier, the *Citizen* reported, if Cuban officials hadn't requested that the flight crew—Hugh Wells, pilot; Ed Musick, navigator; and John Johansen, engineer—fly over Morro Castle and other historic points before landing.

The special *Clipper* issue featured stories about current employees. The Personnel Department provided me with a list of the ten most senior employees at Pan Am at the time, those who had worked for the company the longest. I set about to interview each of them. Dave Taylor, who in 1977 was working as Director of Special Projects in Austin, Texas, had more years with Pan Am than any other employee. He had joined the airline forty years earlier, in 1929. Next in seniority was Andres Medina, Director of Uruguay Operations, who had come on board in 1930. Also among the "top ten" were three Miami mechanics, William Edmundson, Richard Miles and Lawrence Swazey; New York File Coordinator Eleanor Muller; Hong Kong Dispatcher Sherman Glass; San Francisco Duty Service Supervisor Robbie Robinson; and Katherine Eason, a Miami cash clerk. Eason, who had been hired in 1935, told me, "I decided I was going to work for an aviation company when I was 12 years old. My mother took me to a parade for Lindbergh in 1928. I was so taken with all the excitement that I decided right then and there—sitting on the curb of Flagler Avenue in Miami watching Charles Lindbergh ride by—that I was going to work in aviation...I had my application on file with Pan Am more than a year before I graduated from high school."

And rounding out the list of ten employees with the most seniority was a man well known and highly respected not only within Pan Am, but throughout the entire aviation industry. John Borger, Pan Am's Vice President and Chief Engineer, had joined the company in 1935 shortly after graduating from M.I.T., and had gone on to an illustrious career with the company. (John sadly passed away in August, 2011.)

Needless to say, I wanted to include an interview with John Borger in my "top ten" story. I called Borger's office and explained to his secretary that I would like to set up an interview with her boss. I would be happy to come to his office at Kennedy Airport, I told her. The next day, Borger called me. "I don't like looking back," he started the conversation. "I still have a lot to do here at Pan Am. I am a 'forward-looking' guy," he said. And besides, he told me, "I really don't have much that's going to be of interest to anybody."

Well, I knew something of John Borger's background, and I recognized that probably more than any other employee working for Pan Am at the time, Borger had stories that could top all others. He had served as Pan Am's chief engineer for years, and had helped in the development of virtually all the airline's aircraft, from the Martin 130s in the 1930s to the Boeing 377 Stratocruisers in the 1940s to the 747s. I asked a colleague in our public relations office, Jim Arey, who frequently worked with Borger, to intercede on my behalf. He called Borger.

Soon, Borger called me again. "OK", he said, he was willing to see me. "But it won't take long, because I really don't have much to say," he added. So off I went to Kennedy, tape recorder in tow, to meet Borger in his office at Hangar 14. He began to talk. Some two hours later, his secretary interrupted us to tell Borger he was due in another meeting. "Well," said the man who had forewarned me he didn't have much to say, "I guess we'll have to continue this another day." Here is how the legendary John Borger started our conversation, in his typical matter-of-fact manner:

"Just four months after I was hired, I was sent to Wake Island to help set up the base there for transpacific flights that were to come later. There were fifty-eight of us who went to Wake on the steamer North Haven, which also carried crews to build bases at Midway and Guam and set up facilities at Honolulu and Manila.

"When we arrived on the island, there was nothing...nobody...it was just barren. We had to land cargo from the open sea, haul it across one island with bulldozer-pulled sleds and barge it across a lagoon to another island.

"The plans had been carefully drawn up in New York with Navy hydrographic charts and a National Geographic article, virtually the only sources of information about Wake. The base, of course, had to be built completely from scratch. The water supply, power and refrigeration had to be installed before the ship could sail on. We lived in tents until we could build living quarters.

"I stayed there six months and returned to San Francisco on the first (eastbound) flight of the *China Clipper*.

"It was an adventure..."

Yes, it was an adventure, for sure, and probably one of the greatest that any Pan Am employee ever experienced. But like John Borger, all Pan Am employees have adventures to tell. They may not be as exotic and groundbreaking as Borger's story, but working for Pan Am left all of us filled with memories, some wonderful and exciting, and others touching and heartrending. Yes, we all have tales to tell—whether a cash clerk in Miami, a dispatcher in Hong Kong, director in Montevideo, or...editor of the *Clipper* newspaper.

Pamela worked for Pan Am for 19 years. She later went on to posts at Sheraton Hotels, United Airlines, and American Express. Now a writer, she and her husband, Charles, live in New York City and Naples, FL.

Courtesy of the Author
Pamela Hanlon

MOTHER TERESA

By Ron Marasco

Meeting Mother Teresa

It was a strange beginning that would bring us to India where over the years we had the great privilege of meeting a number of times with Blessed Mother Teresa of Calcutta.

Courtesy of the Author

In the fall of 1978 I was at lunch with Ernie Mitchell who was the International Vice President of the Transport Workers Union which represented the mechanics and much of the ground staff at Pan Am. At the time I was the management representative on the contract negotiating committee. As in most of these meetings between the union and the company, Ernie Mitchell and I agreed on very little, but I had come to know Ernie quite well and we shared some common interests in life. In the middle of one of these heated labor/management "discussions", I remember him yelling at me "Marasco! You're coming to Calcutta with me next week!" That "invitation" and the Pan Am connection greatly influenced my life until this day.

Ernie had a cousin, a Sister Cecilia Kenny, who was the Mother Superior in northern India of a missionary order called the Sisters of Saint Joseph of Cluny. The order is represented throughout the world, but particularly well in India. Sister Cecilia was based at a boarding school for girls called Lavinia House in a very poor section of Calcutta and just about a mile up the road from Mother Teresa's Mother House. We were going to visit her!

Flying Pan Am to Bombay (now Mumbai) and then on to Calcutta (now Kolkata) via Indian Airways in those days, even for experienced airline people, was quite an experience. Time and space does not permit a complete description of these trips but in the late 1970s they were quite eventful. On our first trip we arrived at Lavinia House around midnight after an eventful taxi ride from the airport. That trip was the beginning of dozens of visits we'd make to Calcutta, Lavinia House and Mother Teresa's Mother House over the next 33 years.

While our involvement was with the Sisters of Cluny, Mother Teresa and many of her Sisters were great friends with the Sisters who taught and managed Lavinia House. As a result of their loving friendship and close cooperation with Mother Teresa's Missionaries of Charity, we were very privileged to have a number of private visits with Mother over the years. We always met with Mother in a small room just off of her living quarters in the Mother House for the Missionaries of Charity. Mother was small in stature with a humble demeanor and she would always greet us warmly and affectionately. She was a good conversationalist and would put us at ease. But during these visits we were always in awe and in admiration of the many works of charity her Sisters performed in Calcutta and throughout the world. Through sheer untiring work and devotion, Mother and her Sisters were a huge physical presence throughout the streets of Calcutta.

At the beginning of our visits to Calcutta we brought many boxes of all kinds of things. All of this was made possible with the assistance of the Pan Am's cargo people and the many station people who helped us along the way. What we brought with us in those early years would be impossible to do today. In later years and today our help has been primarily financial, made possible by many family members and friends. However, in this type

John McCoy Watercolor of Inaugural Boeing 747 Flight

of environment even small contributions go a long way in touching many people. But apart from material things, most importantly we've shared this bond of love with many of these saintly Sisters for over 30 years.

Our Lavinia Sisters were very aware that our many visits and involvement were made possible through Pan Am and many of them flew Pan Am when they traveled out of the country. In fact, in later years and before her death, Pan Am provided Mother Teresa with free travel throughout the world. Until Pan Am stopped flying in the early 90's Pan Am airplanes were always a comforting symbol to people traveling throughout the world, especially in far off places like India. I vividly remember my youngest daughter on one of our trips to Calcutta, which was slightly intimidating for a young girl, saying to me when we boarded the aircraft in Bombay, "Daddy I'm so happy to see our 'Blue Ball' again!"

Ernie Mitchell and I, the respective labor and management representatives were indeed a very "unholy alliance" of characters. So it was ironic that we were able to be involved with a 20th century Saint in a "holy alliance" in a distant place in the world like Calcutta, India, all of which was made possible by the generous heart of the people of our beloved Pan Am.

A Segue:

Whenever individuals and companies are faced with great challenges they often seek various aspects of motivational or inspirational support. The beginning of Pan Am's Boeing 747 operation definitely required a deep and abiding faith in its future operation both from its people and the company, that someone like Mother Teresa exemplified throughout her life.

It is probably a stretch to say that without Pan Am there would not have been a Boeing 747 aircraft, but clearly without Pan Am it would have been many years later. Pan Am was the lead airline customer that triggered the production of the aircraft, and in fact Pan Am took delivery of twenty-five 747 aircraft in less than one year after the aircraft was in production. During the 1970s Pan Am was the largest 747 operator in the world.

A snowbird, Ron is retired and lives in Easthampton, Long Island in the summer and Florida in the winter.

Courtesy of the Author

NO LONGER "THE CHOSEN INSTRUMENT"

By John McCaffrey
Pan Am and Deregulation

I joined Pan Am in 1978 midway through my 40 years with the airline industry after spending the first 18 years of my career with American Airlines. Bruce Cunningham, Pan Am's System Director for Airline Planning, had worked with me at American and urged me to join Pan Am. He thought I could help the airline cope with the challenges it would face as a result of the expected deregulation of the industry.

I remained with Pan Am for 13 years, until it filed for bankruptcy in 1991. During my time at Pan Am my focus was on expanding the carrier's domestic and international route structures through route awards,

Courtesy of Jamie Baldwin

The old Civil Aeronautics Board Building, Connecticut Avenue, Washington D.C.

mergers and bilateral agreements. My most memorable projects were the 1980 Pan Am – National Merger, the 1981 acquisition of the New York – China route, and the development of the routes between the USSR and the United States from 1986 to 1988.

As anticipated, airline deregulation arrived soon after I did when President Carter signed the Airline Deregulation Act of 1978 on October 24, 1978. For many years, Pan Am had enjoyed its position as the "Chosen Instrument" for US foreign air routes. Pan Am had served the US government well in a supportive role internationally and had become accustomed to receiving governmental support during the Cold War years. The price it paid for its unique international position was continual rejections by the Civil Aeronautics Board (CAB) of its requests to acquire domestic routes.

Pan Am alone, among all the US carriers, had been the strongest supporter of deregulation because it believed deregulation would allow it, for the first time, to compete freely in the US domestic market. What it did not fully understand was the government's intention to end Pan Am's international advantage and to have it compete on its international routes, not only with foreign carriers, but also with domestic carriers. Under the new rules, Pan Am's protected international base was also to be open to competition.

Thus, the US government now wanted Pan Am to compete against US carriers internationally. Pan Am had great strengths in the US, but its large 747 fleet, which was particularly well suited to international traffic, was not well suited for the thinner domestic routes. In addition, Pan Am was not well positioned to meet the challenges of the more competitive domestic market place that was emerging. It was accustomed to receiving traffic from other carriers for feed at its major distribution points in Los Angeles and New York, but it had been denied any route rights within the continental US In addition, to an antiquated large equipment program based on 747s and L-1011s and an antiquated automation system, the rigid work rules imposed on its labor force, which was represented mostly by the Teamsters Union, made it even more difficult to function within its new environment.

During the transition to deregulation, the Civil Aeronautics Board was under the leadership of Alfred Kahn and Elizabeth Bailey. Kahn, who at one time said, "Pan Am can go to hell," was no friend of Pan Am. Although he and Bailey were both delighted to receive support from Pan Am where needed, both saw Pan Am as a distinct threat to the increased competition they wanted to foster in the international arena. The CAB was reluctant to grant Pan Am the authority to establish internal gateways to feed its international routes. Pan Am's US competitors had already established their own hub systems at internal gateways, such as Chicago in the case of United, Dallas/Ft. Worth in the case of American Airlines, Atlanta in the case of Delta, and Houston in the case of Continental. It was from these virtually impenetrable hubs that each offered growing resistance to any feed that Pan Am wished to acquire to support its large 747 fleet. As a result, Pan Am had to compete for feed at its international gateways in Los Angeles, San Francisco and New York, but was denied authority to feed passengers by the domestic carriers from the internal gateways.

Because of the domestic barriers it continued to face, Pan Am's initial efforts after deregulation focused on increasing its access to its coastal gateways. The first case we worked on after my arrival at Pan Am was the application to the CAB for the rights to flow traffic from coast to coast within the US from New York and Boston to San Francisco and Los Angeles. The acquisition of these rights was critical to its ability to compete in the new world of deregulation.

The important players in Pan Am' struggle against its domestic barriers were Pan Am's law firm, Verner, Liipfert, Bernhard, McPherson & Hand, Pan Am's senior vice president, Elihu Shott, and its general counsel, Tom Cody. The Verner, Liipfert law firm had enormous regulatory experience and had the political connections needed to get the job done. Elihu was not only a bright and able lawyer, but had an incredible skill at making words flow quickly, concisely and with great passion. Tom was a skillful attorney with good political instincts and the ability to enhance Pan Am's domestic opportunities.

Pan Am's bid to acquire the transcontinental routes was successful. Unfortunately, it was not sufficient. Pan Am needed a domestic feeder base that would support its domestic flights within the US. It appeared that the only way Pan Am would be able to establish a domestic feeder base would be to acquire another airline that already had a domestic feeder system. Pan Am chose National Airlines among various contenders. It acquired National Airlines for $400 million in 1980 after a fierce bidding war with Frank Lorenzo's Texas International Airlines and Frank Borman's Eastern Airlines. The consummation of the acquisition and the subsequent merger of the two airlines required the consent of the CAB. Again, with the help of Verner Liipfert, Bernhard, McPherson & Hand, Pan Am succeeded.

The merger of Pan Am and National was not an unmitigated success. It was complicated by the unhappiness of the employees of both carriers. A caller to reservations who identified himself as an employee of the airline would be asked whether he was blue (for Pan Am) or orange (for National). The answering time would largely depend on the answer he gave. Service suffered immeasurably. In addition, Pan Am's fleet which consisted mostly of wide bodied international equipment was incompatible with National's DC-10s.

In 1980 China and the US signed a bilateral aviation agreement. Under the agreement, only one US airline would be permitted to fly to China during the first several years after the agreement was signed. A number of US airlines, including Pan Am and Northwest, competed for the right to fly to China. The first step in the process was obtaining CAB approval. The second was to obtain President Carter's approval. In approaching the White House, Pan Am faced its old enemy, Alfred Kahn, who had left the CAB and was now one of President Carter's advisors. Pan Am's lawyers at Verner Liipfert, Bernhard, McPherson & Hand were able to rally the support of significant Democratic Senators. As a result, Pan Am was selected.

As relations between the US and the USSR began to improve in the mid-1980s with the advent of Perestroika, President Reagan and Soviet General Secretary Mikhail Gorbachev reached an agreement to resume commercial air service between the United States and the USSR. Service began in April of 1986 and consisted of flights to and from major cities in the US to Leningrad and Moscow, with stops in Frankfurt. Between 1986 and 1988, I, along with other Pan Am representatives, including Ivan Dezelic, negotiated with Aeroflot representatives to improve the service between the US and USSR. Ivan had an amazing background that gave him unique insight into the problems we faced. He played such a dominant role in developing Pan Am's position that at one time, Mikhail Gorbachev said, "I do not know Mr. Acker but I do know Ivan Dezelic."

The Soviet market was a tough one. But Pan Am did better than break even on it. And in addition to the financial advantages the US - USSR routes brought to Pan Am, the routes enabled Pan Am to play an important role in the emigration of Soviet Jews from the USSR in the late 1980s.

In the end, nothing we were able to accomplish was enough. It is difficult to point to a single cause for Pan Am's failure. Despite the efforts of a great many talented individuals, Pan Am was never able to successfully adjust to a deregulated environment.

John is retired and lives in New York City and Key Biscayne, Florida.

BREAKING THE ICE IN CHINA

By Sho Ohkagawa

Re-Starting Service to China

When asked what event was the most memorable in my 36-year airline career, I would have to say that it was the trip to China in 1977 on which I accompanied Pan Am Chairman William T. Seawell. Chairman Seawell was invited to visit The Peoples' Republic of China by China International Travel Service (CITS).

At that time, the United States did not have formal diplomatic relations with China. Pan Am was honored to be the first US carrier selected to be guests in the formerly inaccessible country. Our group of 12 included Chairman Seawell, two senior Pan Am executives, the Chairman's son and daughter, directors of Pan Am's China Affairs Department, several spouses, and myself.

Courtesy of the Author

Courtesy of the Author

To reach Beijing at that time, it was necessary to follow a circuitous route—no direct flights then! We were required to enter China via Hong Kong. From cosmopolitan Hong Kong, we took a train to the Lowu customs point on the Hong Kong side of the border. There we descended from the train and walked across the border to Shenzhen Station. We were provided lunch in a dining room in the station while we waited several hours for the train to Guangzhou. From that southern city we were able to fly to Guilin.

My responsibilities involved the logistics of our group. I was in frequent communication with our hosts to coordinate scheduled activities and ensure smooth group movement. I also handled Pan Am's gifts to our hosts—for the official delegation, a model of the 747SP and for selected individuals, technological novelties from the US. These were digital calculators and digital watches that I purchased on Fifth Avenue at considerable expense. Who knew that one day all of them would be "Made in China!" We also carried along Johnnie Walker Scotch as we had been told it was highly desirable, the only liquor in China being "maotai" and a local vodka.

Aside from the unique privilege of being part of Pan Am's exploratory meetings with CITS and the Civil Aviation Administration of China (CAAC), 1977 was a very special time to visit China. At that time, there were very few foreigners, and tourist sites were not crowded. One could stand virtually alone atop the Great Wall!

Throughout, we were treated as honored guests with considerable hospitality and formalities at each place we visited. Our hosts were eager to showcase their social and industrial progress under Communism. We visited schools, athletic training facilities and rural communes, meeting some of the largest pigs and ducks I have ever seen. We were treated to the Beijing Opera, cultural performances with themes like "Liberation," and a spectacular circus.

We were thrilled to see first-hand the beautiful landscapes of Guilin by boat, the newly excavated life-sized warriors of Xian, the overwhelming Great Wall and Ming Tombs, and Beijing's Temple of Heaven and Imperial Palace (Forbidden City). While viewing these sights, we discovered that we were sights too. Wherever we went, curious and friendly citizens surrounded us. My Polaroid camera was a real showstopper. Like a magician I was able to take and produce a photo on the spot, mystifying and delighting the crowd.

As a result of this trip, Pan Am was the first to be able to offer American tourists the opportunity to visit China. In addition, Pan Am was subsequently authorized to re-establish service to Beijing, a route they had served until 1949. This was the beginning of a fruitful and ongoing relationship between Pan Am and the Chinese airlines. Soon after our trip, we invited our counterparts to visit us in New York. In 1980, under a bilateral aviation agreement between the US and China, Pan Am began scheduled service to Beijing and Shanghai directly three times per week.

Sho was Pan Am's System Director-Protocol.

Courtesy of the Author

Toasting the China Service

112

BOEING 747 INAUGURAL FLIGHT TO CHINA

By George Doubleday

Pan Am Returns to China

March 1979 marked the first appearance of a Boeing 747 in China. It was a charter flight under the command of Chief Pilot Bill Frisbie, carrying the Boston Pops Orchestra to a cultural exchange engagement in Shanghai. It was also an opportunity for Pan Am to demonstrate its serious intent to open service to mainland China, having heeded the official government policy of 'One China' by terminating scheduled service to Taiwan just a few months earlier.

Courtesy of the Author

George Doubleday Receiving Honors in China

113

As the recently arrived Regional Managing Director for Southeast Asia, based in Hong Kong, one of my first official duties was to close Taipei as an on-line station. All of us in the Region regretted the need for this, as passenger and cargo business was good, the Pan Am reputation was very strong, and our operating costs were low. We turned over our reservations responsibility to a General Sales Agent and offered connecting service and through-fares to the USA via points in Japan.

So, it was time to show our interest in serving mainland China and demonstrating the ability of the Boeing 747 to operate there. I led a team of maintenance and customer service personnel to Shanghai to handle our first flight. It was the dead of winter in Shanghai, snow falling softly in a city with few cars, little visible activity, and people dressed in traditional blue Mao jackets. Our accommodations were at the old JinJiang Hotel, a classic Chinese structure reeking of old world personality – dark wood paneling in the somber lobby, subdued lighting, uncomfortable-looking furniture, minimal signage. Bedrooms were basic but functional, and welcoming in their own odd way. I remember thinking how unique this city and this culture were; how fortunate I was to be able to be there just as the country was opening to western tourism.

Our pulses quickened and we bristled with pride as the flight landed and taxied to the ramp, the Pan Am markings and the blue ball logo on the tail clearly visible through the snow. The aircraft, a Boeing 747SP, had been renamed *China Clipper* for the occasion, but due to anomalies in translation, the Chinese characters actually had the meaning *Chinese Scissors*. Wrong kind of clippers...

We stamped our feet to stay warm, gloved hands on our ears, and went about the task of disembarking passengers and securing the aircraft for the night, improvising hand gestures for the CAAC staff who were helping us. As an aside, Captain Frisbie and our maintenance team noted that the entire airport supply of deicing fluid was a four-liter bucket, half full. Our passengers carefully descended on an outdoor airstair that

Pan Am Archives

Pan American World Airways is far from a stranger to the Peoples' Republic of China. Prior to inaugurating US—PRC service, the airline flew a charter flight carrying Seiji Ozawa and the Boston Symphony Orchestra to Shanghai on March 14, 1979, as well as technical flights from Canton and Beijing.

barely reached the aircraft door. They were whisked into buses that took them to the hotel for a quick rest before the evening banquet.

Anyone who has attended a Chinese banquet will appreciate how we celebrated that evening—an amazingly diverse menu (11 or more courses are not uncommon), endless toasts, and plentiful liquid refreshment. Three glasses per place setting allowed the pouring of beer, wine, and Maotai—each glass refilled as soon as a sip was taken, and sip we did – except when toasting, when it was customary to empty one's glass and level it horizontally to show no drop of liquid remained. Maotai is a powerful drink (typically 100 proof), distilled from sorghum, and one of China's official state banquet 'wines' served to visiting foreign guests and diplomats who are usually unaware of its potency. On this evening, CAAC staff circulated broadly throughout the banquet hall offering toasts to US/China friendship, to future business, to cooperation, to aviation, and just about everything else.

Pan Am's point person in China was John Shoemaker, son of missionary parents, fluent in Mandarin Chinese, and well connected in the travel and tourism sectors of China's emerging business community. He was assisted by P.C. Lee, a genial gentleman who related well to the locals and served as alternate translator and go-to person when John Shoemaker was otherwise occupied. P.C. told me proudly the next morning that in the course of matching drinks with our hosts he had consumed 14 cups of Maotai – an achievement which must qualify him as an all-star legend. We speculated that promotion within the Chinese bureaucracy was based as much on ability to drink Maotai as individual business acumen.

There were concerts and tours planned for the passengers who had flown into Shanghai, with departure some days later via local Chinese airlines, leaving our aircraft free to ferry to Hong Kong to resume scheduled service. So our team of slightly haggard handling personnel boarded the aircraft for the return flight, exuberant at the successful introduction of the Boeing 747 to China, and relieved that the Boston musicians would have to bear the brunt of future banquets.

George worked for Pan Am from 1965-1981. His last position was Regional Managing Director – Southeast Asia, HKG

Courtesy of the Author

IRAN ADVENTURE

By Harvey Benefield

Evacuating Pan Am Personnel from Iran

I call this "The Iran Adventure".

To start, perhaps some background is in order: During the winter of 1978-79 the Shah of Iran abdicated. The new ruler and spiritual leader, Ayatollah Khomeini, had yet to arrive and the entire country was in a state of turmoil. Masses of Iranian people had broken into an armory and stolen weapons. Many, if not all, of the people were armed. For the most part, law and order had broken down. In addition, air traffic control at the airport and in the airspaces was nonexistent. It is worth noting this was six months prior to the Iranian takeover of the U.S. Embassy.

Courtesy of Jamie Baldwin

Tehran

In order to keep air traffic flowing, particularly our own, Pan Am operations representatives had been sent from the New York Headquarters to Tehran to set up interim VFR (visual flight rules) air traffic system to get aircraft in and out of the area safely. When the representatives arrived, however, the situation was so bad they were unable to do as much as desired. They later were trapped in one of the hotels in Tehran along with other American citizens and foreign nationals. They were desperate to leave; that how I got involved.

At the time, January 1979, I was on vacation on a skiing trip with my daughter Laura in Colorado and was out of the loop as to what was going on in the world of aviation. Upon my return, the Pan Am Crew Scheduling Office in New York called and assigned me a Boeing 707 ferry flight from New York to Bermuda followed by a charter flight from Bermuda to Brussels. After a layover in Brussels my crew and I were to deadhead to Frankfurt and operate Frankfurt-New York. This first part of the trip was uneventful.

In Brussels, after supper and upon returning to my room, I received a phone call from Pan Am Flight Operations in New York. It seemed that some of our flight operations personnel were in Tehran and could not leave due to the revolution. Flight Operations asked me, First Officer Paul Franz and Flight Engineer Al Bekebrede to ferry a plane to Bahrain and wait there for further instructions regarding an evacuation from Tehran. The proposed ferry flight was designated TE453 from Brussels to Bahrain and once instructions and departure times were received in Bahrain, we were to operate a flight, designated E453, from Bahrain to Tehran for the evacuation and then from Tehran to Frankfurt with a fueling stop in Istanbul, if necessary. In Bahrain, a crew of five cabin crew joined us, pursers Betty Carter and Bob Reinke and flight attendants Laddy Chorwat, Tavi Renzoni and Joyce Horton.

While awaiting instructions in Bahrain, we were told that Flight Operations could not contact its personnel in Tehran directly. The time was not right. We saw on local television a revolution taking place. During a period of three days I contacted Flight Operations in New York on more than one occasion but the word was to wait another day. With a local telephone I was able to contact our personnel in the "crew hotel" in Tehran, and was told of the troubles they were experiencing in the hotel and the ongoing revolution outside. I was told they were waiting for us. We did not know what to expect in Tehran.

The next few days in Bahrain were not hard to take. The country was full of the old and the new, including new hotels and buildings and a lot of the old and ancient places such as bazaars (souks) and such. The only problem was waiting for the time to be "just right". We received daily briefings from New York about what was going on in Tehran. What we saw on the television, however, was another story. New York was unable to get through to the stranded people in Tehran by any means, yet we were able to pick up the hotel telephone and call them in their rooms. Strange.

After about four days, we were given the word to go. Early in the morning I went to the operations office at the airport and was given whatever weather briefing was available. The weather was forecast to be good, however that was little more than a guess. The only weather charts were satellite photos showing no cloud cover. We fueled for our destination, Tehran, takaing on all the extra fuel we could carry. We had enough fuel to make a few approaches at Tehran and then go on to Istanbul, our first alternate. We were properly dispatched and given a route that would take us to Iranian airspace. In my possession I had a letter in teletype form from the Prime Minister of Iran. The letter was to be used in the event we had trouble with the Iranian authorities.

After takeoff, we had an uneventful trip until we arrived at Iranian airspace at a point over the Persian Gulf. Local VHF communication with Iran was not effective. We then entered into a holding pattern at 29,000 feet and tried to contact air traffic control using HF. I think that is when we made contact. We were denied entry into the airspace. I read them the letter from the Prime Minister and after a lengthy delay, was told that entry was approved under visual flight rules (VFR) only. We proceeded to our destination VFR and were out of range of any communication until nearing Tehran. Fortunately, we were visual all the way. The only two frequencies that were available were the AA beacon, which was the outer marker at Merhabad airport and freq. 131.4 which was the local PanOp (Pan Am's operation) frequency. We maintained VFR and descended to the local airport operating altitude. After we called PanOp and told them of our arrival and that we were unable to contact the tower, they relayed most of the information we needed. We were told that the airport was closed and that they would try and open it as soon as they were able, because the runway was littered with trucks and buses. We stayed in the low level holding pattern while the local people tried to remove the vehicles. This was no little problem because the people who parked the vehicles did not leave the keys. After a long period of time, or so we thought, the runway was finally cleared.

After holding for what seemed like an eternity, we were cleared to land. During the holding period, Al, the Flight Engineer, said that he was picking up the sound of "acquisition" radar. I was told that that meant a weapon had locked onto us. For the uneducated about military terminology, a weapons radar system was trying to get a target for its weapons, and that target was us.

We landed. We were instructed to continue to the end of the runway, taxi to a certain area and wait. We did. As our mission was to pick up personnel for the evacuation, it seemed reasonable that the evacuees would be brought to us. The two outboard engines were shut down and we waited as instructed.

School type buses approached and we thought that they would be the evacuees. We were wrong. When the buses stopped, armed military people emerged and were directed by a senior military person to surround the aircraft. Within a short time, the aircraft was surrounded. I asked the other cockpit members to place their hands on the cockpit glare-shield to show we were unarmed. The commanding officer gave us the signal to cut the engines.

Before long the military people pushed a boarding ladder to the forward entrance door and a group of them boarded the aircraft. They were heavily armed. They searched the aircraft. When they were satisfied the Marines were not on board, we were allowed (told) to leave the plane. We stayed as a group under the wing of the plane and were questioned by a senior military officer, one of two who spoke English.

There were many questions as to why we were there and what did we want. After much discussion among themselves, they decided that we were to get on to one of the buses and go into the city. When asked why, no one seemed to have an answer. That is the last thing I wanted to do. I told the commanding officer that we were a civilian aircraft and we, the crew, were not leaving the airport. We were to go to the terminal to pick up passengers. After some hesitation, he seemed to agree with us and we were told we could start only two engines to taxi to the terminal and no more. One of the armed militia stayed in the cockpit during the trip to the terminal. The buses with the militia followed us to the terminal. The only casualties thus far, were suffered by militia members in one of the buses. We were later told that the bus had overturned when driving too close to the jet exhaust—lack of airport driving training, I guess.

Upon arrival at the terminal, the militia again surrounded us and a set of air stairs was pulled up to the aircraft. The Pan Am passenger service personnel at the terminal were in the process of completing the passengers' necessary paperwork for boarding the aircraft. There was a mix of people. Most were Pan Am personnel, including flight operations staff whom we were to pick up, plus a number of others. We also had Inter-Continental Hotel people and people from the press.

I wanted to check in with the Pan Am operations people but was told by some armed person at the top of the stairs that I could not get off the aircraft. I told the armed person that I was the Captain and I was authorized to do whatever I wanted. He seemed to agree. It turned out to be a worthless exercise. The passenger service personnel were trying to do their best to handle the chaos.

As mentioned before, radio communications was almost non-existent. We had originally planned to be at the terminal for about an hour, but by this time, a few hours had elapsed. I felt that I should tell the company what was happening. In the cockpit a number of radios and radio equipment were available. One that we used was the earpiece and lip mike. Most observers cannot tell whether we are talking among ourselves or speaking on one of the communications radios. We dialed "Berna" radio, a commercial unit in Europe on the HF band

and had them open a line to Pan Am Operations in New York. We spoke to them in a normal voice as if we were speaking to each other and brought them up-to-date, all the while with a weapon-toting person looking at us in the cockpit. At some point during this time, the officer in charge of the militia disappeared and was not a factor. More of an inconvenience.

Loading the passengers was becoming a problem, and no one seemed to be able to make up his or her mind. First, no Iranians. Then an American husband with an Iranian wife was allowed. Then an American wife and an Iranian husband were not allowed. During all this, a couple of people of whatever nationality were able to slip on the plane and sit on the floor in the back. I do not know whether they were found out or not; did not care, either. All evacuees were searched and all camera film was confiscated. Much was harassment.

As the passengers were boarding the airplane, we re-calculated the fuel necessary for the next flight leg and decided to fly nonstop to Frankfurt, bypassing Istanbul. Time on the ground in Tehran had been in excess of four hours. It seemed much longer. Maybe an eternity. We received "startup" clearance and taxied rapidly so as to avoid the chance that someone might change their minds about our departing. We departed the airport with no air traffic control clearance. We departed VFR and contacted Istanbul on the HF band and received clearance while airborne. After takeoff, the passengers started to applaud. When we passed the Iranian border, an announcement was made to that effect and the celebration really started. The bar was opened. Alcohol helped.

We touched down in Frankfurt six hours later. We were interviewed at the terminal by the news media and then we went to the hotel for rest. It had been a long day. Upon arrival at the hotel, the press and the IHC people arranged for a banquet to which we were invited. Many stories were told about the previous few days and the adventures experienced. Many that were funny now, were not so funny then. The chilled champagne, delivered to each room, helped. A few speeches later, we found out just how happy the evacuees were to get out of that place.

After that the trip home was uneventful. I deadheaded back to New York, then on to Miami. I had been gone from my home for ten days.

Courtesy of the Author

Harvey lives in Miami and is very active with PAHF events and Clipper Pioneers.

DEATH AT 35,000 FEET

By Tom Kewin

A Passenger Dies in Flight

We often talked about the possibility of a passenger dying on the airplane and what we would have to do if it ever happened. With 400 people on a jumbo jet, the odds increased and they caught up with me in 1979 on a flight between New Delhi and Tehran.

The captain had just informed the passengers the flight was over Afghanistan when, with a "ding," the cabin call light came on. The Purser said, "Tom, I need some help! A passenger has collapsed and I think he is dying. Can you come to the L-2 area now?" I checked the Engineer's panel and switched the fuel supply to the main tanks and after a word with the pilots, went downstairs.

When I got to the L-2 area, the Purser was loosening the passenger's necktie and feeling for a pulse. There was no pulse. I asked her to get on the PA system and ask for a doctor. Surprisingly, three doctors came

Boeing 747

Photo by Ted Quackenbush (airliners.net)

120

forward. All agreed the passenger was gone, and there was nothing they could do for him. While we raised the armrests on a triple seat and stretched the passenger out under a blanket, the purser took his wife to the First Class cabin and sat with her, holding her hand and talking quietly.

Back on the flight deck, I told the captain what had happened and he asked me to contact the Tehran operations office by radio and advise them we would need a doctor to sign a death certificate and someone to handle the remains. Upon arrival in Tehran, after the passengers were disembarked, a doctor came on board with a team from a morturary and things were soon sorted out. An hour later, our flight, Pan Am *Flight One*, resumed its westward voyage. Our crew and the widow went to the Sheraton Hotel where the Purser insisted the widow share her room.

The next morning most of the crew and the widow met in the hotel dining room for breakfast. This was shortly after the Shah of Iran had been deposed and anti-American feelings were very high. We could expect to wait an hour in an almost empty dining room before a waiter would take our order. However, I guess the word about the death had reached the hotel staff as they were very attentive, for a change. The station manager joined us and explained that the Khomeini government had shut down all foreign telephone service, but we could wire New York any message the widow wanted to send. He wrote down the information on her two children and told us that someone in New York would contact them and he would list her on *Flight One* from London to New York after a one-day layover in London.

The couple was from New Jersey, and upon the late husband's retirement, had set out two months earlier on a trip around the world. It had been everything they had hoped for, and they were looking forward to a week in England before going home. The following day we took the widow and the casket to London where she again shared a room with the Purser. She was also able to call her children.

The flight service team was Los Angeles-based and scheduled to leave the next day for Los Angeles, but the purser was able to trade trips with a New York purser so she could deliver the widow to her waiting family in New York. She was not about to leave the woman alone in her grief. I do not remember the purser's name, but she certainly deserved a medal for compassion. It was not part of her job; it was just the way she felt she should handle the situation.

Tom's book, *The Pan Am Journey*, available on amazon.com

The PAN AM Journey

Thomas Kewin

Tom, a true professional flight engineer, flew in the third seat for 40 years and still lives in the same house he has lived in for 54 years in Mill Valley, CA.

LAST FLIGHT TO TEHRAN 1979

By Johannes Pigmans

Last Evacuation Flight From Tehran

In 1959 I was fortunate enough to begin my career with Pan Am and I traveled the world. I started as steward, purser and then on the Boeing 747, I became an in-flight director. Pan Am was a prestigious airline and we certainly made the going great—literally. My most memorable flight was Pan Am's last flight to Tehran in February 1979. I do not think I need to go into the mess that was the Iranian Revolution, Jimmy Carter losing re-election, the oil embargo, the abdication of Shah of Iran, and the taking of power by Ayatollah Khomeini. However, there were expatriates in Iran who needed to return home.

When Pan Am asked volunteers to extract the last remaining ex-pats out of Tehran, I was front and center and I think I can say the same for the crew. The flight was to operate from Frankfurt to Tehran. I wish I could recall the *Clipper* name of the 747 we flew from Frankfurt. (Pan Am named every one of their planes a *Clipper*.) In any event, the crew and I flew as regular passengers to Frankfurt aboard Pan Am and stayed in a hotel that evening.

The mood of the crew was upbeat as most of us had met at the bar and then had a bite to eat the night before departure. As we left for the airport the next day, we might as well have been staring into an abyss, as this was uncharted territory for most of us and we would definitely be stepping out of the box of our training manuals. We knew we had a large plane filled to the brim with food and that we were leaving Frankfurt to evacuate the last stranded Americans in Iran—as for the rest, we were just winging it.

After a seven-hour flight, officials parked us on the tarmac in a remote area. A fully armed brigade of the Revolutionary

Courtesy of the Author

Tehran from the Inter-Continental Hotel

122

Guard met us. Clad in their keffiyeh (Arabic head dress similar to the one that Arafat wore), they boarded the plane and performed a thorough security check of the airplane—what they were looking for was anyone's guess. Most of us watched in amazement and fear, as we did not know the protocol for this type of event.

All the while, I told the crew to move to the onboard upstairs lounge as guards escorted the pilots off the airplane to brief the flight plan in the terminal. The heat was unbearable and here we were not only far away from the terminal, but far from anything civilized. So as the pilots were away, I looked at the two issues I was facing: (a) how to get people aboard orderly and safely and (b) how in the heck I was going to deal with the armed Revolutionary Guards that quite honestly, scared me. I decided having just one door as an entry and exit was the most prudent way to go about this and that door was to be L5. Well prudent might be a strong word here because the ramp they provided us could only reach up to that door.

So here I was, with one part of the plan executed. Passengers were going to enter into the rear door of the 747 on the left side. I then reached out to Iran Air (the official airline of Iran), to see if they could assist me in safely boarding the passengers. They refused as they were equally dumbstruck by the situation and were not quite sure which side of the revolt they were on—or supposed to be on. To make matters worse, I noticed there were several Iranian Air Force soldiers guarding the aircraft. It is important to note they were loyal to the recently exiled Shah of Iran. For some reason, they seemed more trustworthy than the Revolutionary Guard, as I knew they were trained in the US.

So here went nothing.

I approached what looked like the leading officer and requested or pleaded with him to assist me with boarding. Call me crazy, but somehow asking the Air Force as opposed to dealing with what appeared to be the all too trigger-happy looking Revolutionary Guard brought myself and the crew a sense of ease. They say a Coke and a smile can go a long way and in this instance it was the case as I bribed the Air Force officers with cans of Coca Cola. This seemed to really break the ice and bring calm to a tense situation.

Shortly after the pilots returned from their briefing, we went through the painstaking process of boarding the passengers. Each passenger was thoroughly screened to make sure they had the right documents to leave Iran. The entire process of boarding more than 300 passengers took more than four hours. Finally, as the plane's wheels released from the tarmac in Tehran, almost every one of those passengers broke into tears of happiness. All I knew is that the crew, myself included, breathed a sigh of relief as our chests filled with pride for the great service we had provided to these fellow citizens of the world. What better gift could we have given than the ideals of freedom—the American way and that day it was the Pan American way.

Courtesy of the Author

This is just a short glimpse into what was the most incredible airline ever to exist. Pan Am, besides providing exemplary service and allowing millions to see the world, really believed in America so much that they jumped at any opportunity to help. This was so much at the core and the essence of the company that the entire crew was recognized personally by the President of Pan Am at the time. To tell you the truth, I still have that "President Merit Award" framed and mounted. It is less of a monument to our actions on that day, but more of a reminder of the days that the best airline in the world existed and the pride I have to have been a part of it.

Johannes (Han) lives with his wife Kari-Mette in Florida and New York.

RESCUE FROM ISLAMABAD

By Anne Sweeney

Monitoring Another Pan Am Evacuation Flight

In 1979 when I worked in the Public Relations Department at Pan American World Airways, Iranian militants overthrew the Shah and took the staff of the American Embassy hostage. These people were abused and held for more than a year. President Jimmy Carter launched one effort to rescue the hostages. It failed miserably.

To show solidarity with the Iranians against the Great Satan, Muslim fanatics in Islamabad, Pakistan, overran the American Embassy compound attacking American civilians, including women and children. The embassy was forced to evacuate most personnel and all families.

As it had done during similar uprisings around the world, Pan Am sent aircraft and crew to evacuate these Americans. The pilots and cabin crew volunteered to take a 747 into Islamabad and fly out about 300 people.

I was duty officer that weekend. This meant I was the link between the company and the media and had to be available on a 24-hour basis in case of accidents, incidents, and everything in between. On previous watches, I had handled a number of situations—a bomb in a locker at the JFK Worldport, the resignation of the company president, and Sean Connery's lost luggage.

This was different. On a Saturday morning, I sat in my apartment on the phone to Pan Ops. This was the nerve center of the airline, hidden somewhere in the depths of JFK at Hangar 14. All Pan Am aircraft were tracked from there. My job was to follow the progress of the evacuation flight and once it took off and cleared Pakistani airspace, send a statement to the media. Communications were fairly complex—the phone lines went from me to JFK to London and then by radio to Pan Am in Istanbul and finally, to Karachi.

Remember, this was 1979. The information came in spurts. The aircraft is approaching...it's touching down.... the ramp is coming up...the door is open...Pakistani troops are surrounding the aircraft...they are letting the passengers board.... boarding complete.... doors closed...they're taxiing.... airborne! And later, those very welcome words—the plane has cleared Pakistani airspace.

I had many moments in my Pan Am career, but I was proudest of that one—for being a part of something that was important and something that Pan Am people did many, many times over the years and at far more risk than I incurred. I interviewed the crew for the company newspaper—they had all volunteered to fly into Islamabad and took the passengers as far as Frankfurt.

124

"I was proud of the crew and proud of Pan Am," the captain said. The purser quoted a passenger who told him how frightened the Americans had been.

"But when we saw that Pan Am plane coming for us, it was a symbol of freedom."

But I look back on that day in 1979 so I can feel an emotion that has become very rare in this not-so-brave New World.

Pride.

Anne lives in New Jersey and is busy running a public relations company and doing great work for World Wings International.

Courtesy of the Author

Anne Sweeney today

MERGER WITH NATIONAL AIRLINES

By Mike Clark

Domestic Routes..... Finally

As the decade of the 70s drew to a close, US airline executives burned many thousands of gallons of midnight oil as they planned their various strategies for taking advantage of opportunities presented by the new deregulated domestic airline era that was triggered by the Airline Deregulation Act of 1978.

Those strategies manifested themselves in many ways. Strategic measures ranged from Braniff International applying for hundreds of "dormant route authorities" and actually inaugurating more than a hundred new routes on a single day, almost doubling its size overnight, to National Airlines, based in Miami, one of the smaller of the dozen "trunk" airlines of the pre-deregulation era and also one of the few consistently profitable airlines over the years, doing the exact opposite.

Headed by President Ed Dolansky, a former chief financial officer, National reacted to the passage of the Deregulation Act by developing a strategy of, in effect, circling the wagons, paying down debt and hoarding cash, figuring it would have a war chest that would enable the airline to outlast more aggressive airlines whom National believed would overspend on expansion, thus weakening their ability to resist National's own expansion at a later, more opportune time.

Prior to the passage of the Deregulation Act, US government regulators had never allowed a hostile takeover in the US airline industry. That prohibition was erased in the act and was virtually unnoticed by National. This oversight in National's planning came to light suddenly when Frank Lorenzo, chairman of tiny Texas International Airlines (TI) in Houston, announced that TI had acquired a significant number of shares of National and offered to buy more to gain control and merge the two airlines. National was suddenly "in play."

Courtesy of the Author

**Re-Painting the National Fleet
after the merger**

In the ensuing months, National sought out Pan Am as a "white knight," but that strategy was thwarted when Eastern Airlines jumped into the fray – with speculation rampant that it was not a serious suitor, but was merely attempting to force a bidding war to hike the price for Pan Am, thus rendering it a weakened competitor. The bidding did escalate, with TI essentially bowing out early, up to the point where Pan Am finally offered $50 cash per share, at which point Eastern withdrew its bid. National's fate was sealed on July 10, 1979 when the Civil Aeronautics Board voted to approve a takeover of the Florida airline. Pan Am closed on its purchase of National in January 1980 and NAL chairman Lewis B. "Bud" Maytag, who was slated to become vice chairman of the combined airline, suddenly declined the office and retired to his family property in Colorado.

Planning for the implementation of the merger moved forward on many fronts, and many reasonable and responsible decisions were made by joint task groups of Pan Am and National executives and managers. October 26, 1980, was chosen as "Single Identity Day," at which time National's identity would cease to exist and the two carriers would be operated as one under the Pan Am name and colors.

But by and large, National personnel were unhappy with the loss of "their" airline and resisted at every front the imposition of new operating philosophies and rules. On "Single Identity Day," in Houston, the entire former National airport staff refused to wear their new Pan Am blue uniforms and showed up for work in National brown. From the Pan Am New York headquarters came orders to send them all home to change into the Pan Am uniform before being permitted to work. Local Houston executives recognized how devastating such an action would be, as Pan Am had but six flights daily at the city and National had more than 30, and pre-merger staff sizes were proportional. Without the former National employees, schedule disruptions would have been extensive and customer satisfaction seriously damaged. So the brown uniforms were permitted to stay and the day passed successfully and uneventfully. The next day, the brown uniforms were retired.

Former National personnel continued to resent the imposition of stringent work rules upon a work force more used to making decisions on the spot to keep the airline running smoothly. Likewise, the Pan Am people considered the National staffers little more than provincial loose cannons with no respect for the long worldwide experience of the mighty Pan American World Airways.

Open warfare between the two forces was often barely contained. Anecdotal examples of the discord are rife, but are of no value in this article. Suffice it to say the tension was almost palpable.

Photo by Bob Garrard (airliners.net)

Then, on Friday, July 9. 1982, tragedy struck. Flight 759, a former National Boeing 727, crashed into a Kenner, LA, neighborhood adjacent to the New Orleans International Airport while taking off in a thunderstorm on a flight to Las Vegas. All 147 on board and eight on the ground were killed, including "mixed" cabin crew made up of flight attendants from both airlines. Pan Am quickly pulled together task forces representing employees from virtually every aspect of the company's operations, men and women chosen not by which airline they came from, but based solely upon their demonstrated expertise and experience. The teams dispatched immediately to New Orleans contained experts in flight and cabin crew operating, training and compliance functions, experienced accident investigators, compassionate and capable customer service personnel to help the families of the passengers cope with the aftermath of the loss of their loved ones. Operations people, knowledgeable about the technical aspects of flight, weight and balance specialists, weather mavens, communications experts, and this writer, a media relations specialist, all worked side by side at the accident site and at the hotel which served as command central for the investigative endeavor.

Literally hundreds of the combined Pan Am's personnel worked long, hard hours both in New Orleans and in the airline's New York and Miami headquarters offices, as well as in offices worldwide. They had no time to waste by asking previously unknown fellow employees if they came from the "Blue" side or the "Orange" side of the merged airline. One's co-worker's pre-merger heritage simply did not matter; all that mattered was that the work was done properly and promptly, and that communications between the various task forces was maintained.

The New Orleans operation, and the support of the on-site staff received from headquarters, was truly inspirational. Employees from the Blue and the Orange factions alike gained great respect from their fellow workers. It became very obvious that any tensions that might have existed before were erased from the minds of those of us tasked to Flight 759. Respect for our colleagues was heartfelt.

I am convinced that the spread of that respect would continue to foster once all of us returned to our regular tasks and began sharing our Flight 759 experiences with our colleagues. Unfortunately, time simply ran out for Pan Am before the effects of that magnificent effort could be fully felt over the worldwide Pan Am system.

Perhaps, if we'd just had more time...

Mike is still working and lives in Fort Lauderdale, FL

Courtesy of the Author

TRAVELS WITH JIMMY

By Irene Lindbeck Tibbits

Traveling with the White house Press during the 1980 Election

When Pan Am closed its flight service base in Washington, DC in 1980, the JFK base again had the opportunity to work the White House Press Charters, as they had done prior to opening the base in DC. President John F. Kennedy had started the Press Charters and Pan Am was the chosen one. As luck had it, I was fortunate enough to be asked if I was interested, and it took about two and a half seconds for me to jump at the chance. Who wouldn't? At that time I already had spent 15 years with Pan Am and had had the good fortune to work many special flights, but even the regular flights I worked were for me not only an adventure, but also an incredible learning experience about the many countries we flew to and the people we encountered. Living a champagne life on a beer budget, staying at luxury hotels in world cities, but also at modest places in the jungles of Africa and the Pacific Islands, not that there weren't moments to complain about; one is human after all.

Courtesy of the Author

Pan Am White House Press Charter Crew

At that time the presidential campaign of 1980 was in full swing. President Carter was running for re-election and Ronald Reagan was his opponent, and we, as the crew following or preceding Air Force One with Carter, were really put to the test as far as our stamina was concerned, because the president started early and quit late in his quest for a second term in what was to be a losing battle. We joked that President Carter's day was from 5 a.m. till 11 p.m., and Reagan's from 11 a.m. till 5 p.m., and we of course reported for flight earlier than

129

that, as we also had to come from home base to Andrews Air Force base in advance. No one complained, we were too excited to be part of the historic events of the day that were covered in the evening news and the morning newspapers. And who needs a full night's sleep anyway?

For those not familiar with how these flights worked and who our passengers were, here is a bit about the operation. Air Force One at that time was a Boeing 707 with limited capacity for passengers, unlike today's Boeing 747. We carried the White House press (also international press and foreign dignitaries on trips out of the country) in addition to the White House staff and Secret Service. Air Force One carried a small press pool of about eight journalists. However, we soon found out the press had more fun with us, but they had to do a job, after all.

The intensity of the campaigning got stronger as Election Day came closer. We were covering as many stops as possible during the day, serving hot meals during one hour flights and barely getting the galleys secured before landing. But the passengers needed food and that was sometimes the only time they had to eat. The aircraft also served as a filing center for the press during the fairly brief stops where there were no proper facilities. In addition, we and the aircraft had Secret Service clearance and it saved time.

One day when we were in Omaha, I believe, something special happened. Pan Am usually landed ahead of Air Force One so that the press and staff could be on the ground for the arrival of the latter. On this day, however, the aircraft stairs for disembarkation were delayed and Sam Donaldson, yes, that Sam Donaldson, decided to jump to the tarmac to be the first, competitive as he was. He made it safely. Upon seeing Donaldon's jump, a young lady whose name escapes me, decided to follow suit, but that didn't end so well as she broke her ankle.

Another wonderful day was Halloween; we decided that because we were on the road we should not be deprived of fun, so everyone did their best to drum up costumes. The airplane was decorated with witches made of Kleenex hanging from the light buttons and some of us were dressed as the characters from ET, i.e. Yoda, etc., Bumble Bees and and more. President Carter enjoyed our fun when we appeared near Air Force One.

From this fun event in Jackson, Ms. we continued to Chicago, where we were to have the luxury of a two night stay, and the opportunity to have laundry and cleaning done. We were getting a bit 'ripe' at that point. After an evening arrival, we headed for food and some fun at the disco at the Hyatt at the Chicago airport. We stayed up late, thinking we could sleep in and enjoy a relaxing day. It was not to be. At 4 a.m. we got telephone calls and knocks on the door with urgent messages to get ready ASAP. President Carter had gotten word the Iranian hostages were to be released, so we were heading back to Washington. It was a mad scramble to get ourselves, half asleep, out the door as fast as we could. Our laundry and cleaning was somewhere, so we put on whatever was available, a mix and match for passenger and crew alike. Of course, there would be no catering although somehow we got some doughnuts, and coffee was available on the aircraft. Our laundry somehow did arrive and the last packages were literally tossed onboard as we taxied out. The White House Travel Office later told us it took months before all were claimed, as in the flurry of excitement, laundry was the last thing the press cared about. As it turned out the release was a false alarm.

Reagan, of course, won the election and he gracefully asked Carter to go to Wiesbaden, Germany to greet the hostages when they arrived there after their release. Again, it was Air Force One and the Pan Am charter that went and my crew and I were so excited to be a part of that. Upon arrival in Frankfurt the press was transported to the hospital in Wiesbaden where the hostages were taken for checkups before being brought to the US The cabin crew was given the choice of going to a hotel for a few hours of sleep or going to Wiesbaden. Needless to say we chose Wiesbaden. It was a freezing cold evening and we stood outside waiting for the hostages to show themselves in windows or balconies, which they eventually did to our delight. The cold feet were worth it. On the flight back across the Atlantic it was a very exhausted group of journalists and crew alike, but with a fresh crew of pilots, a skeleton crew took turns to be on duty as everyone was getting some deserved rest.

My life with Pan Am continued, working the Press Charters during the Reagan Presidency. We went to the G7 Summit, the D-Day 40th Anniversary, another very moving and special event in our lives, and met Gorbachev for the first time in Geneva. We also visited Bitburg, Ireland, South America, China and other places. I continued this until I chose to go on to another career. I enjoyed twenty-two years of fun and hard work, with colleagues from a multitude of nations that were interesting, well educated, with good senses of humor (very necessary) and passengers from all corners of the globe who gave me more knowledge about the humans of the world than one could possibly imagine.

Irene continued working the Press Charters during the Reagan Presidency. She went to the G7 Summit, the D-Day 40th Anniversary, and met Gorbachev in Geneva. She also visited Bitburg, Ireland, South America, and China. She lives in San Francisco and continues to travel to exotic locations.

Courtesy of the Author

PAN AM'S WORLD TOURS TO CHINA

By Jeanne Bayer
Escorting Tours to China

In 1979 when the People's Republic of China began to issue visas permitting foreigners to visit the country I was thankful that I had maintained my connection with Pan American World Airways through the philanthropic organization of former flight attendants, World Wings International. It had been 20 years since my last trip as a Pan Am stewardess, hired in London three years previously when the airline's experiment to recruit candidates who spoke a second language resulted in fifteen of us being selected from over 3,000 applicants. What an honor! My dream job!

In keeping with its pioneering approach, Pan Am's World, a tour-organizing component of the airline, was one of the first companies to offer group tours to China. With its usual high standard of consideration for passengers, a Chinese expert, who knew the history and spoke the language, accompanied each group. Additionally, the escort was responsible for the well- being of the travelers. The company chose many ex-flight attendants for this second dream job, because they were well experienced with the affluent passengers who signed up for these 2- or 3-week journeys.

As an escort, our responsibilities included ensuring each member of the group was comfortable. We assigned hotel rooms on a rotating basis so everyone had a chance to enjoy the best view or amenities. We checked that luggage was labeled correctly for the next destination and divided the daily outing groups between sightseers, history buffs, and those who preferred spending time hunting for souvenirs in local department stores or the official Friendship stores. Knowing where the "western" toilets were located at the Great Wall was also useful.

Courtesy of the Author
Forbidden City

132

Among the most memorable destinations was a visit to the newly excavated terracotta warrior army surrounding the tomb of Emperor Shihuangdi in Sian. Our group was among the first to see this amazing discovery and it was a challenge to make sure no one tried to take photos, which was absolutely forbidden, and would have resulted in a trip to the local jail.

Travel within China was mostly by train or plane, with daily outings on Japanese buses, which we found poorly designed for tall Americans. Breaks were necessary for everyone to stretch their legs from time to time. Overnight train trips were a special adventure in elegant velvet-upholstered sleeping cars with lace curtains, and pillows filled with corn husks! One particular journey required our group to walk past a large wooden tub containing live fish placed in the corridor en route to the dining car. Two men were constantly aerating the water, which spilled onto the floor due to the motion of the train. By next morning, the spilled water was several inches deep.

Inter-city flights on Russian-built aircraft were sometimes quite hair-raising as flight crews frequently ignored safety procedures and on more than one occasion, they assigned seats for more rows than actually were on the plane. Our Chinese hosts were always gracious and well-meaning. They regularly presented gifts to everyone, but not always the most practical items. For example, upon boarding one flight each person was handed a large glass box containing a beautiful handmade doll—far too large to fit into anyone's carry-on luggage.

Pan Am's emphasis on quality ensured the best accommodations at each destination, although in those early days hotels in some more remote cities were quite Spartan. This would be balanced by the pleasure of staying in luxurious official government guest houses previously reserved exclusively for dignitaries.

Among the highlights of these trips were visits to specialized schools where the young children trained as gymnasts or acrobats performed for us. Conversations with language students at Tianjin University were especially interesting. They informed us they enjoyed American movies; the latest one they had seen was "Gone With The Wind."

Occasionally we would arrive in a city where our group became the center of attention—as much of an attraction as the local people were to us. In places where everyone had black hair and dressed in Mao-style jackets and trousers, the sight of blond or redheaded "round-eyes," and ladies with knee length skirts and painted nails caused crowds to gather and stare. We felt like movie stars! Polaroid cameras were endlessly fascinating to the Chinese, especially to children who marveled at the magic of instantly developed photos.

In most of the cities we visited, the local residents treated us to the regional cuisine, and many tour members gamely tried to use chopsticks, with varying success. A few decided to request a fork at every meal after they became frustrated and hungry. Breakfast each day was either Chinese style, or the Chinese idea of American—on one occasion featuring chocolate pudding and apple pie along with the scrambled eggs. In each city there was at least one grand banquet dinner featuring local wine, beer and/or strong liquor for the many toasts offered by our local hosts. Fortunately, many of these events took place at our hotel, as several participants would become quite

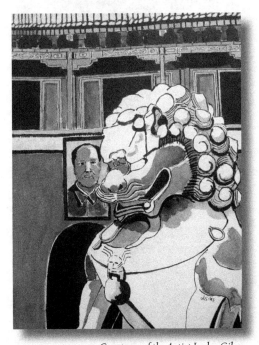

Courtesey of the Artist Lesley Giles

Painting of Lion with Mao-Tiananmen Gate, Forbidden City

133

inebriated by the end of the evening. A very memorable meal was served at a restaurant in Guilin after a pleasant day spent on a boat trip down the scenic Li River. The pathway to the establishment was lined with cages containing various animals and reptiles, which we were unable to identify — and which turned out to be the ingredients of our dinner.

These days, I fondly remember some of the highlights of these long-ago trips when conditions in China were quite primitive in many places: Visiting a people's commune near Shanghai where we were served a multi-course luncheon was voted as best-of-the-trip by members of our group; or inspecting the one-room mud-floored homes in communes where several families shared cooking facilities and where there was no electricity or indoor plumbing. I will always remember visiting Chengdu, in the Sichuan province known for providing the country with medicinal herbs and calling in at the thatch-roofed dispensary of the "barefoot doctor," who successfully treated patients with acupuncture. There was the seaside town of Quingdao, world famous for its German-style beer, its elaborate pier, and Alpine chalet architecture. We enjoyed touring Suzhou, known for its canals, and moon-gated courtyard homes, and the most beautiful women in China. Watching women cultivating rice paddies wearing special large straw hats with long black fringe to ward off the flies while on the train ride from Hong Kong to Canton (now Guangzhou). We will never forget experiencing the magnificent Forbidden City, the Temple of Heaven, and the Summer Palace in Beijing. And, of course, seeing bicycles everywhere.

The contrast between the sophistication of Hong Kong or Tokyo, where our trips began and ended, and the cities of The People's Republic of China, was stark. We flew from New York to Tokyo on the latest non-stop Special Performance modified jet plane, the Boeing 747SP, only to feel as though we had traveled back to a previous century once reaching the Chinese mainland.

Today's China is a very different place; the memories of those early trips will last forever.

Jeanne was a flight attendant based at New York from 1956-1959. She is active with the World Wings International, a philanthropic organization of former Pan Am flight attendants. She lives in New York City.

Courtesy of the Author

TRAVELS WITH RICHARD

By Bruce Haxthausen

Pan Am's Trendsetting Role in Global Air Cargo

Sometimes overlooked in the hubbub of an airline's carriage of people from Point A to B is the role cargo played. Beyond the old standbys of baby chicks and fresh strawberries, live animals and fresh fish, airfreight carried in an aircraft's belly compartments can make the difference between a passenger flight that is profitable and one that is not. Over the years, some passenger carriers even added aircraft dedicated to cargo—freighters that carried shipments on the main deck as well as in the hold. Pan Am was one of the trendsetters in air cargo as in so many other areas, with a fleet of 747 freighters that grew to six in its heyday, the largest such fleet operated by a so-called combination (passenger/cargo) carrier.

Courtesy of Jamie Baldwin

Pan Am's Nose-Loading Boeing 747F

"Advertising is what you pay for, publicity is what you get for free." Like all public relations departments in global industries large and small, Pan Am's PR department worked long and hard to develop publicity campaigns for new routes, lower fares, new passenger amenities, new aircraft, and even new flight attendant uniforms. "Clipper Cargo" could have been lost in the shuffle. After all, the target audience for news about air cargo is rather small compared to that for consumer news benefiting passengers.

But it wasn't lost. Working with the cargo-marketing folks, we in PR gained publicity breaks for Pan Am as a shipping industry leader with its large 747 freighter fleet and a worldwide network offering 747 services to more destinations than any other passenger carrier (and probably more than most of the all-cargo carriers). For publicity, longtime Pan Am staff photographer Paul Friend took great shots of unusual shipments like a giant sculpture, art from the Vatican, Panda bears or an oil well drilling rig that had to be loaded through the 747's upturned nose.

But the constant challenge was how to reach the small group of decision makers at major shippers with news that would continuously promote the size, scope and expertise of the Clipper Cargo operation—and make those leaders think of Pan Am for their shipping needs.

Richard Malkin, an air cargo journalist for the Journal of Commerce in the 1970s and '80s, was one of the true supporters of the air cargo industry going back to the 1940s. Dick and I spoke frequently about Clipper Cargo and developments in the airfreight industry, which he chronicled in interviews with Pan Am cargo execs. He had a marvelous way of speaking and writing in plain English about trends in the field of air cargo, especially focusing on what new shipments were going by air in order to gain the time benefits over surface transport.

It came to light in one of our chats that he was considering writing an in-depth piece that would track a 747 freighter from origin to destination, interviewing local station managers and detailing the commodities carried in and out of various destinations. He wanted to do this on location. I said the best way might be to ride a freighter as a passenger and observe the entire operation first-hand, if we could get permission from the cargo department. Somewhat skeptical at first, the cargo folks warmed to the idea provided a PR person accompanied the journalist. That would be me!

After further consultation with the cargo department, the Chicago-Brussels route (a Pan Am exclusive at the time) was selected as a prime example of Clipper Cargo 747 operations and a good way to highlight Pan Am's service, with a side visit to Frankfurt as well. Flight Ops approved the rather unorthodox carriage of two non-crew members aboard the freighter, which had several rows of economy seats installed on the upper deck aft of the cockpit. Telexes flew back and forth as we sought the cooperation of cargo managers along the route, briefing certain staff members for Malkin to interview and requesting ramp access to observe the loading and unloading process. Special ticketing was required for insurance purposes. Inflight amenities would be limited to the same meals as those provided for the flight deck, warmed up in a mini-galley just behind the cockpit.

Dick and I met in Chicago and drove out to O'Hare for the first segment of this transatlantic odyssey. He did his interviews, observed the loading sequence and then we met the flight crew and clambered aboard the 747. About eight uneventful hours later, we repeated the process on the ramp at Brussels, where after greetings by local staff, we were taken to a superb local restaurant where Dick revealed an unusual mealtime preference: Never mind the foie gras and quenelles, his favorite was always the desserts. (I was glad he wasn't tasked to write a restaurant review.)

The operation went off without a hitch and Malkin's Atlantic article duly appeared in the Journal of Commerce. That account was successful enough that we ended up replicating the project by visiting Pan Am cargo operations centers around the world, traveling together mostly on freighters to South America and then Asia. We hit Sao Paulo, which at the time had its own airport just for cargo, and later Singapore, all during a period of about three or four months. Malkin was a real pro, armed with a standard set of questions for managers everywhere. It was revealing to watch him elicit all manner of information on commodities and logistics from managers who quickly realized that this was a man who knew the business inside and out, oftentimes better than they did.

A total of four of Dick Malkin's first-person accounts appeared in the JOC from mid-1980 to early '81, one for each region we visited. Unfortunately, his articles could not appropriately include experiences like the many fine meals (and desserts) we enjoyed with local Pan Amers during the course of the project, nor such once-in-a-lifetime moments as coming upon a nighttime view of Caracas from the cockpit, city lights twinkling through scattered clouds as we flew northbound above the beginning of the Andes. But I won't forget them.

Bruce was a manager in the headquarters PR Department from 1973 to 1981. Later, he assumed the same position at Air France, returning in 1997 to take up freelance aviation writing for several years. He lives in New York City.

Courtesy of the Author

Courtesy of the Author

Young Bruce at Pan Am's First Office

137

NIGHT FLIGHT TO MOGADISHU

By Ian James (Jim) Duncan

Flying Munitions to Somalia

Late in August 1982, I was part of a volunteer crew who took a Pan American 747 Freighter on a highly classified Military Airlift Command (MAC) Mission from Little Rock, Arkansas to Mogadishu, Somalia. At that time, I was a 747 Check Airman and held the title Manager of Flying of the New York Base at JFK Airport.

Courtesy of the Author

Mogadishu

It began with Bill McCarthy, the Duty Director in Pan American's Operational Control Unit informing me a request had come by way of the Department of Defense, the State Department, and possibly the CIA. The request was the ferry of a 747 cargo freighter to Little Rock AFB to take on an extensive load of Class A munitions (rocket-propelled grenades, .50 caliber bullets and T.O.W. —Tube-launched, Optically Wired controlled missiles). The cargo was to be transported non-stop to Ramstein Airbase, Germany with continuation, after a short crew layover in Frankfurt, via Cairo for refueling, to Mogadishu, Somalia. Ramstein's main runway length of 9300 feet would not allow enough fuel, given the heavy cargo load, to make the flight nonstop to Mogadishu. Bill also cautioned me that the nature of this operation required strict confidentiality until the end of the mission.

My initial call was to my wife who did not take well to the idea.

"Are you insane?" she screamed into the phone. "Have you forgotten we have small children? Why you?"

"It's something I need to do," I replied, assuring her that this was not any different than some military missions I had flown in the past. "Plus, there will be added life insurance" I joked.

Obtaining a crew was a challenge. The ALPA Union office only needed to hear—military charter— class A explosives—flight to Mogadishu – to react briefly: "Find volunteers, and if you have to use Management crew, pay appropriate hourly tracking to the MEC (Master Executive Council of ALPA) account." A call to the Flight Engineers Association resulted in a similar answer.

Courtesy of the Author

Ian and Ilona Duncan

Most of my appeals to fellow crewmen were immediately scoffed as I explained the nature of the assignment. Ultimately, the Manager of 747 Flight Training at our Miami Training Center, Capt. Dwain Turlington, would join me for the initial segment to Ramstein. As though it were ordained, my good friend Jack Meyers walked into my office to shoot the breeze before leaving on a flight to Frankfurt. Without blinking an eye, Jack agreed to operate the second part of the mission out of Ramstein. When Flight Engineer Gene Turner, a commuter from the West Coast, who was at JFK on stand-by looking to fill out his monthly flying hours, teamed up, our crew was completed.

At sun-up the following day, the empty, overpowered 747 Cargo Liner lifted off the runway at JFK like a jet fighter and rocketed to our cruise altitude of 39,000 ft in a matter of minutes on its way to Little Rock AFB. Later that day, after arrival and a few hours rest, we closely inspected the Dangerous Goods Manifest. "Looks like a mega load of fireworks," Dwain commented sarcastically as we checked the secure tie downs of hundreds of boxes in the lower cargo compartment. In addition to the flight plan, weather and wind forecasts, we were handed a special advisory to steer and remain clear of British and Belgian airspace. European and African countries had allowed "only by exception" the overflight of any aircraft carrying class A explosives. This came about as a result of an Air Force B-52 dropping nuclear weapons into the Mediterranean Sea off the coast of Spain in January 1966 after colliding with a tanker aircraft. We were further cautioned to clarify any alteration in our flight path to ensure that we were not knowingly crossing the threshold of any country which prohibited our overflight.

We took off into the evening sky crossing over the Atlantic to overhead at Quimper, France in the early morning hours and continued on a straight path to land at Ramstein AFB, in Southwestern Germany. An Air Force "Follow Me" truck in bright yellow colors guided us to the Dangerous Cargo loading ramp where six

Armored Personnel Carriers were added to the upper deck cargo compartment. A Mercedes taxi took us to the InterContinental Hotel in Frankfurt, where, after a beer and a bratwurst, we got some well deserved sleep.

Over breakfast the following morning, Jack, Gene, and I speculated how they would route us from Ramstein to Cairo, as the result of the denial of overflight rights over Austria, Italy, and Switzerland. We were to be picked-up at the hotel at 3 p.m. for a late afternoon departure. However, back in our rooms we were further perplexed by a phone message stating that our departure from the hotel had been moved up by one hour to allow time for a military classified security briefing. The puzzle was solved at Ramstein when we heard the words of the Air Force intelligence officer: "From Cairo Southeast bound to Mogadishu you must fly radio silent. Do not answer any transmissions, don't use your transponder; what's more important, you will not obtain the usual Air Traffic Control clearance!"

That was big news to me.

"Were you told any of this before?" inquired Jack.

"I had no idea, honestly," I replied.

"Yeah, right," Jack answered.

Despite this unsettling information, we agreed to stick with the plan and take off on our night flight to Mogadishu. Soon we left France behind and looked down on the dark waters of the Mediterranean flying around the boot of Italy southeast to land in Cairo. During refueling we scrutinized our flight plan once more at the operations office. We were to fly a southeasterly track along the center line of the Suez Canal and the Red Sea. The airspace to the east of our course was Saudi Arabia and Yemen, to the west, the Sudan, Ethiopia, the disputed territory of Eritrea, and finally Somalia. At the mouth of the Red Sea, to make it appear on radar that we were destined somewhere else, we were to fly one hundred nautical miles off-shore, and around the Horn of Africa.

"We are going to be pretty much on our own for most of the night without any air traffic control contact," I noted. "Let's take on a bit of extra fuel in case we have to divert to Nairobi."

The Pan Am freighter lifted off once again into the night sky. The city lights of Cairo gave way to the darkness of the desert below. Thirty minutes into the flight, 150 miles southeast of Cairo, the heavy plane was still laboring to reach its cruising altitude. The termination of all communications with the Egyptian air controllers created an eerie stillness. The only contact we could safely make was an hourly call to contact Pan Am Dispatch via Berna Radio in Switzerland on the high frequency single side band radio: "Pan Am Clipper Operations Normal."

Somewhere over the Red Sea, Jack speculated: "What do you think will happen if someone gets wind of us?"

"Whatever we do, let's stay clear of Yemen and Ethiopia," Gene warned.

"The worst area is at the mouth of the Red Sea," I said, recalling the words of the intelligence officer.

"Yeah, ground to air missiles," Jack chuckled.

We continued to monitor the local VHF air traffic control frequencies for information on other air traffic nearby and overhear various aircraft reporting their positions.

"Good, no altitude conflicts," Jack remarked.

"With the extra fuel we could speed up transiting this godforsaken place by using a higher cruise Mach air speed," Gene suggested.

"Let's do it."

As we approached 200 miles north of the mouth of the Red Sea, we eased the power up to hold Mach .88, cutting our transit time by ten minutes. A blind warning call came over the radio: "Aircraft heading 140 degrees at high speed 65 Miles NW of Addis Ababa, identify yourself."

"Let's see if they have anything to catch us," Jack exclaimed.

"As far as I recall, they have no aircraft capable of intercepting us according to the Intelligence Officer," I remarked.

"I hope he was right." was Gene's comment.

As we were not responding, the warnings came repeatedly from Addis Ababa and Sanaa. "Strangest flight during my Pan Am career," I remarked as a visible shrug of relief is felt by all three of us once the plane has turned further to the East to carry us out over the Indian Ocean and around the Horn of Africa.

"We conquered the worst," Jack said smiling, as he poured a cup of coffee out of a thermos.

More than four hours after leaving Cairo, we made our first radio call to Mogadishu, where we would arrive forty minutes later.

On the ground and from the ramp we watched men unload the Armored Personnel Carriers. "Do you think we could take one for a spin around the ramp?" Jack asked the Somali officer. "If you think you know how to drive it, go ahead," he answered.

It was a small reward for the Pan Am family having performed the assigned task. Pan American had supported our nation in the past. We were merely filling another square.

Jim was a New York based pilot from 1964-1988. He also served as JFK Base Manager, System Chief Pilot and V.P. Flight Operations.

Courtesy of the Author

LONDON LORE

Edited By Mike Sullivan; Written by Roger Freeland, Ron McBride, David Samson, André Allsop-Menist and Dave Turvey
Stories from Across the Pond

Buggies at Heathrow

In the 1980s, Ken Freeland was Director of Passenger Service for Pan Am at Heathrow and Chairman of the Airport AOC (Airline Operators Committee). One day he was approached by a company which made electric golf buggies proposing to give Pan Am a few buggies in our colours and logo in order to try them out as terminal transport for disabled and late passengers. He thought this was a great idea and he put the proposal before the British Airports Authority (BAA) which owned the airport.

Photo by Jamie Baldwin

Pan Am Flight 2 at London Heathrow Airport

142

The BAA was well known for its bureaucracy and immediately rejected the idea on safety grounds. Later, however, at his monthly meeting with the BAA, he said in the nicest and kindest possible way that the BAA should consider the immense benefits to the airport and passengers, and not worry too much about the problems, as these would be resolved during the trial period. Pan Am was reluctantly granted a three-month trial.

A few weeks later the then British Minister for Transport, Michael Heseltine, came to Heathrow to officially open the new British Airways Concorde Lounge in Terminal 3 and, surrounded by scores of flunkies, was walking down the walkways of Terminal 3 toward the opening ceremony. The walk was over a quarter of a mile, so Ken saw an opportunity and drove the buggy alongside the Minister. "Would you like a lift to the Concorde Lounge, Minister"? he asked. Michael Heseltine was astonished with the sight of the buggy and immediately accepted a lift, leaving the flunkies behind.

Courtesy of the Editor

Michael Sullivan was Formerly Director, In-Flight Services at London Heathrow Airport.

After a few minutes chatting, Ken said, "Minister, we are being blocked from introducing this service to our passengers and the airport by the BAA, which does not seem to see the great benefits to the customers. We would love your support. So what do you think of the buggy?" Michael Heseltine seemed tremendously impressed.

When the flunkies reached the lounge some 10 minutes later, the Minister sang the praises of the buggy idea, only to be told sheepishly by the out-of-breath BAA executives they were thinking of approving the plan. The Minister instructed them to accept it on the spot. Thus Pan Am became the first airline at Heathrow to operate a buggy fleet in its terminal. Within a few years, most airlines had them and now they are a part of the infrastructure at Heathrow, assisting thousands of disabled, elderly and late show passengers reach their departure gates in comfort and on time.

—*Roger Freeland (son of Ken)*

A Difficult Passenger

This story stems from the early 1950's. The Government in its wisdom had decided to locate the main airport serving London at Heathrow Heath, adjacent to two large reservoirs. In those days before such measures as the Clean Air Act came in to force, it was an all-too-frequent occurrence for Heathrow to be closed in fog for days on end. Navigation aids to assist landing aircraft in difficult weather conditions also lacked the sophistication and accuracy of those available to pilots today.

This story started on just such an occasion. Heathrow was closed in fog and it was decided the westbound Round the World Flight, *Clipper One*, be diverted to Hurn, near Bournemouth on the South Coast of England. Five of us went by car, in itself a rather difficult task in the conditions, to look after the passengers when they arrived at Hurn.

Shortly after the arrival of *Clipper One* in Hurn, the weather there also deteriorated and the decision was made to send the London-destined passengers to London by coach and to overnight the transit passengers at a hotel in Bournemouth. The former was accomplished without delay—not so the latter. When we checked the number of passengers to go to the hotel, one was missing. We found an elderly lady still sitting on the aircraft and refusing to budge. She spoke no English nor any other language known to us, but having established that she had boarded in Istanbul, we found a paper that had been given to her indicating the length of time she should expect to remain on the aircraft before arriving at her destination, which was New York. Since that time had not yet elapsed, she wanted to remain on the aircraft.

After vigorous sign language and pointing to the fog that was by now very thick, she joined the other passengers on the coach to go to the hotel. After a meal at the hotel, she was shown to her room and we relaxed. This was a mistake! The time forecast to get to New York had elapsed and she now thought she should leave. She was escorted back to her room and my colleagues Anne Harcourt together with Adrienne Corbishley stood guard. Several times she tried to leave, but finally she went to bed and Anne and Adrienne locked the door.

The next morning the other passengers boarded the coach to return to the airport which was now open. Not this lady! First she jammed the main rotating door of the hotel so that nobody could enter or leave. When this was resolved, she wrapped her arms around some railings. The other passengers watched in amusement as another colleague, Ken Freeland, and I tried to pry her away. With her build of an ox and strength to match, this was no easy matter.

Courtesy of the Author

Ron was formerly Director of Terminal Services, London Heathrow Airport.

At that moment a deep voice said, " `Allo, `Allo and what have we here then?" A member of the Constabulary had arrived. He gently took her by the arms and led her to the coach to the cheers of the passengers. She obviously recognized authority! We thanked the policeman, who then asked the identity of our airline. When we told him, he suggested, "Perhaps more training would be in order if that is the way you treat your passengers." He then departed at a measured policeman-like pace.

Three weeks later *Clipper Two* arrived eastbound. Transit passengers were waiting in the Final Lounge, and among them was the lady from Istanbul. She saw Anne Harcourt and started to brandish her fists, so Anne beat a hasty retreat. Later there was panic at the airport as there was a person on the runway and flights were being held. You guessed it! The lady from Istanbul! Police were dispatched to detain her, but it was decided to take no further action other than to make sure she was on the flight with the hope we never saw her again!

—Ron McBride

Pan Am Flight 001 (*Clipper One*)

Pan Am was unique among the airlines at London Heathrow as most of the flights were transit rather than originating or terminating. This resulted in situations requiring resolutions or handling, generally not experienced by the other airlines. One specific situation I had to deal with as a duty manager in the early 1970s relates to the transit of *The Round the World Flight PA001, Clipper One*. The flight arrived on time and the arriving passengers disembarked with no problems. I was just about to go below and check the ramp activities when the purser requested that I go and speak to a transit passenger who was insisting that he disembark in London. As we would have to locate and offload his baggage, it would most probably delay the flight departure. I went to see the passenger who was a male in his thirties and had boarded at Istanbul.

He spoke poor English and was mumbling, making it even more difficult to understand what he was saying, but we did understand he wanted to disembark the aircraft. After several questions as to why he wanted to disembark, he finally managed to explain he was en-route to meet his girlfriend in New York and could not meet her in his present condition. Apparently after leaving Frankfurt he had gone to the lavatory and somehow lost his false teeth down the toilet and was unable to recover them. He could not meet her without his teeth! As the toilets had already been serviced in Frankfurt, there was no requirement to service them again at London. After briefing the purser and captain, and requesting the passenger remain onboard while I sought to resolve the problem, I contacted the toilet service crew and asked them to attend to *Clipper One*. As time was critical, they agreed to drop the rear toilet and hope to get lucky. Meanwhile, the ramp crew was attempting to locate the passenger's baggage.

Eureka! They located his set of dentures which was a great relief. I went back to the aircraft, informing the purser and captain of the situation and took a sick bag back down to the ramp with me and placed the dentures therein. Meanwhile, boarding had commenced. With the dentures in the sick bag, I approached the passenger and told him that he could now proceed to New York and meet his girlfriend. To my utter amazement he took them out of the sick bag and put them straight into his mouth without even a thank you.

In the best Pan Am tradition, the flight departed on time, with one very satisfied but—unhygienic—passenger.

—**David Samson**

Courtesy of the Author
David

An Immigration Problem

Pan Am Heathrow personnel over the years had become used to dealing with all sorts of odd situations. One such situation was to be served by an HM Immigration Officer with an order to arrange for the deportation of a non-violent immigration refusal that had arrived by Pan Am.

Over the years the rapport between HM Immigration and Pan Am was one of great understanding and cooperation. In the case of a possibly troublesome deportee, the Immigration Officer would contact the Association of Retired Police officers who would supply one of their group to accompany the deportee from wherever he/she had arrived. Over the years, Pan Am at Heathrow also became involved in the returning of non-violent deportees with Pan Am staff volunteering to carry out these duties on overtime. I was lucky enough to fulfill some of these trips and in most cases, quite enjoyed them.

One immigration case, in particular, comes to mind. A particular gentleman from one of the West African countries had arrived at Heathrow and was to be detained by HM Immigration in order to complete a full investigation into his documentation. From experience, it is fair to say an official investigation could take some time. In general, immigration officers would bend over backwards and really put themselves out to try and make it possible for passengers to be let into the UK. However, this particular passenger ended up with an official refusal and thus the airline would become responsible for arrangements to deport him. I was asked by my superior if I would be willing to accompany this gentleman through London in order to go to his Consul and be issued with fresh documents of his country. (His original documents had been destroyed by person(s) unknown, prior to landing at Heathrow.) As long as he carried his documents, Immigration would allow him to travel on to the United States, for which he carried a visa. There would be no need for anyone to accompany him on the flight.

I agreed to accompany this gentleman across London to his High Commission in South Kensington. It was quite a pleasant trip for both of us. Upon arrival at the High Commission, the passenger was told to obtain some passport photos before they could do anything. We jumped back into the taxi and decided to proceed to the photographers at Harrods and have the necessary photos taken. As they needed a wee while to prepare the photos, I took the gentleman for a snack in the Harrods café. All very pleasant indeed, he enjoyed moving around the glamour of London. He was really a delightful gentleman of certain intelligence!

Returning to the High Commission, the personnel there were most helpful whilst putting this Pan Am passenger through the procedures required for the issue of a fresh passport and documents. Both of us were impressed with the charm and sheer happiness of the staff. The answer to this little world of happiness became clear to us. In the process of dealing with the application for a fresh passport, several drawers had to be opened to retrieve official forms for filling out. My passenger and I were a little surprised to see, quite openly, that each drawer that was opened carried at least one bottle of gin. The passenger was even offered a wee drop of this evidently enjoyable liquid and that put a smile on his face. Now I understand why some passport offices in the UK are much happier than others......

—André Allsop-Menist

An Encounter with Air Force One

I remember being on relief in Hanover, Germany, when Pan Am was operating DC-6Bs when British European Airways (BEA) was flying the much more modern Vickers Viscounts on the Berlin routes via the strict Berlin corridor over East Germany. This all changed later, during another of my relief spells there, shortly after the Pan Am Boeing 727s began flying between Hanover and Berlin Templehof. I was waiting in our operations office for the arrival of our mid-morning flight, when we heard the Pan Am crew call up and request permission from ATC to pass the little old propeller BEA aircraft, so that they could land ahead of it. Permission was given to the *Clipper* and this prompted the BEA Captain to request permission to talk to the *Clipper*. Again permission was given by ATC, and in a very stiff upper lip British accent, the BEA captain replied to the *Clipper*'s comment, "It's quality, old chap, not quantity that counts." This raised quite a laugh to those of us in the Ops office!

In June 1984, I was sent to Shannon to handle two Pan Am Press charters for the visit of President Reagan to Ireland. As usual, one of the Press aircraft, a DC-10, arrived ahead of Air Force One with the President, followed by the second Press Charter, a Boeing 747. I was invited to join the tarmac welcoming ceremony, along with the Air Force One and Pan Am crew members. I remember being surprised how small Nancy Reagan was compared to the President. Afterwards, I was invited to join the Air Force One crew that evening at Bunratty Castle where they were going to enjoy the famous Medieval Banquet. Unfortunately for me, the Boeing 747 had an engine generator problem and by the time I had acquired spares from London, it was too late to attend. The aircraft repositioned a couple of days later, to Dublin, from where the President was to depart Ireland. Again, one Press Charter took off ahead of Air Force One. After the departure of the President, I boarded the DC-10 with the remainder of the Press pack. Bottles of Irish Whiskey were handed out to all the Press at the foot of the steps, this time my luck was better; as I got to the foot of the steps, I, too, had a bottle thrust into my hand.

—Dave Turvey

Courtesy of the Author

Dave

LAST ROUND-THE-WORLD FLIGHT

By Merle Richman
The Final Chapter

They say when French writer Jules Verne wrote *Around the World in 80 Days* in 1873 it was during a financially difficult time for the classic adventure novelist. Compared to Pan Am's travails, it was no sweat. He couldn't have been as financially bad-off as Pan Am was over a hundred years later when the airline decided to end its historic Round-the-World Flights One and Two. But whether it was Verne's novel, which I had read many years earlier, or perhaps Nellie Bly's 1889 epic 72-day tale which she wrote for her newspaper, the *New York World*, I was awed by their feat and saw the last Pan Am RTW flights as my final opportunity.

Courtesy of the Author

Merle's children at departure on the last Pan Am Round the World Flight

So it was on a fall evening in 1982 during dinner with my family that I announced that I was going to fly around the world that coming weekend, leaving October 28, 1982 and listened as my 14-year-old daughter Diana quickly ask if she could join me, followed later by my 12-year old son Dwight. Not sure that they understood the magnitude of the undertaking, I explained that the curtailing of Pan Am's Flights 1 and 2, which had been operating since June 17, 1947, represented surrendering what many considered the most symbolic aspect of the airline. No other airline in the world had previously ever even attempted to make round-the-world service commercially viable. And we would be on the last flight!

Courtesy of the Author

Diana and Dwight on board the Boeing 747 with Dad

Not only would we be on the final flight, departing Los Angeles that Friday at noon, I told Diana and Dwight that if anybody in recent history had boarded Flight 1 and remained with the plane for the entire duration of the flight until it landed at JFK in New York on Sunday afternoon, I and others I queried, were unaware of such a back-breaking marathon.

With the advent of jet service in 1958 with the Boeing 707, Pan Am switched the departure city of Flight 1 from San Francisco to Los Angeles. Thus the route of the flight would be Los Angeles-Tokyo-Hong Kong-Bangkok- Bombay-Dubai-Istanbul-Frankfurt-London-New York on a Boeing 747.

And so on Friday, October 28, 1982, with Capt. Carl Wallace in the left hand seat, we joined the world of Verne and Bly albeit in a lot more comfortable environment than Phileas Fogg, and certainly easier than that of Henry Bensley, who in 1908 on a wager, set out to circumnavigate the world on foot wearing an iron mask! Certainly the venture gave plenty of time for reflective thought. Phileas Fogg was depicted by Verne as a rich English nobleman. But by 1982 it would not require the wealth of a man like Fogg to circumnavigate the globe. Pioneering Pan Am had on occasion offered round-the-world promotional fares in the area of $2,000 and purchasers could get on and off the flights at desired stops and re-board the daily flights days later. Those who worked for Pan Am, however, with the inherent travel privileges, could see the world for "peanuts," to borrow from Southwest Airlines. For Diana and Dwight, the RTW trip was an unparalleled emotional and educational experience.

Some two full days after takeoff from Los Angeles, we landed in New York on a brilliant sunny fall day. We made it in one piece after 56-hours of flying. We had eaten the best airline food in the world (more breakfasts than dinners when you fly west to east), pasted GO PIRATES stickers (supporting the West Windsor-Plainsboro High School, NJ marching band) somewhere in most of the airports we landed. And yes, Diana and Dwight even did some of the homework they brought with them.

Altogether, the flight covered 18,647 miles in 39 hours and 30 minutes of actual flying time. And who knows how many steaks! Worth every bite!

Pan Am Archives

John McCoy Watercolor of Pan Am's
First Round-the-World Flight

Merle enjoys globetrotting from his base in Amelia Island, FL.

148

PAN AM'S MARATHON MAN

By Rod Dixon

Winning the New York Marathon for Pan Am

My father, Royd Leslie Dixon, was a consultant to the South Island Tourism Promotion Association. He had travelled extensively in Australia in the late 1930's giving lectures on New Zealand and promoting the idea of New Zealand as a tourist destination. I remember him telling me he was in Auckland, New Zealand in 1940 when the first Pan Am flight from the USA touched down on the Waitemata Harbor. It was one of the Pan Am Clipper Flying Boats. This excited him and he realized at the time, the potential for tourism for New Zealand with and through Pan American World Airways. I remember as a small boy, he always had a Pan Am bag with tourism material ready to give to anyone who would listen.

Courtesy of the Author

Rod Dixon wins the New York Marathon

In 1976 New Zealand athletes John Walker (Olympic Champion), Dick Quax and I talked with the Director of Sales and Marketing for South Pacific Television about developing an International Athletics Tour for the European and USA Athletes to enable them to come to New Zealand and Australia for competitions. These would take place during the New Zealand Summer Month of January. From these talks, South Pacific Television engaged Pan Am as the co-name sponsor of the series to be known as the Pan Am South Pacific Television International Track Series. I was very involved in the development of the series and convinced Pan Am and South Pacific Television to have an international track and field meeting in Nelson, my hometown.

The series developed with three events in Australia and four in New Zealand during late 1976 and into 1977. Pan Am was the Official Airline and carried the best athletes from all over the world to New Zealand and Australia. The success of the International Track Series continued in 1978 and again in 1979.

Through television, competition among the best athletes in the world was brought into homes all around New Zealand and Australia. South Pacific Television achieved the highest ever ratings in the history of the channel. Pan Am also enjoyed the best consumer awareness ever for the airline in the region and also assisted our Olympic Athletes with favorable travel discounts for our travel to the USA and Europe—some of the very first support we ever received.

In 1979 as I prepared for my European campaign of training and racing towards selection for the New Zealand Olympic Team for the 1980 Olympic Games in Moscow, I approached Mr. Wayne Stenning, General Manager of Pan Am, New Zealand, for assistance with travel to the USA and onwards to Great Britain and Europe. He was very supportive with discounts on many flights, easing the burden of my European travel expense. I performed so well that I returned to New Zealand undefeated and ranked #1 in the world in my classification. From then on, I carried the Pan Am logo on my training equipment, and competition shirt, and travelled the world. The success of this sponsorship resulted in a very close working relationship between myself and Pan Am.

In 1980, following selection to represent New Zealand at the Olympic Games, again Pan Am supported me in my plans to seek competitions in Europe in preparation for the games. In May of 1980, however, the New Zealand Olympic Committee announced our country would not send a team to Moscow because of the Soviet boycott. I immediately decided I would focus on the USA Road Running Series and again approached Pan Am for their support in my quest to achieve my goal as "The Number One Ranked USA Road Running Champion." Pan Am decided as "one of their people," I should be part of the head count as a Special Employee with the New Zealand office. Mr. Richard Elliott, who in 1980 was the General Manager of the Pan Am office in Auckland, was a huge supporter. Together with all the staff, he gave me assistance whenever and wherever I travelled and competed.

During 1980-1981-1982, I was traveling almost every weekend within the USA, running and winning races from the 5k through to the Half Marathon, and in every race, I carried the Pan Am logo on my shirt. I began appearing in running magazines, in fitness and health magazines, and on television. I even had a running shoe named after me. The American runners knew who I was. I was also known as the Pan Am Athlete.

I would often visit the Pan Am offices and managers at various locations to meet and greet staff, who were now starting to follow my running successes and feeling proud that I was representing them. Whenever I travelled on a Pan Am flight anywhere in the world, I would always send my greetings to the captain and the flight deck crew. The flight attendants were always so supportive and excited to know I was one of them. On a good number of flights, the captain would invite me to the flight deck to discuss running, fitness, and health. Pan Am flight crews were always very conscious of their health and fitness, and I developed special friendships with many of the flight crews around the world. Everyone was committed to serving Pan Am in the most professional manner.

In March of 1982, I finished in third place at the World Cross Country Championships, won the Auckland New Zealand Marathon, and later in September, set the world record for the half Marathon at Philadelphia. I started receiving calls from New York City Marathon Race Director Fred Lebow to run the New York City Marathon. I knew the marathon distance required special training and with time and patience, I was prepared to train exclusively for the New York City Marathon. I discussed this with Mr. Jeff Kriendler at Pan Am Public Relations and told him I would go into the most intensive training I had ever done and I would totally commit myself to competing in the 1983 New York City Marathon. Jeff told me everyone at Pan Am was fully supportive and would continue its support during my preparation.

Four days before New York City Marathon, I remember taking a Pan Am flight from Philadelphia to New York, knowing this was the best prepared I had ever been for any of my previous races. I was confident of a great performance. On arrival at JFK, Pan Am Staff members met and escorted me to the Pan Am helicopter, a special flight for a special Pan Am Ambassador. The staff at JFK all cheered and gave me best wishes for the marathon. I felt like every Pan Am staff member was on My Team and I really did feel honored and privileged to be a part of the Team. I carried the Pan Am patch on my competition shirt every mile of the 1983 New York City Marathon. Amid the cheers of the thousands of spectators, I often heard, *"Go Pan Am!"* I was running the race of my life with the support of every Pan Am employee and felt proud to know we were together in this, a race to the finish line, to be crowned New York City Marathon Champions.

Later, I was overcome with pride when it was announced that a 747 would be named Pan Am Clipper Rod Dixon and would fly the skies between New York-Los Angeles-Auckland and Sydney. I had the privilege and pleasure of traveling many, many times on my "own" 747.

I had an amazing relationship with Pan Am spanning 12 years.

Rod (right) was a Special Consultant and Ambassador to Pan Am from 1979-1990. He finished 10th in the marathon in the 1980 Olympics and also guided a blind runner in the 1985 Bay to Breakers in San Francisco. Today, he devotes his time from his Southern California base to the health benefits of running—especially for children.

LIVING MY DREAM

By Ivan Dezelic

From Immigrant to the Pan Am Executive Suite

It was the mid 1960's on a small island of the former Yugoslavia. The communist regime under the dictatorship of Marshal Tito was at its peak, and I was a young man indoctrinated by the Communist Party to serve my homeland country—and Tito himself. Being young, restless and driven, I had other plans and ideas in mind rather than becoming a member of the Communist Party that was working its way from Asia across Europe. I wanted to follow so many other young men I had heard of who were escaping in droves from the stronghold of Communism over the ever more protected borders of Yugoslavia to the New World of America and beyond.

Thus, before I knew it, the day had come when I had an opportunity to escape to neighboring Italy and I seized the moment! I was on my way towards my new freedom and destiny as I had imagined and dreamed. But never did I envision what great opportunities would soon be filling my life. I spent the next couple of years moving around through various refugee camps awaiting my final destination. Finally, the time had arrived when my life would change forever. I received my American immigrant visa and soon after, I boarded an Alitalia charter flight to the new land of opportunities. I arrived in New York City without a penny to my name or a family to lean on, ready to embark on this new life I had so desired and dreamt about while working on the farms of a small village and struggling with the forces of a communist military life.

Interestingly, as luck would have it, I was able to obtain a job working in the restaurant located on the lobby level of the Pan Am Building on Park Avenue. While there, I had the most incredible experience of meeting the Pan Am man himself, the legendary Juan Trippe! He saw potential in this young man; he saw drive, and a desire to capture the world. The day I met this CEO was the day my life started moving upwards.

Courtesy of the Author

Ivan (left) and his family.

152

He offered me the chance to grow, to learn the business and become a member of the most precious family, Pan Am employees. I learned directly from him, and from that day forward as I not only moved from floor to higher floor, climbing the corporate ladder and advancing to higher positions along the way, I was always afforded a unique opportunity to become a close confidant of every CEO of Pan Am until its very last days in service.

While my new home, family and career in America provided me the chance to start living my dreams, to learn and develop new skills, working tirelessly on developing various new projects for the betterment of my great employer, I never forgot the far-off land, from which I came. Consequently, one day I suggested to my then current boss, Ed Acker, that Pan Am should fly and offer services to the countries behind the Communist Iron Curtain. As a salesman for Pan Am at the time, I worked in various markets directly with our competitors, such as Swissair, KLM, Lufthansa, JAT and other European carriers who were monopolizing the Eastern European markets. There was no US carrier service available in the region. Ed was intrigued with the idea and was inspired to make a visit to my homeland country and village where I grew up. He, along with his wife, Sandy, joined my wife and me for a visit to Yugoslavia, to experience the quaint village where I was born, along with a few other major cities within the country.

In those days, it was customary for the visiting head of an airline company to pay their respects to the country's national carrier, which was the Yugoslav National Airline, JAT. While JAT had already been operating services between the Yugoslav national capital, Belgrade and the United States, there was an evident need for services to other major cities of Yugoslavia, such as Zagreb, today's capital city of Croatia, and the eternal and renowned city of Dubrovnik. Thus here was a unique opportunity for our company, Pan Am, to begin services in this region while avoiding direct competition with the national carrier.

Soon after, we were visiting Dubrovnik and having a courtesy meeting with the executives of JAT. A discussion of the country's capability to develop tourism was the hot topic on the table. The head of the JAT delegation was about to reach across the table for a butter plate when Ed Acker dropped a bombshell! He announced that Pan Am would start service to the Republic of Croatia that coming summer and would be flying into Zagreb. The table suddenly got chaotic as the JAT man pulled his hand back so quickly that he lost his balance, and he and his chair went tumbling backwards. No one could have ever believed the weight of those precise words on the JAT team. Pan Am not only started service to Zagreb the following year, but also to Dubrovnik and later to Belgrade itself. All of this was made possible because of the tremendous capabilities Pan Am had at its Frankfurt hub, to begin spreading its wings. My involvement in developing not only the Yugoslav market, but the rest of Eastern Europe and the former USSR as well, was well on the rise.

Another great opportunity to help launch the brand new services to Yugoslavia was just around the corner, as Pan Am became the official airline carrier for the 1984 Winter Olympic Games. The hard work and efforts of the great Pan Am team and my many fond co-workers had just begun.

The Provincial Capital of the Republic of Bosnia and Hercegovina, Sarajevo, was elected to be the host of the 1984 Winter Olympic Games. Here in this Republic, as well as for the whole of Yugoslavia, was a once-in-a lifetime opportunity to showcase its national and regional capabilities, its people and culture to the rest of the world. This was also an exclusive opportunity for Pan Am and its family of employees to show off the best they had. We assembled a team of experts in all fields of services to ensure every area would be covered with precision. We established fully functioning capabilities to operate an airline in a city with very scarce air service and little know how to receive thousands of foreigners from all walks of life who were about to arrive and witness the world's most competitive sporting event ever held in the Balkans. We trained airport employees, worked hand-in-hand with government officials, representatives within the Republic's organizing committees and local folks themselves. Pan Am's team members were the stars and pride of the town.

There was nothing that we asked of the locals or officials that would not be done for us as reciprocity for how we treated them and helped to organize this most special event. There were days when American visitors arrived without the necessary visa to enter the country. All they needed to do was say that they were Pan Am customers and they were granted unlimited entry into the country on the spot. Such was our relationship with the hosting government.

Our marketing team produced special Pan Am Olympic pins for the Winter Games. These Pan Am pins became the hottest item to trade around the Games, and quickly became, and still are, a collector's item. Pan Am operated the first ever daily service between New York and Sarajevo, Yugoslavia. No snow storm, bad weather conditions nor other complications stopped our team from performing.

To our amazement, on the approach for landing, if a major snowstorm was in progress, which was often the case, the locals, with the coordination of our experts, plowed the runways so that no flight was ever cancelled or diverted. Pan Am made history as the world's carrier with this momentous occasion. There were so many proud moments of my involvement in this project and so many outstanding men and women on our team who worked day and night to make Pan Am's extraordinary service known the world over. It was truly an emotional experience for me to return to the country of my birth in the limelight of such a public presence, an experience and life that only Pan Am could provide.

So, here I stand today, now as a retired airline employee, the dream still alive within me as the day I emigrated from the remote village on an island off the coast of the present day Croatia, remembering Pan Am and all of the great members of this family, who offered me the opportunity to live and develop the real American dream!

Pan Am, I salute you, your humble and grateful employee, Ivan Dezelic.

Courtesy of the Author

"Ivo" retired from Delta and now stays active at his Miami base. He and his wife, Kathy, see their children and grand-children in the States, and his relatives in his beloved Croatia.

Courtesy of the Author

RE-ENACTMENT OF THE CHINA CLIPPER FLIGHT

By Cass Meyers

Planning for an Historic Event

Contrary to what one might think, the original Pan Am *China Clipper* did not fly to China. The flight originated in San Francisco and terminated in Manila, Philippines. On the way, it stopped at Honolulu, Midway Island, Wake Island and Guam before arriving in Manila. It then returned by the same route.

To celebrate the *China Clipper*'s 50th anniversary it was decided to "re-enact" that flight with a flight departing on November 22, 1985 from San Francisco. The flight would be operated with a Boeing 747 but would follow the

Official First Day of Issue

China Clipper   USAirmail 33

SAN FRANCISCO, CA
FEB 15 1985
94188

FIRST DAY OF ISSUE

LOADING THE MAIL

China Clipper
ArtCraft FIRST TRANSPACIFIC AIRMAIL
© USPS 1985

Pan American Archives

Commemorative Envelope

155

exact route of the original *China Clipper* with stops (and festivities) at each of the waypoints of the original flight. The 1985 version would even carry a US Postmaster who stamped and posted letters and cards along the way.

Pan Am marketed the seats on the flight commercially and there were many celebrities participating, including author James Michener, an astronaut, and other dignitaries such as Charles Lindbergh's four grandsons. The Manila Hotel on Manila Bay was also nearly taken over for the group where two days of fun was planned.

Two outside factors made the re-enactment especially interesting: (1) United Airlines had already purchased Pan Am's Pacific Division and was scheduled to take over flight operations as United Airlines in early February 1986; and (2) the President and First lady of the Philippines, Ferdinand and Imelda Marcos, were on their last legs as rulers, both literally and figuratively. In a couple months, the world would know that Imelda Marcos owned 2,000 pairs of shoes!

Being based at the Pan Am Regional Office in Hong Kong, I was fortunate to be among those responsible for the setup on the ground in Manila for the arrival, greeting and hotel transfer of the passengers, as well as the ceremonies and entertainment that followed.

The event itself was what was expected and more! The arrival went without a hitch. The Pan Am Country Manager, the late Joe Basso, even managed to locate the same bugler who, in 1935 was a Boy Scout, and who, at 58 years of age, played the same bugle for the arrival. Needless to say, a great time was had by all but it was, in a way, bittersweet, as Pan Am's presence in the Pacific was rapidly coming to an end.

To deflect their negative reputation at the time, the Marcos' became involved and the Pan Am *China Clipper* event became national news (the news media at the time was controlled by the Philippine government, i.e., the Marcos'). It also took away attention a bit from the deteriorating political situation in the country. There were daily demonstrations of "People Power" throughout Manila, the same People Power that would eventually lead to the overthrow of the Marcos' Government.

The day after the flight arrived, Pan Am hosted a black-tie banquet—with Imelda being the honored guest. She even sang several songs for the packed ball-room, accompanied by a 25-piece orchestra. Lady Gaga she was not! They (Ferdinand and Imelda) also decided to host a gala sunset cruise in Manila Bay (unplanned) for the passengers to get some positive publicity. The thing was, there was already an event scheduled to be held on a Philippine Navy ship (obtained by Pan Am for some first class tickets to a few admirals). The Marcos decided that selected guests should attend their party on the Presidential Yacht (which was as big if not bigger than the navy ship). So there ensued some scrambling and the making of an A list and a B list of those who would go on the navy ship and those who would go on the yacht. I opted for the Navy ship and am glad I did—it was a blast!

Courtesy of the Author

Cass Meyers (top right)

Cass was with Pan Am from 1982-1985 as Regional Director, Sales-Southeast Asia, based in Hong Kong. He now lives in Singapore.

In the end, it was an enormous success for Pan Am and probably the last event of its kind in aviation history—unless United Airlines wants to re-enact the 80th anniversary in 2015, in which case I'll be glad to help!

CHINA CLIPPER II

By Ann Whyte

Retracing the Route of the China Clipper in a Boeing 747

"You swept away forever the distance which separated the great continent of America and the Philippine islands," said Manuel L. Quezon, President of the Commonwealth of the Philippines in 1935 when the inaugural transpacific airmail flight arrived from California. Pan American Airways was the first airline to accomplish this incredible feat using a seaplane called the *China Clipper*.

Photo by Don Boyd (airliners.net)

Boeing 747 – *China Clipper II*

It took four years for Pan Am and the Glenn L. Martin Company to design and build the Martin M-130. It was the first aircraft in the world that could cross an ocean with a payload and it cost under $500,000. Its range was 3,200 miles fully loaded, which meant to get to Asia via the Pacific Ocean, it would have to make several stops to refuel. After survey flights and a lot of planning and construction, four islands, Honolulu,

Midway, Wake and Guam, were identified as stepping stones for this trip. The inaugural flight left San Francisco on November 22, 1935.

Now how did I get involved in anything to do with this historic flight? I was invited to join a reenactment for the 50th anniversary in 1985—a trip from San Francisco to Manila with stops at four islands. Who wouldn't be thrilled about that? I was on board because I worked at Pan Am as Manager-Public Relations, and one part of my job was to answer questions about Pan Am's history from the media, from people writing books, as well as the general public.

I took over this interesting area from Pan Am historian/curator Althea (Gerry) Lister, who retired in 1974 after 45 years and six months of service. She had worked longer for the airline than any other employee except founder Juan T. Trippe. At her retirement gathering, Chairman William T. Seawell told Gerry the historical records and museum stood as a tribute to her accomplishments. A private pilot, historian, secretary and associate to some of the giants of Pan Am's past, Gerry was an icon who gathered up Pan Am memorabilia whenever and wherever she could.

So, I arrived with great anticipation at San Francisco airport on November 22, 1985.

Pan Am selected a Boeing 747-212B named China Clipper II, for the reenactment.

The 1935 China Clipper, piloted by Captain Edwin Musick, departed from Alameda and stopped in Honolulu, Midway Island, Wake Island and Guam before finally landing in Manila. The 8,210 mile trip took 59 hours and 48 minutes flying time. Our 747 would follow the exact route. The revenue passengers, in addition to many VIPs, were composed of members of our frequent flyers program, others who yearned to be a part of aviation history, and those who wanted a package tour to the Pacific.

Excitement and expectancy were evident at our airport ceremony that included music and speeches. The son of James A. Farley, Postmaster General in 1935, was there. His father had delivered a message from President Franklin Roosevelt, who said, "Even at this distance, I thrill to the wonder of it all." San Francisco Postmaster

Pan Am Archives

John McCoy watercolor of Pan American Airways First
Flight to Asia, Martin M-130, Philippine Clipper.

158

Mrs. Mary Brown told us a special China Clipper international stamp had been issued at Treasure Island in February 1985 and the original flight carried 100,000 letters to the Philippines. Also, 5,000 envelopes which had received philatelic treatment were on board our flight and would get special cancellations at each stop. Flight attendants paraded in the various styles of uniform worn since the early days. We cheered members of our flight crew when they were introduced. It was a festive event.

Then it was time to "cast off," and our Chairman Ed Acker reminded us that in 1935, the flight made contact with the five stations by telegraph key and radio operators translated the transmissions into voice response. The voice hook-up transmitted to make sure that all five bases were ready and standing by for orders. They were. Over 150,000 people were at Alameda to see the original seaplane take off with thousands more lining the shore. The China Clipper, fully loaded with fuel and mail, strained to gain altitude and had to fly under the unfinished Oakland Bay Bridge.

For the 1935 flight, the San Francisco to Hawaii leg was the most dangerous. It took 21 hours for the seaplane to fly over the 2,397 miles of open water. There was no radar, no voice communication. The flight navigator had to climb out of a hatch several times at night to take star sightings with a sextant. Harry R. Canaday, a pioneer captain on board our flight, remembered that in the early days, even with the best equipment available, it was what they called "flying by the seat of your pants." Shure V. Sigfred, another pioneer captain on board, was astounded by the number of people and amount of cargo carried on our modern 747. "We loaded the ship according to the weather and weighed every ounce," he reminisced.

But on our flight, there was a party atmosphere. It took just five hours for us to reach Honolulu. I was eager to see each island for a different reason. I had the opportunity to look at photographs and read accounts of those early days in the archives. What I saw were pictures of enthusiastic crowds, flowers, song and dance waiting to greet the M-130 crew in Hawaii 50 years ago.

I could feel the hospitality as soon as we landed. To me, Hawaii signifies music, dancing, singing, fragrant blossoms, romance and exotic fruit. We received a warm Aloha welcome of leis, song and dance. Next, the organizers whisked us away to Pearl Harbor where they honored us with a ceremony to dedicate a plaque commemorating 50 years of commercial air service at the location where the original China Clipper landed, Middle Loch, Pearl City Peninsula. That evening, it was thrilling to be part of the reception, testimonial dinner and entertainment at the Royal Hawaiian Hotel where our pioneers were recognized and applauded.

The real adventure started for me as we took off for Midway the next morning. After visiting Easter Island in 1975, I had a special interest in remote islands. Now ten years later, I was going again to a place way off the beaten track. We accomplished the 1,309 mile flight in under three hours and were welcomed by officers of the US Navy. We were on a tight schedule and we were to be in Midway for one hour. I helped passengers get a stamp so that they could send a card or letter home from this atoll.

Midway is half way around the world from Greenwich, England, and is a bird sanctuary. Many of our group wanted to see the nests of the Laysan Albatross, known as the gooney bird because of its antics. After they have reared their young here, these large seabirds are out over the ocean for four months. They mate and return to Midway each October to the same nesting ground. Graceful in flight with their long wingspan, changing wind currents can sometimes make them comical to watch when they take off and land. It was a sight many of us had never seen before. We ended up spending an extra hour in Midway.

During our next leg to Wake, we crossed the International Dateline. It was now November 24th. A distance of 1,182 miles, the flight was just under three hours. The first thing I noticed upon arrival was a sign which read, "Where America's Day Really Begins."

John Borger, retired Vice President and Chief Engineer who was on board, knew all about the effort it took to prepare this island for the seaplanes. At Wake, I wanted to reflect on the hazardous mission Pan Am staff had faced all those years ago. Six feet of clearance from the surface of the water was needed for the seaplane to land. The lagoon had to be cleared of coral heads and blasted with dynamite. Lumber, pipes, food, carpenters, cooks, plumbers, electricians, steel workers were brought by the freighter North Haven as everything had to be built from scratch. Vegetables were grown hydroponically without top soil. This speck of flat land presented the biggest challenge to Pan Am, to feed, house and service the crew, aircraft and eventual passengers. We had two canaries with us to bring song to the island. The original flight carried 25 canaries and 25 pounds of birdseed.

The flight to Guam, a distance from Wake of 1,503 miles was three and a half hours. I remember seeing in the records that Guam in the 1930s was known as a picturesque isle full of coconut trees and Poinciana flame trees. Again, we were eagerly welcomed. However, we had fallen behind schedule because of an enjoyable longer stay at Midway and Wake. By motorcade, we were taken on a scenic drive to Apra Harbor, the US Naval Air Station, and Sumay Cove, where the original Clipper landed. The US Navy had arranged comfortable chairs under a tent for us. There were speeches of welcome by Governor Ricardo J. Bordallo and proclamations and resolutions. A commemorative monument was unveiled by the First Lady of Guam, Mrs. Madeleine Bordallo. It was a radiant sunset at 5:24 in the evening. Unfortunately, entertainment arranged by the Guam Visitors Bureau could not take place as it was dark almost immediately.

I knew that in 1935 the survey flights had gone no further than Guam. When the China Clipper reached Manila six days after leaving Alameda, it was the first aircraft to arrive there via the Pacific Ocean. There were 250,000 people waiting to see the flying boat, ships in the harbor, and escort planes in the air. Our flight reached Manila late to a huge welcome, a distance of 1,597 miles and three and a half hours flying time. It had taken us two days from California with the overnight stop. We walked past singers and an orchestra under an archway decked with flowers and a sign that read "The Filipino People Welcome The China Clipper As The Dove Of Peace And Goodwill. Mabuhay." In 1935, Captain Musick and his crew had passed under the same type of arch with the same words. The next evening we attended a sumptuous dinner with many dignitaries present. The Bayanihan Dance Troupe performed. First Lady of the Republic of the Philippines, Mrs. Imelda Marcos, spoke of the long friendship between the two countries. And she even sang a few songs for us.

On our last night, we enjoyed a reception aboard a sunset cruise. Blue and white balloons were released. We all sang; there was haunting saxophone music. There were many vivid memories to take home from Pan Am's first transpacific destination. Charles and Anne Lindbergh in 1931 had surveyed a route for Pan Am to Asia via Alaska and reported that such a routing was feasible. But when needed, landing rights could not be obtained from Russia. The only alternative therefore was the route across the vast Pacific. Passenger service started in 1936 and the route was extended from Manila to Hong Kong and Macao.

Brilliant minds had conquered the challenges. Courageous and dedicated people had conquered the ocean. Now 25 years after that reenactment flight, I still feel so proud of the past and the pioneers. Pan Am led the way and literally shrank the globe.

Courtesy of the Author

Ann was Manager, Public Relations in New York. She worked for Pan Am from 1968 to 1987 and lives in New York.

SALE OF THE PACIFIC ROUTES

By Diane Vander-Zanden

Crews React to the Loss of the Pacific Division

After a one-night stay at the Hyatt Hotel in Seoul in late April of 1985, I awoke early to get ready for a morning departure to Honolulu with two stops in Japan; Osaka and Narita. Since it was to be a long day, it was routine for most of the crew to go to the hotel's beautiful dining room for an early breakfast. The maitre'd was aware that the crew members liked to gather at one of the few long booths which looked out on the city below and reserved it for us.

On this particular morning, most of us had already gathered when the Seoul Station Manager, Abe Gonzales, made an appearance. Abe is a cheerful fellow and always had interesting stories or jokes to share. This morning, he looked less cheerful than usual. He told us that Pan Am had just sold its Pacific routes to United Airlines. There was a pause before one of the pilots asked, "What's the punch line?" We all expected Abe to come up with something funny. You cannot imagine the consternation when he responded somberly, "It's no joke. It was announced this morning in New York."

We were all aware that the Pacific routes were the major source of Pan Am's revenue, so the shock was twofold: What was going to happen to the rest of the company without the Pacific routes? What was going to happen to us? This latter question was especially heavy in the minds of the flight attendants present as we were all based in Honolulu in the middle of the Pacific.

I had actually begun my career with Pan American in Honolulu where I was teaching several mathematics classes at a private high school during the 1962-63 school year. One evening I saw an article in the Honolulu Advertiser announcing that Pan American World Airways was going to be in Honolulu looking for stewardesses. The article said the company was especially interested in young women who could speak Asian languages but all were welcome to apply. The next day, I called the number given in the article, and was told

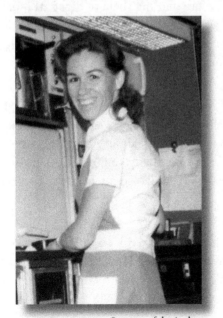

Courtesy of the Author

**Diane Vander-Zanden working
in the galley**

161

the interviews would be conducted in downtown Honolulu in a suite at the Alexander Young Hotel on Bishop Street. (A Pan American sales office was located on the ground floor of the hotel.) I was scheduled for a 15-minute interview in the morning and was greatly surprised that it led to a second interview. I was impressed with how very nice the Pan Am people were. I left the second interview with a lot of hope, and about a week later, received a letter with the Pan American logo on the envelope, telling me I was hired pending passing a physical. This was in spite of the fact I did not speak an Asian language. The Pan American letter arrived when I was mid-way through my second year teaching. I could not believe my good fortune in getting such an exciting job. I was assigned to a mid-June class in San Francisco after the school ended.

Most of my fellow classmates at the Pan American training center in San Francisco shared the same feelings about our good fortune. Most of us were not from well-to-do families and were thrilled at the opportunity to travel. We soon discovered that working on Pan American's 707's, in spite of the long hours, was interesting in itself. We also found that we had become jet-setters, which was beyond the means of many Americans, as well as beyond the dreams of most of us.

By April of 1985, I had been flying almost 22 years, most of them in the purser position. The sale of the Pacific routes was not just a shock to employees. When we arrived in Osaka from Seoul, we had a short transit time. When we were preparing to leave, I took my position at the main cabin door, to greet the oncoming passengers. Over the years I had not only developed friendships with other employees but also with many of our regular business travelers. The tenth passenger to board was a Canadian Nisei friend whose business was based in Tokyo. The first thing he said was, "Diane, is it really true? Is Pan Am selling their Pacific routes?" Sadly, I told him it was true. Later we only had time for a brief chat but he told me that all the TV stations in Japan were frequently making breaking news announcements and almost continuously scrolling the news across the bottom of the screen during their regular programming. On a flight to Sydney, five days later, I engaged in conversation with many other loyal customers who shared their dismay at hearing news of the sale. Even though the sale would not be completed until the following February, we often heard this reaction from our passengers who seemed to be as shocked as we were.

The Honolulu-based flight attendants soon learned they could be part of the sale if they wanted to work with United Airlines. This was because part of the agreement provided that United would hire 432 Pan Am pilots and 1202 flight attendants. There were no pilots at the Honolulu base but there were a little over 500 flight attendants. Pan Am had asked United to offer jobs to all of us before offering them to flight attendants at other bases. They did not want to pay for our moves to the mainland, as required in a forced transfer. Emotions ran high at the base. Pan Am was such a part of our lives that there was a feeling of abandonment. Many flight attendants put in for transfers immediately because they feared they might have to take the job with United if they stayed in Honolulu. Some of us found it hard to make a decision. I selected to go with United.

It was not an easy decision, though the main "pro" was that it allowed me to remain in Hawaii. The biggest "con" was that I would have to leave the Pan Am family where I had worked with many wonderful people in all departments. Though I was hired in Honolulu in 1963, I did not speak an Asian language and therefore, was originally assigned to the San Francisco base. When the company removed that language restriction from the Honolulu base in 1973, I transferred to the islands where I finished my Pan Am years with the sale of the Pacific routes.

I had qualified for the purser position just 19 months after I finished flight attendant training and was in that position for most of my nearly 23 years with Pan Am. I was also fortunate to work on occasional "special assignments," mostly writing training programs or teaching newly hired flight attendants. These assignments included three months in New York and several months in Miami, and many more non-flying assignments in Honolulu where the In-Flight Training Center was located during the late 70s and early 80s.

Since both Pan American and Aloha Airlines are, sadly, no longer around, I will confess I also wrote a one-day training class for Aloha Airlines. Writing materials for another airline was strictly prohibited, but one of my

Pan Am classmates, Mae Takahashi, had resigned in late 1969 and taken a position as head of the Flight Service Department at Aloha. Mae said she had a bit of an attitude problem with her senior flight attendants and asked if I could write and conduct a one-day training session for her. I agreed to do it as Mae was a colleague I highly respected and also a good friend. When I taught the class, I very much enjoyed meeting the senior ladies, especially one who started the day with a bit of a challenging attitude but ended it with enthusiasm and a sense of humor. Her name was "CB" Lansing. Unfortunately, several years later, in April of 1988, Aloha's Flight 243 had an explosive decompression and CB was swept out of the aircraft, the only fatality in the incident.

I continued my airline career with United for more than 19 additional years, retiring in 2005. Today I am still active with Pan Am groups in Hawaii. I am currently on the board of the Aloha Chapter of the Pan Am Association and I am also active in the Hawaii Chapter of World Wings International.

Courtesy of the Author   *Courtesy of the Author*

Diane's career began in 1963 at San Francisco as a Stewardess and Purser. She transferred to Honolulu 1973 where she remained with Pan Am until the sale of the Pacific Routes to United Airlines. She lives in Hawaii.

BEGINNING OF THE END OF PAN AM

By Joe Hale
The End of Pan Am

The demise of Pan Am began many years before the actually final date shown on its death certificate.

For all of us associated in the Pacific, and particularly in Japan, the beginning of the end was in February of 1986 following the unbelievable announcement in Spring of 1985 of the company's decision to sell the Pacific Division to United.

My Pan Am journey made possible with the support of my wife Marge and our children was one of excitement and pride working as we did for the recognized world leader in aviation. Even with its sad ending, to this day, that we were the professionals of the industry is not in dispute.

My road to Japan started with my first job in Washington, DC as a junior ramp agent with National Airlines at Washington National Airport loading and unloading baggage and in charge of the lavatory truck. Shortly thereafter I joined Pan Am in the city as a cashier. That was July 18, 1958. In October of that same year I attended the christening of the Pan Am 707 in Washington, DC.

Later I became the sales rep covering the State of Virginia and then to District Passenger Sales Manger; District Sales Manager in Cincinnati; Director-International Affairs in the Washington executive office, and Director Passenger Sales in Honolulu.

In mid 1980 I was surprised though honored and happy to have been named Director-Western Japan based in Osaka. For me personally it was a bit like coming home since I was born in Yokohama.

Pan Am Osaka was a station where that Pan Am professionalism exuded. Not large by

Courtesy of the Author

The Clipper Club at Tokyo Narita Airport, after the last flight had departed. Mr. Morita is in the back row, center.

164

any standard with limited number of flights, it was staffed, nonetheless, by people who were sales minded, aggressive and with a keen sense for the Kansai customer behavior. It was my good fortune to have been assigned there. I learned a lot.

In my opinion, Pan Am Osaka was for too long in the shadows of Tokyo when it was really a shining example of a station with a can-do spirit and deserved to be recognized.

Having said that, Pan Am Japan overall had earned the recognition of its sophisticated ability as a world-class operation among the Pan Am system. To have been part of that was a privilege and to have had a turn as the regional managing director for Japan, Korea and China and to have headed a great team was an honor I still cherish.

There are too many episodes one recalls to list in a note of this nature. However, there are a couple of them which define the uniqueness of Pan Am in different ways.

After the sale of the Pacific to United, I was visited by an official from UA and instructed to arrange for the transfer of the Pan Am Sumo trophy to them. I consulted the Chairman of the Sumo Association and explained about the Pacific route sale and what had happened. I advised them that the new carrier had asked that they take over the Pan Am Sumo trophy. The Chairman said that because of the long relationship of the Sumo Association with Pan Am that they would prefer to have us continue with the seasonal trophy presentations. We did so for several years until the company was no more. The value of the depth of relationships in Japan and the high regard for Pan Am prevailed much to the shock of the folks in Chicago who had not yet at that time learned that fact.

Another quite different story also shows our true colors.

Osaka was a small operation with limited staff. Yet we had managers and supervisors who took their work seriously. One such manager was in charge of training and making sure all the staff received their instruction. Since it was not possible to have everyone come into a classroom at one time, he met with small numbers over a period of days.

One evening after the flight to Honolulu had departed, I watched this manager set up a flip board with some printed materials in preparation for his session. In this rather cluttered back room at Itami Airport, at this late hour, the manager conducted his session--for one agent who had been sick when the training was originally given.

I was deeply moved by his dedication and his Pan Am professional character.

The historical fact is that the sale of the Pan Am Pacific Division really did take place.

By early 1986 all of the required approvals both from the US and Foreign Governments for the sale of the Pan Am Pacific Division had been received and a date for the actual change was set for February.

Pan Am Archives

The official date for the finalization of the transfer of the Pan Am assets in the Pacific was to be on 11 February 1986. However due to requirements of normal airline scheduling, the final three Pan Am flights from Tokyo's Narita Airport were to be on 12 February.

We made arrangements to hold a brief send off ceremony at the departure gate area and invited both US and Japanese officials plus Mr. Akio Morita, Chairman of Sony who was a corporate Board member of Pan Am. To say he was shocked with the decision to sell the Pacific would be an understatement. Over time in my position as head of Pan Am in Japan, Mr. Morita and I met regularly to chat about the company and have lunch at his Tokyo office. He always wore a Sony windbreaker whenever we had lunch from their company cafeteria. Mr. Morita said selling the Pacific was a huge mistake.

Today the conventional mantra among the US carriers is to have a significant Pacific presence.

In our many discussions on the decision, Mr. Morita and I wondered why a group of smart executives could not see the value of the Pacific to Pan Am's survival.

The transatlantic markets after the 1978 Deregulation Act brought in virtually all major heretofore US domestic carriers with the ability to carry passengers from their well developed domestic route system from hometown America to points in Europe competing more effectively against Pan Am. However, the governments in the Pacific, especially Japan, had not accepted the idea of open skies. Pan Am and also Northwest thus enjoyed unique traffic rights not only to carry passengers between the US and Japan but points beyond as well where at that time the economies of the major countries in Pacific Asia were booming. Today the conventional mantra among the US carriers is to have a significant Pacific presence.

The final flights on 12 February all departed Narita in the early evening. Due to the fact the deal closed on February 11th in the US, our former Pan Am employees at Narita belonged to United and in fact had already been issued new uniforms. Thus we had to request United to allocate sufficient staff to handle our final departures. They agreed.

I made some remarks at the departure area and it became clear to everyone around that our former Narita employees assigned to our flights all put back on their Pan Am uniforms to check in passengers and to handle the boarding process.

When the final flight began its push back and everyone had moved against the glass wall of the terminal and looked at the tarmac, spontaneously the entire crowd of well wishers began to sing Auld Lang Syne and many waving pen lights which I had brought.

Amid this scene was the distinctive white hair of Mr. Morita waving with penlight singing with tears in his eyes. In Hawaii, we call this a chicken skin moment.

The next day we had arranged to place an ad in the major local newspapers. It read:

"Thank you.

As our half century of flight operations in the Pacific comes to a close, we want to express our deep sense of gratitude to all of our friends in Japan.

We thank our customers, our associates in government and industry and especially our employees for giving Pan Am the best fifty years any airline ever had.

Although we'll no longer be flying to this part of the world, we will maintain offices in Tokyo and Osaka and in other major cities throughout the Pacific, to help with your travel arrangements on our routes in the U.S., Central and South America, Africa, the Middle East and Europe.

Once again, thank you. It has been a wonderful journey."

It was my honor to have been part of the greatest division of Pan Am and for the classy way we managed a terrible corporate mistake.

Life is full of curves and bumps and we all look back and have private thoughts about what if.

This practice, I have found, may be hazardous to your health. It is perhaps better to know clearly what happened and to assess what part we had with the final outcome. Hopefully we can say with certainty that we in Pan Am Japan did all we could to support the company because we knew that if the company was not well we could not be either.

As we look at the aviation industry, admittedly from a somewhat biased perspective, Pan Am was a major force and recognized as everyone's airline in countries across the world. However, its disappearance must have meaning. I suspect that each of us has tried to search our heart and mind to arrive at that answer.

KARACHI HIJACKING – RESCUING A 747

By Hart Langer

Rescuing a Hijacked Boeing 747

It was *not* the proverbial "dark and stormy night." In fact, it was a beautiful autumn morning on September 4, 1986 in Hamburg, Germany. I had arrived in Hamburg the day before on an A-310 non-stop flight from New York JFK having given IOE (Initial Operating Experience) on that aircraft to Captain Ed Cywinski, our Chief Pilot at the JFK Base. The entire crew had gone out to dinner the night before and was all together in the dining room of the Hamburg InterContinental Hotel enjoying breakfast. The weather was beautiful from Hamburg all the way to JFK and everyone was looking forward to an enjoyable flight.

Right in the middle of breakfast, however, a hotel porter came in to the dining room and said that there was a call for me from Pan Am Operations in New York. Captain Jim Duncan, then our System Chief Pilot, was on the phone and told me that a Pan Am 747 was hijacked on the ground at Karachi, Pakistan. The hijackers had taken control of the airplane, and during the confusion that ensued when they got on board, the Pan Am crew in the cockpit wisely used the cockpit escape devices and exited the airplane through the escape hatch in the ceiling of the 747 cockpit. (Incidentally, this was the first and only time that these escape devices were *ever* used in the 747!)

A 747 without a crew was useless to the hijackers, and they demanded that Pan Am provide an Arabic-speaking crew to fly them where they wanted to go. Jim Duncan, through his contacts in IATA, called Captain Jazza Ghanem, the Vice-President of Flight Operations at Saudia (Saudi Arabian Airlines) to see if they could help out. Captain Ghanem was willing, but unfortunately was overruled by top management at Saudia.

As a result, the consensus at System Operations Control at JFK was that if Pan Am could find a volunteer crew, negotiations with the hijackers could possibly get them to release all of the passengers in return for flying them to another location. Captain Duncan wanted to know if Captain Cywinski and I could head to Karachi and fly the 747 to wherever the hijackers wanted to go, in return for releasing all 390 passengers. We agreed: The HAM (Hamburg)/JFK flight was cancelled, and Bob Huettl, a check Flight Engineer who was laying over in LHR (London), also volunteered.

Ed and I hopped on a Lufthansa flight from HAM to FRA (Frankfurt) and Bob got on a Lufthansa flight from LHR to FRA. Airway chart publisher Jeppesen, which has a major office in FRA, assembled a package of approach charts for all Mid-East airports and met us with it when we arrived in FRA. We boarded a Swissair DC-10 for Karachi (KHI).

As it turned out, the APU (Auxiliary Propulsion Unit) that was supplying electrical power to the 747 in KHI had a small oil leak, and the Tech Center at JFK had predicted exactly when it would shut itself down and stop providing power to the 747. When it finally happened, the airplane went dark, and the hijackers thought they were under attack. They herded all the passengers into the over wing area, began shooting people at random, and set off numerous explosive devices. At that point, the Pakistani army did indeed attack the airplane and finally overpowered the hijackers.

All of this happened while we were en route to KHI. Captain Duncan was able to get in touch with the Swissair DC-10 using a phone patch and HF radio, and informed us the hijackers had been arrested. When we arrived, we had a chance to inspect the airplane. The carnage was unbelievable and the airplane had numerous bullet holes in the fuselage as well as structural panels destroyed in the area of the wheel wells. Pan Am dispatched a crack team of mechanics from LHR to KHI, and in five days they had the airplane in a flyable condition – which is remarkable, considering there were fifty-seven bullet holes in the fuselage. Ed, Bob, and I waited in KHI and then flew the airplane back to JFK with a fuel stop in FRA. We were surprised in FRA to find that Captain Don Pritchett, our Vice President—Flight Operations, had traveled to FRA to thank us and accompany us on the flight back to JFK.

We flew the flight from KHI to FRA to JFK at 25,000 feet—quite a bit below the 747's normal cruising altitude—because Boeing restricted the airplane to a 5.6 psi pressure differential due to the temporary repairs to the aft pressure bulkhead.

The most memorable moment of this entire episode was a conversation I had with Bob Huettl, our Flight Engineer, who I was sitting next to on the Swissair DC-10 en route to KHI. We were discussing various ways in which we might be able to deal with what was to come when we arrived in KHI, boarded the 747, and confronted the hijackers. At one point I asked Bob why he volunteered to do this. His answer remains with me to this day.

Bob said that he had flown for Pan Am for more than thirty years and that he had always been senior, made good money, flown the best and newest airplanes, and had the best schedules. Now, he said, it was time to give some back. What a guy!

I had many exciting and challenging flights over my Pan Am career, but being able to work for so many years with countless numbers of Pan Am people like Bob Huettl will be what I remember the most.

Courtesy of the Author

Pan Am may have had its problems, but in the day-to-day operation, the coordination and cooperation between Maintenance and Engineering, Flight Service, Flight Operations, Dispatch, System Operations Control, and countless other departments was positively inspirational and an absolute pleasure to be a part of.

Hart lives in the Atlanta area.

KARACHI HIJACKING – PAN AM's CARE TEAM

By Liz Morris
Pan Am's Care Team

Five armed terrorists hijacked Pan American World Airways Flight 73 en route from Bombay to New York via Karachi, Pakistan, and Frankfurt, Germany, on September 5, 1986. The fanatics hijacked the airplane while on the ground at Karachi and held it for 18 hours before authorities stormed the aircraft, capturing the terrorists. Twenty passengers and a purser died in the terrifying event—among them Neerja Bhanot, a 22-year senior flight purser who assisted a number of passengers by escaping via a chute while she laid down her life shielding three children from bullets fired by the terrorists.

At that time, before Federal law required airlines to establish Care Teams to assist families and survivors of crashes and other disasters, Pan American used a one-on-one process to assist such survivors. The company selected me as one of 50-100 volunteers to meet the Boeing 747-121 upon its arrival with some 300 survivors at John F. Kennedy Airport, New York. We were instructed to stay with our designated passenger or family and do everything possible to assist them with ground transportation, telephone communications, re-bookings, etc. (All immigration formalities had been attended to, via passenger listings, before the aircraft's arrival, we learned.)

I was first in the line to receive my special passenger or family, perhaps because of my 20-year seniority or because I worked in Special Services, which dealt with such situations. I assumed they would assign me to the first passenger out of First Class, a celebrity or VIP of some kind. Imagine my surprise when, as we lined up in the large and spacious JFK arrival hall to greet the traumatized passengers of Flight 73, I suddenly saw a skinny young Pakistani teenager break from the oncoming crowd and run toward me shouting "Mrs. Morris, Mrs. Morris!"

As he approached me, I recognized him. Through several of the preceding years, he had come to my office as the unaccompanied minor VIP son of an influential Pakistani family. The first time I met him, he was a sad little boy weeping profusely. I had ascertained his family had enrolled him in a top-notch Connecticut primary school to prepare him for a further first-class US education. But, he was already homesick, had not wanted to leave his family and friends, and I had a difficult job consoling him until the Connecticut school representatives arrived to take charge of him.

I thought much of him in the months following that first encounter. At the end of his first term, he came again to my office, assigned to me, before his flight home. That time he arrived smiling, ... carrying with him the book, The World's Dirtiest Jokes. I laughed and joked with him that he had obviously adjusted and was no longer homesick. He agreed, and two or three times a year, he would look me up in the Special Services office--even after the age of 16 and no longer qualified as an Unaccompanied Minor.

Now, on that fateful September day 25 years ago, as the young man ran up to me, still small and slender, I immediately recognized him as my young friend but couldn't comprehend that he had been on Pan Am Flight 73.

"What are you doing here?" I asked him, thinking he had arrived on another flight from Pakistan to begin a new school year.

"I was on Flight 73 when the gunmen came on board," he answered.

"Oh, my God," I exclaimed. "What happened?"

"I was very, very scared," he replied, "but I was able to slide under a three-seat row in Economy Section because I'm small and skinny. I didn't eat or drink anything for days during and after the attack and I could hear all the threats and commotion, but I have been liberated and am on my way back to school--glad to be alive, unlike some fellow passengers."

Like the others, my young friend received the VIP treatment from the Pan Am staff on the receiving line. His Connecticut school was on the ball. Pre-notified of his arrival, they had a car and counselor waiting at the terminal gates. I was able to assist another Flight 73 family but cannot recall too much about them.

My dominant memories of the tragedy are of my young Pakistani "unaccompanied minor" and his successful fight for life.

Liz works for Delta at JFK.

Courtesy of the Author
Liz Morris

PAN AM SHUTTLE

By Kelly Cusack

Competition for the Eastern Shuttle

After completing the merger with National Airlines Pan Am picked up many new domestic destinations from New York. The domestic schedule with single or double daily flights wasn't sufficient to appeal to the average New York business traveler. With the advent of frequent flyer programs it became essential for Pan Am to create a stronger domestic presence in the New York market knowing that once customers had domestic miles with the WorldPass program they would likely fly Pan Am when traveling internationally.

An opportunity to expand Pan Am's domestic presence in New York arose in 1986 when Frank Lorenzo purchased Eastern Airlines which had been operating The Eastern Shuttle on the Boston – New York (LaGuardia) – Washington, DC route since 1961. Lorenzo also owned New York Air which competed directly with Eastern on these routes. In order to win regulatory approval for the Eastern acquisition Lorenzo had to sell the New York Air slots and Pan Am was excited to have a chance to compete in this highly visible and lucrative domestic market.

Courtesy of the Author

Kelly (second from right) and Jane Namakamal
at the Marine Air Terminal, LaGuardia.

The Pan Am Shuttle was launched in the Fall of 1986 from the Marine Air Terminal which had been built by Pan Am in 1940 for Trans-Atlantic flying boat operations. An extension was added on to the original terminal allowing it to accommodate up to 5 jets and hourly service (on the half hour) to Boston and Washington, DC was offered from 6:30 am to 8:30 pm (Washington), 9:30 pm (Boston).

Pan Am's goal was to compete with service and not price, offering leather seats and in-flight beverages and snacks. In order to allow customers to enjoy the in-flight perks Pan Am offered advance ticketing unlike the Eastern Shuttle that only ticketed in-flight. Another unique amenity of the

171

Pan Am Shuttle was the Pan Am Water Shuttle, a ferry service from a pier at the Marine Air Terminal to Pier 11 serving Wall Street in Manhattan. Because of the layout of LaGuardia Eastern could not match this service. The Water Shuttle reduced travel times significantly from LaGuardia to lower Manhattan during rush hours. Pan Am also introduced a "Business Center" in the modified Marine Air Terminal with fax and copier service. Within the terminal Pan Am offered a wide range of complimentary newspapers and magazines conveniently placed so customers could grab them as they dashed to catch a flight.

Pan Am used both A300-B4 and Boeing 727-200 for the service. The Airbus fleet was factory delivered to Pan Am while the 727 fleet came to Pan Am from both People's Express and Lufthansa. The Airbus fleet only served for a few months due to noise abatement rules at Boston Logan Airport. Once the former Lufthansa aircraft joined the fleet they were predominantly used in the Boston market as their engines met the noise requirements.

The Passenger Service (ticket agents) group was composed mainly of Reservations Agents from the Pan Am Building. Their extensive knowledge was always evident when a customer with a complex international ticket that included Shuttle segments needed to make changes.

The Fleet Service (ramp) and Maintenance group were mostly transfers from JFK airport. Coming from Pan Am's busiest station with many connecting flights and a preponderance of wide-bodied aircraft the Fleet Service and Maintenance groups felt they had been put out to pasture as many Shuttle customers were day trippers with no checked luggage.

Pilots were domiciled at JFK and could report to LaGuardia for Shuttle rotations that could last for 2 or 3 days. Flight Attendants too were initially domiciled at JFK with multi-day Shuttle assignments but eventually Pan Am opened flight service bases in both Boston and Washington in order to save hotel costs by creating trip patterns that allowed crews to begin and end their day at their home base.

The Pan Am Shuttle had an unusually high percentage of Hawaiian Employees working in Passenger Service. With the sale of the Pacific routes to United in March of 1986 there was a surplus of agents in Honolulu. These agents used their union "bumping" rights to secure positions at the Shuttle. There were 8 transfers from Honolulu. They shared a house and a car. They worked shifts for each other allowing each of them to get home to Hawaii about once a month for a week or more. They were lovely, warm people and their presence at the Shuttle was uniquely Pan Am.

Being a small and dedicated work group there was an excellent rapport between the terminal and ramp staff. We all knew each other well, took meal breaks together and worked effectively as a team. There was less of the traditional "not my job" at the Shuttle and that was well reflected in the high on time performance of the Shuttle and the team spirit of the Shuttle employees.

The Shuttle became an instant money maker for Pan Am as the yields were very high for such a short flight. The outstanding on time performance of the Shuttle also raised the overall Pan Am on time performance. Finally the Shuttle succeeded in providing Pan Am the visibility and presence in the Northeast Corridor and both New York and Washington DC based Shuttle customers were more likely to fly Pan Am internationally in order to take advantage of the WorldPass, Frequent Flyer Program. There was less impact in Boston for at the time Pan Am's only international flight from Boston was to Bermuda.

Though I had been working for Pan Am since 1980 various reorganizations and reductions in staff found me working in the Fleet Service group at the Shuttle. Just out of college and quite enamored with New York City night life I chose the afternoon shift and worked from 2:00 pm to 10:00 pm with enough seniority to get many weekends off. There were days when the sun was shinning that I couldn't believe I was getting paid to have so much fun at work. I was at the Shuttle for approximately one year before moving onto Reservations and becoming Pan Am's youngest Reservations manager at the age of 28.

When Pan Am first launched the shuttle we were at a disadvantage as our last flight to Washington DC was at 8:30 pm and Eastern offered a 9:00 pm departure. We could not offer a 9:30 pm departure as our 727 jet equipment would arrive into the DC area after the night time noise abatement curfew was in effect. Customers not sure if they would make our 8:30 pm departure would often just head over to Eastern not wanting to risk missing that last flight to DC. I had noticed Pan Am Express, formerly Ransome Airlines acquired in early 1986 to feed Pan Am at JFK, had a Dash-7 turboprop that arrived at LaGuardia from Providence, RI every evening at 8:30 pm. The flight delivered passengers to the main terminal and remained overnight.

About a month into our operation I suggested to one of the Shuttle managers (who had been recruited from Eastern) that the Dash 7 inbound from Providence arrived sufficiently early to make a 9:30 pm departure to Washington and the turboprop engines on the aircraft were not in conflict with the Washington noise abatement restrictions. A few weeks later it was announced that the Dash 7 would begin flying a 9:30 pm departure to Washington. Suddenly, traffic on the 8:30 pm Shuttle picked up as customers knew there was a later Pan Am departure to fall back on if they missed the 8:30 pm. Even better, Eastern customers now began heading over to Pan Am if they weren't sure they could make Eastern's last flight at 9:00 pm. My idea of using the Dash 7 for the last flight of the day was never acknowledged by management but I didn't care. I was proud to have made a useful suggestion that increased revenues for the company and gave us a competitive edge against Eastern Airlines. Eventually, hush kits were added to some of the 727 fleet allowing that aircraft to perform the 9:30 pm flight to Washington.

One happy Shuttle memory that always makes me smile involves TV newscaster Connie Chung who was flying to Washington DC one evening. She was early and was discreetly sitting in the gate area. I happened to spot her as I walked through the terminal. Against my usual pattern of not disturbing customers I opted to say hello. At the time Connie Chung was one of the few women featured on national network news and the only Asian. We spoke for about two minutes and she was very gracious. I left her to go on with my duties. By coincidence I wound up at the aircraft door to assist with oversized luggage for Connie's flight. As she came down the air bridge Connie greeted me by name and thanked me for the nice conversation. The look of shock on the faces of the customers in line around her was priceless as they pondered how Connie Chung was on a first name basis with a Pan Am Shuttle ramp agent.

The Pan Am Shuttle was sold to Delta in September 1991 as part of the Atlantic Route Sale and still operates from the Marine Air Terminal.

Courtesy of the Author

Kelly Cusack

Kelly lives in Florida and is the proprietor of www.everythingpanam.com.

PAN AM PROTOCOL

By Shim Lew
Protocol Department

Pan American World Airways, to the best of my recollection, always had a Protocol Officer. In fact, it was the only airline to have such a position. For most of its history, Pan Am only flew to international destinations. In addition to the two daily round-the-world flights—one eastbound the other westbound, Pan Am flew to most of the world's major capitals. Whether it was to Europe, Asia, Africa, or South America, Pan Am's famous "blue ball" could be seen parked at most of the world's major airports.

Every year in September, with the opening of the United Nations General Assembly in New York, Pan Am's John F. Kennedy (JFK) terminal became a frenzy of activity centered on the world's diplomatic community. Whether it was an ambassador, foreign minister, or head of state, the Pan Am terminal was second only to the United Nations in the total number of diplomats passing through. Considering the security details and entourages of these dignitaries, all with diplomatic immunity and harboring the highest of expectations, one could only imagine the complex handling situations that arose from time to time. In spite of the challenges, Pan Am gave each dignitary the level of service he or she came to expect and deserved. That's what Pan Am Protocol was all about.

Pan Am was unrivaled in its ability to carry off this annual and extraordinary feat year after year. It was in the person of the Protocol Officer—the Chief of Protocol—to which credit is due. The fact that diplomats and heads of state from around the world often chose Pan Am over their own national carriers, was a testimony to Pan Am's reputation for excellence. I had the privilege of working

Courtesy of the Author

Shim Lew with Mother Teresa

174

as Pan Am's Deputy Chief of Protocol from 1987 to 1991 alongside Mr. Sho Ohkagawa who was then the Chief. It was my job, not only to meet and greet these individuals—the most obvious part of the job—but to plan, orchestrate, and in a sense, choreograph their way through Customs, Immigration, and the baggage claim processes and facilities. At times the achievement was rather challenging, considering the multitudes of exhausted and weary travelers who were vying for the same limited space and facilities.

Somewhere along the way, our special handling list began to expand way beyond the diplomatic community. Requests to handle "celebs," the moguls of Corporate America, various politicos, and sundry "others" kept pouring into our office. The list became a veritable "who's who" of Hollywood, the sports world and even the religious establishment. Constant pressure and some anxieties may have been an apt way to describe our daily regimen. After all, Pan Am's reputation among the "elites," was, to a certain extent, in our hands. Nevertheless, it was a quite rewarding profession. When I look back on the individuals I came in contact with, I realize just how worthy the effort was. No adequate understanding of our job could be appreciated without some mention of those who passed through our hands at Pan Am's JFK Worldport. Their names are, and remain, a historical testimony to the high esteem in which Pan Am was held. Some of the more famous and recognizable names include Al Pacino, Elizabeth Taylor, Douglas Fairbanks Jr., Sidney Poitier, Burt Lancaster, and Sophia Loren.

What was particularly satisfying, actually flattering, was when some of them came through and asked for me by name. In addition to those icons of the movie industry mentioned, other celebrities included some real superstars and legends: Michael Jackson, Madonna, Elton John, Billy Joel, and several of the Beatles. On one particular day, I was awaiting the arrival of Michael Jackson who was connecting to our London flight. Word came ahead requesting discreet handling as Michael shunned publicity in venues such as airline terminals. I was sure we could make it from his arrival gate to our Clipper Club (Pan Am VIP Lounge) without calling much attention to ourselves. I positioned myself right at the door of his arriving aircraft and as the passengers deplaned, my eyes caught sight of a giant of an individual who stood about six-feet six and wearing a black stovepipe top hat. That was Michael's bodyguard. Michael was wearing a leather flight jacket with Burberry scarf, sunglasses, a medical face mask, and a hood pulled over his head. Not the most inconspicuous trio, we made our way through the terminal unscathed as everyone stopped and stared.

As expected, royalty also enjoyed flying on Pan Am. Our terminal was graced by the likes of Princess Margaret of England, Prince Rainier of Monaco and his children, Caroline, Stephanie and Albert, who were all regulars on Pan Am. Then there was Jackie Kennedy Onassis who was about as close to royalty as any American. Our list also included an array of princes and princesses from several Middle Eastern kingdoms, and sheikhdoms, and then there was the family of the former Shah of Iran.

Not to be undone by the likes of royalty, many business leaders also chose our airline: Bill Gates, Donald Trump, and Malcolm Forbes, who once pulled up to the terminal in a Lamborghini Jeep, were not unfamiliar at the Pan Am terminal.

It was not only the foreign heads of state we handled. There were many of our own ex-presidents who came through: Richard Nixon, Gerald Ford, Jimmy Carter, and the senior Bush. Jimmy Carter stopped by our office on several occasions and I can only describe him as a 'regular guy.' Then there was Boris Yeltsin just before he became President of Russia and Mikhail Gorbachev right after he left office. Shortly thereafter, Gorbachev embarked on a worldwide speaking tour in which he represented an environmental foundation. In his many travels, whenever he could, he chose Pan Am and always made it a point to visit our office.

Shimon Peres and Benjamin Netanyahu also traveled on Pan Am. Like their Russian counterparts, their travels signaled shifting tides in Israeli politics. It was an exciting time in history and looking back, one cannot help but feeling part of it, or at least privy to it. I served in that position during the last years of the Cold War and most of the world leaders I mentioned were indeed, part of that history. I think of myself as having stood by on the 'sidelines' of history. Each person I handled, in one way or another, was at the time making history. When I think of them, a particular historical context comes to mind, much like an old song conjures up feelings of a bygone past.

This is only a sampler of the "famous" who chose to fly Pan Am. But not even a sampler would be complete without mentioning something about the world's prominent religious leaders who also flew with us. There were many, and they ran the gamut from the Dalai Lama to Mother Teresa. Cardinal O'Connor, Archbishop of New York, was a regular on the Rome flight. The Patriarch Alexis, head of the Russian Orthodox Church, also flew with us.

One of my most memorable moments was meeting Mother Teresa for the first time. She arrived at the Pan Am terminal on a cold and wintery day for a flight to Rome. She was wearing only her habit and sandals, so I made arrangements for her and some of the sisters from her order to relax in a private area before flight time. She always seemed to be most happy with her "sisters" who were dedicated to serving the poor and those afflicted with AIDS. They had a care facility in the Bronx and Mother Teresa often came to New York to visit. When I walked in to escort her to the gate, she was giving a blessing to each of her sisters. She gave blessings to everyone she met. Turning to give me a blessing, I told her I was not Catholic, but she said it did not matter, and she blessed me anyway. I cannot describe exactly how I felt, but from that day forward, I knew just how special and unique a person she was. Mother Teresa was also fond of passing out little 'Miraculous Medals.' She would bless them and press them into your hand. They became very popular, especially among the Catholics working at the airport. I would assist Mother Teresa every time she traveled to New York and it was often. She was indeed a regular and frequent flyer on Pan Am.

The 'name dropping' would not be complete if I did not mention some of the more famous athletes who also traveled on Pan Am and made 'our list.' There were many, but I will stick to some of the more legendary. There was Bob Feller, Whitey Ford and Mickey Mantle, who sometimes traveled together, and Met slugger Daryl Strawberry. And of course, perhaps the greatest of all times—a real American icon—Joe DiMaggio.

I have always considered myself fortunate, and indeed privileged, to have worked for Pan Am, but to have been Deputy Chief of Protocol for Pan American World Airways, in those days at JFK, was indeed, special.

I would not have traded the experience for any other in the world.

Shim is still Chief of Protocol—now for Delta at JFK.

GLASNOST COMES TO PAN AM

By Elizabeth Hlinko Margulies
The Pan Am-Aeroflot Partnership

In 1988, Pan Am and Aeroflot joined forces on a partnership in which the two airlines jointly marketed and operated nonstop Boeing 747 flights between New York and Moscow. The Pan Am planes were staffed by

Courtesy of the Artist Lesley Giles
On the Barricades – Moscow

Pan Am pilots and cabin crews, while Aeroflot placed flight attendants onboard to serve as interpreters and provide branding for Aeroflot. To promote the service, my job was to help organize a media tour of key cities in the United States.

This was the type of history-making project that, as a recent college graduate working in the Public Relations department, I both relished and found surprising. I use the term "surprising" because unlike my mother, who began working for Pan Am during its magnificent rise, I knew I was working for an airline that was rapidly on its final descent and we were all holding on for dear life.

My mother used to tell me stories about seeing Juan Trippe and Charles Lindbergh in the hallway and the great experience of working for a company that at one point, had the most recognizable logo in the world. While I had a completely different experience from my mother's, we both agreed that working for Pan Am was the best job of our careers.

When I was first given the assignment to coordinate this project, I was gently "warned" by some of our Eastern European experts that my life would likely be gone over with a fine toothed comb and that I should not be surprised if I noticed government agents following me. I would, after all, be hosting possible Communists in the US. To this day I have no idea if that was a real warning or paranoia from colleagues, but since I didn't have anything to hide, the idea never really bothered me. In those days, I didn't know if satellite media tours even existed, or if they did, I'm sure they were too costly to consider for promotional projects like this, so ours was a good old fashioned, pound the pavement series of in-person TV and radio interviews in various cities. A Pan Am flight attendant and an Aeroflot flight attendant were chosen to represent the partnership. The Aeroflot flight attendant was accompanied by her "escort," a marketing executive from Aeroflot in Moscow, and I was the Pan Am organizer.

The tour itself was a success, generating substantial media coverage for the partnership. I would like to think the friendship between the two flight attendants from different worlds came across loud and clear during the interviews. I'd also like to think their camaraderie helped to convince people to travel to the USSR on this Pan Am, Aeroflot joint venture.

The story could end here, a successful US media tour, good media coverage, but it does not. In the new era of open discussion and free dissemination of news and information, Aeroflot informed us they wanted to host a similar media tour in the Soviet Union. For me, this truly was an experience of a lifetime. During the US tour, I was the behind the scenes public relations representative. I was responsible for making sure the interviews were arranged and went smoothly. This was, after all, what a good PR person's job was, so that's what I thought would be the case during the Soviet Union media tour.

Imagine my surprise when during the first press conference in Moscow, the reporters turned to me and asked questions like, "How much money do you make?" and "Are you married?" I truly was not prepared for these questions, or for having my photo and interview appear in Russian newspapers. But, after all, this was still the early stages of a new freedom for the Russian people, so looking back now, I probably shouldn't have been surprised at some of the questions.

The rest of the trip was both remarkable and eye opening. I remember being in a hotel room in Moscow with the Pan Am flight attendant as we discussed how much we would like to find some fresh flowers to cheer up the room. We went out for a walk, looking for flowers only to find vases with fresh flowers in our rooms when we returned. It certainly felt like Big Brother was watching!

Another memory that is etched into my mind is when the Aeroflot marketing executive slipped me a couple of dollars and asked me to go into one of the hard currency stores to buy film so she could take photos of us on the trip. Apparently it was illegal for Russians to have hard currency or even go into a hard currency store. Truly eye opening.

Then came the scariest flight of my life. During a flight from one part of the Soviet Union to another, I felt the plane starting to descend slightly. As it was not long into the flight, I knew we were still hours from our final destination. An announcement in Russian came next, followed by all of the passengers getting into the brace position. Obviously something was very wrong, and "our" Aeroflot flight attendant was in the restroom.

Upon her return, we bombarded her with questions and she responded "there's a mechanical problem." As a Pan Am spokesperson, I was used to responding to media inquiries about air turn-backs with "mechanical problem" as the cause. I also knew that answer covered an expansive range of possibilities, and I wanted to know specifically about the mechanical problem. That was not to be the case. Thoughts were racing through my head. Did anyone from home even know I was on the flight? Did I trust that the Aeroflot equipment was safe? Did the pilot even know how to fly the plane? Soon I realized we were circling, and it went on for a while, so I felt a weird sense of calm. It was at that point the Aeroflot flight attendant said she believed there wasn't really a mechanical problem, it was likely the crew wanted to land in Moscow so they could go shopping. While logically I couldn't understand how they would allow that to happen, I was ecstatic we were actually touching down in Moscow, even though the passengers unloaded in the middle of an icy tarmac, dodging taxiing planes as we made our way to the terminal.

While I'm guessing that flying on Aeroflot has improved dramatically since 1988, all I can say is I was extremely grateful for the fact Pan Am operated those joint venture flights, especially the flight that carried me back to New York after my amazing Russian experience.

Photo by Gerhard Plomitzer (airliners.net)

Aeroflot IL-62

Elizabeth worked for Pan Am from Feb. 1983 to Dec. 1991 and was Manager, Corporate Communications from Aug. 1988 through Dec. 1991.

LOCKERBIE

By Arnie Reiner

Pan Am Flight 103, the Lockerbie Bombing,

As Experienced by a First Response Investigator

Pan Am's blue ball logo and the American flag atop the tail of Clipper jets were viewed synonymously around the world as symbols of America. However, to rogue groups and governments with grudges against America, Pan Am's Clippers were also convenient terrorist targets of opportunity traversing the world on a regular schedule. Pan Am Flight 103 would become one of those targets.

It was a routine afternoon December 21, 1988, at Pan Am's flight safety office at John F. Kennedy International Airport in New York. Routine, until the Senior V.P. of Operations' secretary came through the door and announced the airline's system control group had just been informed Flight 103 had disappeared from radar during departure from London. Officials then presumed the aircraft was lost. Soon after that, network news reports flashed word throughout the world that Pan Am 103 had gone down in Lockerbie, Scotland with the loss of 243 passengers, 16 crewmembers and an unknown number of casualties on the ground.

Pan Am immediately activated their aircraft accident contingency plan. Every key department was involved and they established a 24-hour command center at Kennedy Airport to coordinate company post-accident efforts and assign duties. Concurrently, a go-team was assembled primarily from Flight Operations and Maintenance and Engineering with supporting members from other departments to assist in the investigation at the accident site. They would join government investigators from the US Federal Aviation Administration (FAA), National Transportation Safety Board (NTSB), a Boeing representative and a large contingent of investigators from Britain's Air Accident Investigation Branch (AIB). Representatives from the Airline Pilots Association (ALPA) and Flight Engineers International (FEIA) and Independent Union of Flight Attendants (IUFA), unions also flew to the scene to assist in the effort.

As a member of the go-team, I assembled with the rest of the group at Pan-Am's JFK Worldport that evening to catch the evening flight to London. Captain Bob Gould, Senior Vice President of Operations would lead the team. The Worldport was a somber and frenetic scene, swarmed by media reporters with their cameras and lights intent on capturing the sorrow and anguish of relatives and friends gathered there to meet those who would never arrive on Flight 103. Company representatives were on hand to lend what comfort, support and assistance they could at a time of bottomless despair.

The evening flight across the Atlantic was the only opportunity for a short sleep before the early morning arrival at London's Heathrow Airport, which at that time of the year, was five hours ahead of New York time. Pan Am staff met us at Heathrow and whisked us off to a chartered twin-engine plane, which we flew to an airport near Lockerbie. After quickly dropping our bags at a hotel, Captain Gould and I split off from the group and had a driver take us about the town and out into the nearby countryside to take in the scope of the accident scene.

It was immediately obvious from the large debris area in town and out in the surrounding countryside east of Lockerbie that the 747-100, *Clipper Maid of the Seas*, N739PA, experienced a catastrophic in-flight breakup at a high altitude. At the time, all British investigators knew was that the plane disappeared from the Air Traffic Control radar without so much as a peep from the crew at 31,000 feet, flying at a groundspeed of 434 knots on a northwesterly track of 321 degrees.

When we arrived, we found the nose section had broken off and was in a field outside town with First Officer Raymond Wagner and Flight Engineer Jerry Avritt still inside the wreckage. Captain James MacQuarrie lay outside, already covered by a tarpaulin. Debris was visible in the steeply rolling pastures in every direction. A portion of the horizontal stabilizer was off in the distance. An engine lay imbedded in a Lockerbie street. The center fuselage and wings had come down almost vertically, striking a housing area and exploding on impact. Over 10 homes in the immediate vicinity were destroyed and others were badly damaged out to 900 feet. The impact and explosion fueled from the fuselage and wing tanks gouged a huge elongated crater where the houses once stood. Looking down into the scorched impact trench, there were no signs of cabin occupants. About a half mile away, a fuselage section aft of the wing root struck a house and impacted a street leaving passengers and cabin crew tangled and broken in building debris and aircraft structure. Constables guarded the scene. Residents milled about, quietly.

We returned to the hotel, washed up and gathered the Pan Am group for a preliminary briefing. I presented to the group what Bob and I had seen and learned so far: That obviously, there had been a very rapid catastrophic in-flight breakup and the aircraft had come down steeply, shedding parts as it descended. In addition, as far as we knew, there was no distress transmission from the crew before the plane disappeared from radar. Our objective was to keep an open mind about what might have happened, not speculate, and follow the evidence. Privately, my thinking was that by then 747s had been around over 18 years. Pan Am was the driver behind their development. They were structurally damage tolerant, solid planes with robust systems redundancies and in nearly two decades of operating experience at Pan Am, they didn't just suddenly fall apart in midair.

Something else was going on here. I'm certain the structural engineers from the company's Maintenance and Engineering Department who sat at the briefing that evening were thinking along the same lines. Teams were formed by their various disciplines for the following day's investigative work, which we would accomplish alongside British investigators and Scottish constables. With so many investigators from Pan Am, the U.K, the US and others participating in the investigation, a local Lockerbie school was used as a central meeting and logistics point. The school cafeteria was opened and staffed by local volunteers to provide meals. At one point, Margaret Thatcher, the British Prime Minister, came by the cafeteria to lend moral support to the effort.

After the first day in the field, clothing and footwear became an issue. We had all left New York with the clothing basics for light outdoor activity, but the rainy, cold, soggy grasslands of the Scottish countryside presented obstacles to getting around that were untenable in such light attire. The arrival of carton loads of variously sized Pan Am logo emblazoned heavy coveralls, rainwear and ankle high boots normally intended for the company's maintenance and flight line workers corrected that logistical impediment. A flight attendant in our group who was part of the investigation team presented something of a comical picture in this attire, because there were no coveralls in her size. She moved about with sleeves and pants legs rolled up over her lean frame looking like the scarecrow in the Wizard of Oz. But now, properly clothed for our jobs, we went about our work. Daylight itself was a constraint. With winter's onset in the Scottish highlands, sunrise occurred around 8:30 a.m. and sunset at 3:40 p.m., with darkness quickly following. We had to keep moving while we could see.

My group spent day two unproductively in and near the large scorched impact crater in town, which still smelled of jet fuel. The 747's structure was so obliterated, except for charred flap drive jackscrews, that nothing useful was discovered. However, we did determine the fuel-laden wings and a large fuselage section containing the center tank had caused the crater. A few hundred meters from the crater, shards of fuel soaked burning debris had been hurled like flaming arrows, arcing down and sticking in the dirt, leaving a circle of scorched earth where they hit. A lady who looked to be in her late forties sat on a stone wall adjoining a nearby field, staring out into the distance, saying over and over, "Why Lockerbie?" British military aircraft flew overhead photographing the debris fields.

On the third day, three of the groups fanned out east beyond Lockerbie walking the sheep meadows looking for objects of interest, gathering and bagging debris, and marking their locations on maps. I had never seen fog like we experienced in those Scottish highlands. Often the fog was so thick that one could see only 15 or 20 feet ahead. I used a compass to keep from walking in circles. On one hillside, express mail envelopes lay scattered about. On a knoll, a lone constable stood guard in the mist by a clothed, female adult body that had not yet been recovered. She had been hurled free of the falling wreckage and landed flat in the rain soaked sod, compressed it about half a foot and bounced about two feet from the indentation. She had no visible trauma marks and it occurred to me that she might well have survived the fuselage's furious descent, only to die on impact. The constable said he would remain with the body to keep animals from it until it was removed.

From the medical team headed up by Pan Am's corporate medical director, John McCann, we learned the bodies were taken to a nearby ice skating rink and laid out on the ice for preliminary identification. It served as a makeshift morgue, the ice providing refrigeration to limit decomposition. Relatives provided information about birthmarks, tattoos and unusual anatomical characteristics to help the identification process.

Our group's first break, the one confirming our unspoken suspicions, came while walking down a country road. A farmer approached and told us he and his wife had removed a number of suitcases from nearby sheep meadows to keep them out of the rain. He said they were in a shed by his house. There, in neat rows, were about a dozen pieces of passenger baggage. One had distinct scorch marks. Also that day, one of the British AIB team members noted a distinct bowing out of a fuselage skin fragment. Then a constable accompanying our group found a heavily pitted fuselage fragment in the tall meadow grass. It was tagged and bagged by the constable to assure continuity of evidence and taken away for analysis. The following day, the British announced the analysis of the wreckage confirmed an explosion had occurred in a cargo container in the forward cargo compartment. A later investigation revealed forces from the blast breached the fuselage and internal shock waves led to further fuselage failures, which quickly led to the aircraft's in-flight disintegration.

With official confirmation the loss of Flight 103 was a terrorist act, not an accident, our role as accident investigators ended, and one of the most intense forensic and criminal investigations was just beginning.

Arnie resides in Pensacola, FL and is completing a memoir of his time as a Marine Corps helicopter pilot in Vietnam in 1966-1967.

Arnie Reiner today

Courtesy of the Author

Young Arnie Reiner

INTERNAL GERMAN SERVICES

By Eric Fetzer

Pan Am's Services in Germany

Pan Am's Internal German Services (IGS) played a major role in Germany, maintaining a hassle-free access to Berlin (BER) by air. The IGS allowed Pan Am to provide services between West German cities and BER. Pan Am had served these markets since the 1950s and became the dominant airline providing almost endless airlift capacity, reliability and flexibility to the people living in Berlin, to business travelers, tourists, groups, and politicians.

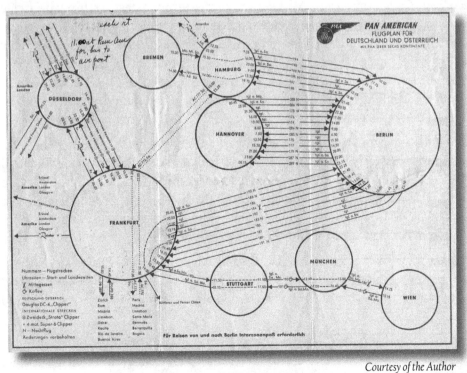

Courtesy of the Author

Plan of Internal German Services

183

Captain A. J. "Lefty" Leftwich meeting Berlin Mayor Willy Brandt, 1961

The years after World War II found Berlin divided into two parts: West Berlin, politically controlled by the former allies, and East Berlin, controlled by the German Democratic Republic, also known as the Soviet Union. West Berlin seemed to be an island surrounded by eastern territory. It was possible to travel on the surface between West German cities and West Berlin, but this involved passing through East German territory. To do so, travelers had to have travel documents and passports, as if entering a foreign country. Frequently, the East German government sent travelers back and treated them quite badly. However, as part of the post-war agreement that divided Germany, three air corridors were set up to allow air transport into West Berlin, flying over East German territory. Only the airlines of the former three allies (US, UK and France) could fly the routes to and from Berlin and they required the aircraft to fly at a minimum and maximum altitude. They did not allow Lufthansa to fly these routes; for travelers to Berlin, this was a real inconvenience.

The IGS became very popular and profitable. And Pan Am was regarded as a home carrier that had the support of the US government. It operated more services than the other allied carriers (BA and Air France). And over the years, many captains based in Berlin even learned to speak German. All the cabin attendants were German-speaking. Pan Am operated a dedicated fleet to fly the IGS sectors and maintained ticket offices in each of the city centers. The service was in high demand, helped by a subsidy paid by the German Government for tickets to and from Berlin resulting in lower prices to consumers.

Over the years, Pan Am operated DC-4, DC-6B and Boeing 727 and 737 aircraft on these routes. In the eighties, the company operated the Airbus A-310 along the routes and expanded international long haul and hub services. The summer schedule of 1985 also introduced a nonstop A-310 between Hamburg-HAM and New York-JFK.

On one of the inaugural flights, a reporter from one of the major German publishing houses was traveling Clipper Class to JFK. There was "minor incident" when during take off a water leakage in the air conditioning system above his seat poured over him and his seat. The passenger was so upset that he insisted he stand up during the entire flight. Even the direct involvement of the captain was in vain. Back in Germany our sales representative, after several attempts, was finally successful in getting a personal appointment with the passenger. All he did was present the passenger with an umbrella. After that no further excuses were necessary and the reporter continued to be a Pan Am Frequent Traveler.

In the summer schedule of 1985, we wanted to rename our A-310s with the names of the German cities served. For the christening of Clipper Hamburg, we invited the Mayor of Hamburg and other officials, the Airbus General Manager Germany, the media and VIPs. We were in a hurry to get the ceremony underway because we wanted to keep the aircraft on schedule. However, I had an uneasy feeling about the aircraft and called flight scheduling to ask which aircraft they assigned for the HAM sector. I was told it was the Clipper Munich. Fortunately, we were able to get the aircraft switched in record time and we christened Clipper Hamburg and avoided a lot of embarrassment.

Eric served with Pan Am until 1989 in Hamburg where he now resides.

Courtesy of the Author

THE BERLIN WALL FALLS

By Don Cooper

Collapse of the Berlin Wall

In the spring of 1977, I arrived in Berlin after eleven years of flying the Pacific from Pan Am bases in San Francisco, Seattle and Hong Kong. After check-in formalities with the Chief Pilot, the secretary arranged temporary lodging for me at the Air Force's Columbia Club at Tempelhof. It was an ideal location, with good connections by U-bahn to Tegel Flughaven where Pan American flight operations were located.

The decor of my room, with its sparse furnishings, high ceilings and tall windows, gave me the impression that I was in a time warp of a bygone era in World War II. Maybe the ghost of *Reichesmarschall* Herman Goering was haunting the corridors! That suspicion abruptly ended about 4:00 o'clock in the morning when I was rudely awakened by the resonating sound of concussions coming from artillery. The Soviet military had a huge firing and tank training area west of the city. I immediately realized that I was not in the Nazi era but one of the Soviet›s making–the Cold War. It was definitely eerie and a little terrifying to hear those loud explosions so early in the morning but it left no doubt in my mind what it was. My unpleasant experience had been the normal routine for years for the war-seasoned West Berliners.

Fast forward twelve years to November 1989. I was eight years into my second tour of flying out of West Berlin. In my life time, I never expected the Berlin Wall to come down or the collapse of communism but there I was, experiencing that special moment. During the days just prior to the collapse of the Wall, the news media kept reporting the events and the numbers of people crossing into West Germany from the East. It was a historic event in the making.

On November 8th, I reported to flight operations at 5 a.m. for a two day trip with a lay-over in Bucharest, Romania that evening. After arriving in Bucharest and going through government formalities, we boarded the bus for the 30 minute ride to the Dunas InterContinental Hotel. Before I left the aircraft, I picked up several newspapers left in the seats by the passengers. I wanted to read them in the hotel that evening. I would return them in the morning for the convenience of the outbound passengers.

The next day, November 9th, my wake-up call came about 4:30 in the morning and pick-up was an hour later. When I was ready, I proceeded to the lobby and waited for the other cockpit members and our three Polish cabin crew to appear. Pan Am used Polish cabin crews on East Bloc flights because they spoke Russian,

186

the common language for Iron Curtain countries. Arriving in the hotel lobby I proceeded to check-out. While I was waiting for the others, the clerk came up to me and he asked "If I was done with the newspapers," which I had under my arm, "If so, could I have them"? From previous trips to the hotel, I knew the secret police were normally around nearby. At first, I said "no" because I thought the secret police could cause problems. The clerk told me "don't worry, there were none on duty." Then he proceeded to ask me "what happened in the West during the last week"? I proceeded to tell him the information I had heard or read. He just shook his head in wonderment. As I boarded the bus, I gave him the newspapers.

Flight time from Bucharest to Frankfurt is approximately two and a half hours. While in flight, it was routine procedure to monitor both the Air Traffic Control and company radio frequencies. As we approached Frankfurt, I kept hearing other Pan Am flights requesting permission for the news media to enter the cockpit to take pictures of the border when crossing into East Germany. Naturally, the company denied their requests. By now, we had suspected the Wall had collapsed, but we wouldn't know for sure until we landed. On that particular day, the continuation of my pattern was to fly from Frankfurt to Berlin, then to Dusseldorf and return to Berlin and then to Nurnberg and finally back to Berlin at 10 p.m. It would be a long day of flying, especially when starting in Bucharest early in the morning. The flights to Berlin and Dusseldorf were both routine.

In Dusseldorf, the return flight to Berlin was booked to capacity. After loading we pushed back and started the engines and then the police came and motioned us back to the gate. They informed us that everyone was to leave the aircraft because we had a bomb threat. Later, we found out that someone called in the threat, hoping to get on board the flight so they could attend the big party in Berlin. After the passengers vacated the aircraft, it was towed to a remote site so police dogs could search the aircraft. The crew had not eaten since early morning. I told them to go get a hot meal and I would entertain the passengers' questions. The crew got their meals, thanks to Dusseldorf's station manager, who had already ordered refreshments and champagne for our inconvenienced passengers.

Courtesy of the Author

There were two TV teams on board, one from Toronto, Canada and the other from Dublin, Ireland. The question everyone asked was if they could come to the cockpit and take pictures of the border as we passed over. Naturally I had to tell them that it was not possible because US law prohibited passenger entry into the cockpit. It was about 2 o'clock in the afternoon when the bomb threat commotion started. The bomb search delayed our departure and it must have been close to 4 p.m. when we finally took-off. In early November, darkness occurs about 4 p.m. in northern Germany, which is located at 54 degrees north latitude. We would fly the center corridor for our trip into Berlin. As we approached the center corridor, I requested for a floor altitude of 4,000 feet to get a better view of the border and point out the sights as we crossed over. As we approached Berlin, I requested a circle of the city before we landed,

Don was a pilot for Pan Am from January 1966 until the last day. He flew a flight from Bermuda landing at New York at 0800 on December 4, 1991, the day Pan Am stopped operations. "Coop" is active in writing aviation history articles when not communicating with his legions of Pan Am friends.

which was approved. The streets of Berlin were packed with people and it was almost like the end of World War II, with rockets and fireworks exploding all over the city. It was truly exciting and one of those lifetime events that people look for and want to be part of and celebrate.

The flight to Nurnberg was routine but the return flight to Berlin was almost a repeat of the Dusseldorf—Berlin flight, except for the bomb threat. People wanted to celebrate and be part of this historic event. Some passengers had driven several hours across Germany to get aboard the last flight into Berlin. Early the next morning, Pan Am scheduling called and asked if I would take a flight to Dusseldorf scheduled for a 6 a.m. departure. "Sure, I will be right out," I said. When I entered the aircraft, I realized the people I had brought to Berlin the night before were the same people I was taking back to Dusseldorf. When they spotted me, they greeted me with loud cheers and waved their champagne bottles and continued to celebrate. What a wonderful time to be in Berlin!

P.S.   For some reason the cockpit door latch was inoperative and the door remained open for the rest of the day. The door latch is not a no-fly item. Naturally, the flight engineer entered the discrepancy in the maintenance log. That night, Berlin maintenance adjusted it with a wipe rag. It ground checked okay.

YET ANOTHER "LAST FLIGHT"

By Roger Cooke and Tom McClain

The Sale of IGS to Lufthansa

Pan Am's prospects looked bleak as the summer of 1990 ended. The fall was typically a soft time for cash generation. CEO Tom Plaskett was concerned that the company would not have the resources to make it to the Christmas holidays when traffic typically picked up and gave the balance sheet a small cushion with which to plod through winter. His close advisors warned him that as fiduciaries, the Board of Directors and

Pan Am's Internal German Service Carries 50 Millionth Passenger

The 50 millionth passenger to travel on Pan Am's Internal German Service (IGS), Edith Wehner of Munich, is escorted from the airplane after landing in Berlin on January 15, 1982. The occasion was marked by a colorful ceremony attended by Pan Am officials and government luminaries, including the Mayor of Berlin. Also on hand was a 30-piece U.S. Army band.

Known as "an airline within an airline," IGS has been in operation since 1946 and provides a vital link between West Berlin and the free world. Today, the IGS fleet of 11 727s flies the air corridors between Berlin and Hamburg, Frankfurt, Munich and Stuttgart, carrying some 6,000 passengers a day. Pan Am personnel assigned to IGS include 183 American pilots and 158 flight attendants, mostly German nationals. The crews are supported by a ground staff of over a thousand residents of the various cities served by IGS.

For 36 years, Pan Am's Internal German Service has provided an important air transportation system to a divided Germany. At the same time, the high volume and yield rate of this unique operation make it an important contributor to Company revenues.

Pan Am Archives

the management team could not run the cash reserves to an irresponsibly low level and then file for bankruptcy. It was essential the bankruptcy decision be made early enough in the process so Pan Am would have enough cash to manage its way through Bankruptcy Court and emerge as a reorganized, competitive enterprise.

Tom imagined it might be necessary to file before Christmas and as early as late September or October. With that in mind, in late August, he instructed me (Roger Cooke,) Pan Am's General Counsel, to assemble a team of accountants and lawyers to meet secretly at the Rockleigh, NJ accounting office over the three-day Labor Day weekend to prepare a petition to the bankruptcy court. Tom would hold the draft in reserve in case he needed it on short notice.

On the Friday afternoon before the weekend, we were making final preparations to begin work the next morning across the Hudson River when Tom called and advised of a change in plan. Tom had just concluded a lunch at the Sky Club with Heinz Ruhnau, the Chairman of Lufthansa Airlines. Tom and Heinz discussed the future of Pan Am's operations at Berlin's Tegel Airport. Pan Am had begun service to Berlin in September 1950 when it acquired American Overseas Airlines from American Airlines. Its service from various West German cities into and out of Berlin was legendary. Residents of the divided city celebrated Pan Am as a lifeline to the West.

With the fall of the Berlin Wall and the unification of East Germany and the Federal Republic of Germany, Herr Ruhnau would be able to realize a forty year dream of flying on a German flag carrier to the former capital of his country. He had previously confided in Tom the sense of unfairness he and his Lufthansa colleagues felt at being able to fly anywhere in the world, but being forbidden by the Allied Command from flying to Berlin. It was a legacy of World War II that was about to be resolved.

There was little doubt Lufthansa would immediately devote substantial resources to its return to Berlin. And there was also little doubt that what had been a stable cash generator for Pan Am—its fabled Internal German Service/IGS—was about to become a "wasting asset." Pan Am would not be able to compete with Lufthansa once it was allowed to serve Berlin. Lufthansa had a lock on the ticket distribution system in Germany and adding Berlin to its destinations would be a cakewalk. The question was whether Pan Am would leave sooner rather than later; it had no future in a unified Germany.

Tom reported that at lunch Ruhnau had agreed to pay Pan Am $150 million for Pan Am to cease its Berlin operations at the end of the day on Saturday, October 27, 1990. Lufthansa would replace Pan Am's service on Sunday morning. The deal included not only Pan Am's internal German traffic rights, but would shift Pan Am's slots and gates at Tegel to Lufthansa. The slots and gates were critical if Lufthansa was to resume service with critical mass. The alternative would have been for Lufthansa to build up its service over time as slots and gates became available from regulators or other airlines. The return to Berlin was Lufthansa's manifest destiny; the question was simply one of time. And Tom very much needed the cash; it would insure that Pan Am could last through the fall to Christmas.

Courtesy of the Author

Roger Cooke

Instead of reporting to Rockleigh, New Jersey, I used the weekend to travel to Frankfurt and brief Pan Am's Vice President of European Operations, Tom McClain, (my co-author) on our assignment. We had four weeks to negotiate an agreement with our counterparts at Lufthansa for the transfer of the IGS.

Tom McClain had joined Pan Am in January of 1990, two months after the Berlin Wall fell and quickly learned the importance of the IGS to Pan Am. Pan Am's leverage with the German government in Bonn and the Ministry of Transport, in particular, was solidly supported by its IGS service and Pan Am's Berlin operations. When negotiating a myriad of issues with the help of the US Embassy, the IGS was routinely the proverbial "elephant in the room." For example, this leverage kept PanAm independent of the Frankfurt baggage systems which would have added a half hour to every Pan Am connection.

There was little doubt that both airlines were highly motivated to complete the deal. It was well known that Pan Am was on the verge of collapse and desperately needed cash—it needed to make payroll! It was equally clear Lufthansa wanted to make a statement with its resumption of service to Berlin after so many years. It needed Pan Am's slots and gates to do so.

The issue that dominated the negotiations was the terms under which Lufthansa would assume responsibility for the Pan Am workforce. All of Pan Am's IGS ground employees were German, including a maintenance staff. The German maintenance team maintained the Boeing 727 fleet, which was used to serve Berlin. In addition, it became a practice of the operations team in New York to rotate Boeing 727 aircraft into and out of the IGS service in order to schedule their maintenance by the German mechanics.

The Pan Am negotiators wanted Lufthansa to bring all the IGS employees over with equivalent wages and benefits, as well as full credit for their Pan Am service. Lufthansa sought flexibility in its handling of the employees, especially in light of the fact that Pan Am was a failing enterprise. They resisted the idea of protecting the jobs of any of the US staff, including the pilots, many of whom had spent their entire careers in the IGS. They succeeded in this effort. As far as the ground staff, German labor law mandated fair treatment on favorable terms.

The negotiations were completed over the four weeks of September with the US negotiators shuttling between New York and Frankfurt throughout the month. Once the agreement was in execution form, Lufthansa put me in the only remaining seat—the cockpit jump seat—of a scheduled flight from Frankfurt to Geneva, so I could brief Tom Plaskett who was attending an IATA meeting on the final terms of the deal. I returned to Frankfurt the same day and delivered the executed agreement to Lufthansa with Plaskett's signature. All that remained was to obtain regulatory clearance and then to close. The regulatory hurdles were cleared without incident.

Had this been a conventional commercial transaction, the closing would have been a routine affair—bankers and lawyers in a downtown conference room exchanging bank transfer receipts and real estate documents. This closing was anything but routine, though. Lufthansa scheduled the closing to occur in Berlin. At midnight on Saturday, October 27, 1990 Pan Am would have flown its last flight to Tegel and on Sunday morning Lufthansa would fly what had been Pan Am's schedule, using Pan Am's slots and gates. In a single stroke, Lufthansa would replace the entire airlift capability that Pan Am had operated for 40 years. For West Germans and Berliners, Pan Am would go from a symbol of Western support to a memory.

Lufthansa arranged for a reception at the Kempinski Hotel in Berlin followed by a dinner for the numerous Lufthansa and Pan Am staff who had worked on the transaction, as well as their guests. The reception would also give invited dignitaries the opportunity to celebrate the importance of the occasion.

Early on Saturday afternoon, Tom McClain joined me and our spouses and colleagues and left Frankfurt for Berlin and the closing ceremony. Gunther Pitzner, Pan Am's regional Vice President was among the group. Gunther knew just about everyone in the German airline industry—airline executives, travel agents, suppliers and government officials. He was stunned to see so many of them at the airport and on the final flights Pan Am would be operating on that Saturday. Many headed to the Kempinski—but many said they simply wanted to take one last ride on Pan Am to Berlin. Again and again, the Pan Am contingent would hear it was the end of an era and the airline community wished to honor the contribution Pan Am had made to the welfare of the German people.

The reception was crowded. The Mayor of Berlin spoke, as did the Minister of Transport. When his turn came to speak, Herr Ruhnau was unprepared for the emotion of the moment. Overcome and unable to speak, he retreated from the microphone and composed himself by pacing the front of the ballroom for what seemed an eternity. When he returned to the stage, he spoke in familiar, rather than formal, voice about the significance of his and his airline's return to Berlin. It was as if the events of the previous few months—the fall of the Wall and the end of the cold war—were replaying themselves at 78 RPM.

Dinner followed for the working group to commemorate the closing; a bittersweet moment for the group from the United States and a celebration for the Germans. Following the dinner, the German contingent headed to the airport to welcome midnight and the end of an era. The Pan Am team was honored to have played a role in the momentous events of the day—the reunification of German air service—but were content for the festivities to end.

Courtesy of the Author

Tom McClain

PAN AM'S COMPASSION

By Susan Westfall

Fulfilling a Lifelong Dream

Merriam-Webster's definition of the word "compassion" is: sympathetic consciousness of others' distress together with a desire to alleviate it.

My definition of compassion is: Pan Am.

Photo by Jamie Baldwin

The Louvre—Paris

193

During my last three years of a joyous and rewarding career at Pan Am, which began in 1977, I worked in Corporate Communications where they dubbed me the "compassionate person." Accordingly, among a number of prized roles, I had the privilege of reading through dozens of letters each month from people around the world asking for assistance, and then determining which "compassionate petitions" we would be able to honor. This was fulfilling both personally and professionally, especially since I always felt that Pan Am was a family that took care of its own, and one that contributed to the global community as well.

These requests spanned the gamut of free airfare for the sick, free shipments of precious cargo, and things that were simply, well, out of the ordinary.

Pan Am granted one such request for free airfare in October of 1990 that, to this day, remains in the forefront of my mind. It is the story of Gerald Jean-Pierre, an award-winning art student afflicted with Duchenne Muscular Dystrophy, a form of genetic de-generation which attacks the muscular system, whose lifelong dream was to visit the famed Louvre Museum in Paris, France. We became aware of this gifted and brave young man through the Southern Florida Chapter of Make-A-Wish Foundation.

Pan Am provided free transportation to Gerald, and to his mother, aunt, and sister (who suffered from Muscular Dystrophy). Their journey began with much fanfare at Miami International Airport with a sendoff and loving support from Gerald's entire art class, family members, representatives from Make-A-Wish Foundation, and a local Miami television news crew. Gerald and his family lived his dream of visiting the Louvre and upon returning home, were full of praise for the Pan Am Passenger Service Agents and Flight Attendants in Miami and at Charles de Gaulle Airport in Paris who helped make their trip a special event they would always remember.

Committed to helping others, Pan Am worked hand-in-hand with organizations, and individuals, to provide gratis transportation to countless needy people. One such recipient was a Russian teen named Olga, whom we flew to the US to receive treatment for leukemia. Another was Frescia, a young, impoverished burn victim receiving more than 15 operations in the US to repair severe damage to her face and neck. Frescia's father became seriously ill, so Pan Am generously flew her home to Chile to be by his side.

This is just a small sampling of stories that speak well of Pan Am's compassion, however, for me it was the many "thank you" notes we received that spoke volumes of Pan Am's kindnesses. After flying a woman from Orlando to London for an organ transplant, her friend wrote, "I have a tendency to think of big companies being 'too big' and 'not caring'. It is nice to know Pan Am has a heart and did help in such a big way." On behalf of a young son whom we flew from Miami to San Francisco for cancer treatment, his parents and siblings wrote, "Words cannot express how we feel and we will never forget all the compassion and special attention that the airline employees showed our family. ... When we left San Francisco we felt like we had received a miracle." After flying a woman from Los Angeles to New York so she could receive treatment for a craniofacial deformity, she wrote, "Thank you for helping me restore the nice feelings I used to have toward others' happiness. After several facial reconstructive surgeries I am also able to feel happiness of my own again. ... Pan Am has been, and will always be, my first choice when flying anywhere, thanks to your caring employees."

One of my most enjoyable memories had nothing to do with free airline travel, as much as it had to do with making a Pan Am 747 at a JFK hangar travel by way of some muscle and strong hands. After being contacted with a rather unusual request, Pan Am decided to help a team of New York City police officers, firefighters, and educators break a previous Guinness World Record for a similar feat that had taken place in London (not involving Pan Am). As reported by Newsday, which covered the event and interviewed the organizer of the "Airplane Pull," this event was organized to "... one-up the British effort, to get city fire fighters and police 'together constructively' and to raise money for several charities." With one big push (or in this case pull!) of support and teamwork by Pan Am and its Operations and Maintenance personnel, the 140-person Airplane Pull was said to have raised $1,400 for a number of children's charities. Pan Am also donated tickets for a fundraiser auction, with a goal of raising an additional $5,000.

Then there was the "Candy Clipper" project, involving the Pan Am shipment of 12 tons of Hershey's Chocolate to Romania on behalf of US Romanian Church officials, and the tireless efforts of Pan Amer Jeff Musheno from JFK. This delectable shipment was destined to find its way into the sweet and innocent hands of neglected orphans and handicapped children who had suffered as a result of Romania's challenging political situation at the time. What may seem to be a small gesture to most of us had a profoundly uplifting affect on the recipients, making their lives just a little bit brighter. A headmistress of a school with handicapped children wrote a thank you note, saying that the chocolate was, "very appreciated by our children who are still at the age when sweets provide moments of real delight ..."

This last illustration exemplifies the goodwill that Pan Am always strived to extend throughout the world, or globe, that through our eyes, always radiated Pan Am blue.

In 1989, Pan Am shipped a three-story tall greeting card from JFK to Moscow free-of-charge, which was the brainchild of an Iowa businessman wanting to demonstrate America's thankfulness and appreciation to Soviet President Gorbachev for his contributions toward world peace.

Compassionate. Generous. Kind. Caring. Enthusiastic. Angelic. These words were among a handful of adjectives ascribed repeatedly to Pan Am and its employees from many of the people whom we helped. These accolades could easily be used to describe the tens of thousands of employees who worked throughout Pan Am's history across all departments and continents, regardless of any personal or corporate struggles that may have been experienced at that time. Countless employees were instrumental in successfully accomplishing Pan Am's compassionate endeavors as highlighted above, and in untold other instances throughout the years. No doubt endless acts of compassion have been carried out by Pan Amers that we will never even know about, done in dedicated service and humble quietude.

These words of praise sent from those we helped also quite aptly describe the numerous Pan Am colleagues who became like family to me and remain lifelong friends to this day. I became best of friends with two such women (Diane Krumholtz and Dr. Cindy Gale, nee Morales) that, 34 years later, remain just as close to my heart. They have brought much love and meaning to my daily life that ultimately resulted in immense personal growth.

As for the example set by Gerald Jean-Pierre and his aspiration to visit the Louvre, I too have an aspiration, and that is to keep compassion alive in my life every day. Gerald presented me with an original drawing (drawn with a pen between his teeth, since he had limited use of his limbs) that serves as a reminder of my Pan Am family, of a courageous young man, and that a day without extending compassion to others, and one's self, is a day not quite worth living.

Though my heart is nourished with fond memories and continued contact even after all these years, I sincerely miss working, and playing, with my compassionate Pan Am family.

Susan owns a public relations firm in Boulder, CO.

Courtesy of the Author
Susan Westfall

195

PAN AM AND CRAF

By Charlie Imbriani
Pan Am's Role in Desert Storm

Saddam Hussein's invasion of Kuwait in August 1990 placed Iraq squarely on a collision course with the United States. By now, that history is quite familiar to most of us. What is not familiar and much less appreciated outside of military and aviation circles is the crucial role US Civil Aviation played in the war.

US airlines flew over 5,000 missions into the Persian Gulf in support of Operation Desert Shield and Desert Storm. It was not only unprecedented in military and aviation history, but was key to the war's successful outcome. Pan American World Airways flew over 300 of those missions and this is part of that story.

Courtesy of the Author

Charlie Imbriani at Military Base in SaudiArabia

196

By August 7, 1990, President George H.W. Bush ordered units of the 82nd Airborne to Saudi Arabia as an advance guard of what the military would later recognize as Desert Shield. Thus began the largest airlift in history, as the rush was on to position a defensive force on the Saudi peninsula. The Military Airlift Command (MAC)—the military's "airline"—did not have sufficient lift or capacity to accomplish this mission. It was inevitable the government would call on the Civil Reserve Air Fleet (CRAF); and indeed, it did, for the first time in its thirty-nine year history.

The CRAF is a voluntary program by which US airlines commit a predetermined number of aircraft and crew to national service in times of war or national emergency. President Harry S. Truman created The CRAF in 1951 by an executive order primarily to assist in bringing American troops to Europe to counter a possible Soviet invasion. His administration created and designed the CRAF for the Cold War. It was never before tested and with a new and totally unexpected mission, the initial activation of CRAF brought with it some apprehension.

Before the official activation of CRAF on August 17, 1990, several US carriers already volunteered aircraft to meet the crisis. Pan American World Airways (Pan Am), in keeping with its long tradition of coming to the nation's aid in times of adversity, was one of the early volunteers. Thus began for me, one of the most rewarding and exciting experiences in my twenty-seven years with Pan Am.

I wore many hats in my Pan Am career, which began on the "Ramp" in 1964, and in a fortuitous way, ended there in 1991 as a Ramp Operations trainer. One of my favorite jobs though, was "Clipper Skipper," a euphemism for a receptionist at Pan Am's VIP lounge, famously known as the Clipper Club. It was truly an exciting job; for on any given day someone from 'Who's Who' passed through our doors.

In 1990, war was imminent, and the activation of the Civil Reserve Air Fleet gave a temporary reprieve to the Ramp Operations trainers; they called on the trainers to support the CRAF operation. You could say by default but in reality, we were ideally suited for the job. Pan Am flew 358 missions into the Persian Gulf, all long-range 747 passenger (troop) flights and freighters. The minimum distance from the continental United States to Saudi Arabia was 7,000 miles. Many flights originated on the West Coast, Texas, and other interior points within the Continental United States, often adding an additional 3,000 miles to the journey. In most cases, the point of origin, the final destination, and in some instances, the intermediate stopovers, were offline, or otherwise, not a Pan Am base. So having an experienced Pan Am representative at these locations made all the difference in the world. That's where we came in.

What I, and the others in my position were required to do, was to go ahead of our arriving flights to any of a dozen or so US military bases. We organized the loading of the troops, their personal gear, and all the equipment they planned to take, which by the way, did include refrigerators and the proverbial kitchen sink. We had to organize working parties, plan the load, supervise the loading, fueling, and complete a weight and balance for the cockpit crew. This is more or less where our area of expertise paid off. Most of my generation, having lived through the draft, were veterans of one military service or another. In my case it was the Marine Corps. Going onto a military base, or I should say, getting onto a military base sight unseen, can be a challenge. But dealing with a Marine gunny sergeant can be unnerving to the uninitiated. For the most part, however, it was all part of our past experience—at least for my partner, Freddy Bissert, and me.

Freddy had been with Pan Am since the late 1950s, and was a real old salt who taught me much. We were from completely different backgrounds—an unlikely, but unflappable pair, who received many professional compliments from the US Air Force personal with whom we closely worked. Freddy and I spent over a month at Cherry Point, NC Marine Corps Air Station where elements of the 2nd Marine Division deployed to the Persian Gulf. We spent Thanksgiving Day, Christmas, and the New Year with the Marines. Pan Am was arriving daily, and after a hard day's work, some of the young Marines, including their second lieutenant, would ask me to tell them about the 'Old Corps.'

One day, at Ramstein AFB in Germany, we found ourselves standing outside the Air Force operations office on the flight line, waiting for our arriving flight. There was a moderate fog but the visibility didn't look to be below landing minimums. Just then, a young Air Force NCO stepped out of the office and asked, "Are you the Pan Am reps?"

"Yep."

"Well, our C-141s are diverting. I'm sure your flight will have to divert to Frankfurt."

I was sure of one thing and not sure of another. I was not sure if the visibility was below minimums, but I was sure the Pan Am captain flying the aircraft was well aware of what he was flying and the destination; and he would be determined to get it there. We walked back into the Operations Office and just then, breaking the silence, we heard a familiar refrain, "Ramstein, this is Pan Am Clipper...requesting landing instructions." I walked back outside and could see the bright landing lights piercing the fog and said to my partner (jokingly of course), "The Air Force is playing in the big leagues now."

If asked to recount my most memorable recollection of that operation, I would have difficulty picking one. Each trip—I did twenty-seven—was in some way eventful. But my last trip into the Gulf does evoke a particular memory. We received word while at our hotel in Kaiserslautern (near Ramstein, Germany) over CNN, the war had ended. Nevertheless we had a flight that day into Bahrain. Once there, I was supervising the offloading of our 747 freighter, and I noticed a small aircraft taxied to the ramp and parked adjacent to us. It was a G-2 (Gulfstream II) and I overheard someone say, "That's General Schwarzkopf's plane."

A while later I saw about ten or twelve US servicemen milling about the aircraft, getting ready to board. I took a picture, not having any idea of what I was witnessing. Once back at the hotel, CNN provided the answer. The soldiers milling about the General's plane were the American servicemen the Iraqis held as prisoners. Once released, General Schwarzkopf personally came to pick them up.

Two years later, I met the General and I showed him that picture. I asked, "General do you recognize this picture?"

He said, "Sure, that's my plane, where did you get that picture?" With a bit of pride building in my chest I told him, "I took that picture."

I often think of those days, wondering about all the people I worked with and shared a bit of history. I wonder what ever happened to those Pan Am crew members, the pilots and flight attendants, the Pan Am mechanics, and the operations representatives who flew and worked those missions. Their professionalism, dedication, spirit of volunteerism, and genuine concern for our troops went way beyond anything I have ever seen or experienced before. I spent hours flying and working with these extraordinary people and can tell you that this was truly one of Pan Am's finest hours—perhaps its last.

They did a brave thing flying into the war zone. There was neither flourish nor fanfare and even less recognition. They did it because they cared. They cared about our nation, they cared about our troops; they cared for each other, and they cared a lot about Pan Am. I was proud to be part of it.

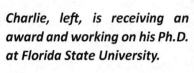

Charlie, left, is receiving an award and working on his Ph.D. at Florida State University.

DESERT STORM

By John Marshall

Flying Troops into Saudi Arabia

It was early in the year 1991. No one knew it at the time, but Pan Am had less than a year to live. The country was about to embark on a military action in the Middle East in response to the invasion of Kuwait by Saddam Hussein's ruthless army. The US military had converted a good part of Pan Am's 747 fleet to support the CRAF missions.

Pan Am Archives

Troops

199

Our jumbos had the keel beams beefed up and huge cargo doors carved into the sides of our passenger aircraft. We could convert our modified airliners to freighters in a matter of hours and pressed them into service at the word from the Pentagon. As Desert Storm took shape and got legs, that is exactly what happened.

The months from January to June were a heady time for the 747 crews who were fortunate enough to fly CRAF missions. The missions ranged from carrying troops and materiel from stateside military bases all over the country across the Atlantic to the war zone, and then a few short months later, astounded by the lightning pace and unexpected success of the war effort, we brought them all back. I was lucky enough to be on both ends of the equation.

The eastbound trips early in the conflict were sober, reflective journeys. The troops were silent and withdrawn, with the introspection of soldiers on the eve of battle. Most of the flights stopped at Kennedy before the eight-hour trans-Atlantic flight to Rome Fiumicino, where the operation was gas-and-go. No one deplaned, except to change the crew, and then on to the picturesque "resorts" in Saudi Arabia. The flight crews slept in Rome, and usually picked up the following day's trip to the war zone. I flew several missions into King Khalid Military City, a name that doesn't exactly conjure up visions of swaying palms and secluded beaches. In fact, the name really didn't do it justice...it was a dirty slash in the endless brown of the Arabian Desert, a no-nonsense operation manned by grim-faced Saudis and hurrying GIs.

Few of the Pan Am captains of my seniority flew in combat—we had been military airmen, but most of us fell into the gap between Korea and Vietnam. This was a wonderful opportunity to feel as though we were really on the front line of the whole operation, making a significant contribution to the war effort. We were all volunteers, but no one made a big deal out of it. It was common knowledge we were flying military operations into a war zone; as I remember, there was a directive from the Chief Pilot's office to the effect that no one had to fly these missions who, for whatever reason, didn't wish to participate, no questions asked. I don't recall ever hearing of anyone refusing.

As we all remember, Desert Storm was one of the quickest, most successful military operations in US history. It seemed as though we had no sooner transported this tremendous infrastructure of men, women and materiel into the furnace of the Iraqi war zone, than we were over there again preparing to bring them all back. That was the fun part.

I flew many flights all over the world in my Pan Am career, but nothing matched the exhilaration, the delight, and the satisfaction that came from bringing those troops home. On one trip I remember, we picked up an airplane full of GI's in Rome headed home. It wasn't long before it was apparent I had coincidentally commanded the flight that flew most of them over to the war a number of weeks earlier. We flew those trips with an open house in the cockpit, which made the crossing immeasurably shorter by the constant stream of men and women in and out, with the happy uninhibited chatter of those who had survived.

One group told me with great relish of an incident that happened to them late in the conflict. They were hurrying down a goat track of a road in southern Iraq when their Humvee got firmly stuck in the soft, drifting sand. The GI's disembarked with their shovels and trenching tools and began digging out. Just at that moment, a large group of Iraqi troops appeared over the hill, rifles in hand. The GI's hurriedly hunkered down behind their rooted vehicle, when it soon became apparent the Iraqis wanted nothing more than to surrender. The GI's huddled for a brief moment, then told the Iraqi leader they would accept their surrender only on the condition they help get the Humvee out of the sand. No sooner said than done. In the cockpit there were chuckles all around as we all laughed at the absurdity of it. I was very happy to be a small part of it all.

But the best part, by far, was landing our 747 back at the military bases from which all these men and women had embarked weeks before. From far across the field, we could see the huge crowds carrying flags and banners, colorfully painted with welcoming words. They were bouncing with eager excitement, scarcely containing themselves until we finally parked and opened the doors. There was always a military band playing non-stop. We usually carried a maintenance guy with us, and as I remember on this day, it was Joe Annuncio, a jolly, well-fed supervisor from JFK. He always carried a huge American flag with him, and as we taxied in, he climbed onto the observer's seat, opened the top hatch, and frantically waved the flag as we made our way to the ramp. What a reception! Shake, stir, and repeat as necessary.

Very few trips gave me such satisfaction and left me with such a good, warm, satisfying feeling. I think of it often. When the conflict had ended and the dust settled, the Air Force gave me a medal and a nice citation that now graces my den wall. I have been asked if I would do the whole thing over again.

Would I?

In a heartbeat.

John attended Deerfield Academy, Stanford University, and served in the U.S. Air Force prior to his career with Pan Am. He was based in Hong Kong, Sydney, Berlin, San Francisco, and served as the chief pilot of the Honolulu base, also known as "The Royal Hawaiian Flying Club." He received the civilian Desert Shield and Desert Storm medal for flying military troops and materiel in support of Operation Desert Storm. He finished his Pan Am career commanding the last 747 revenue flight from Sao Paolo, Brazil, to JFK and then retired as a 747 captain with Korean Airlines. He recently received the

prestigious Wright Brother's "Master Pilot" Award and is enjoying his membership with fellow Quiet Birdmen. John's writings and columns have appeared for a number of years in Smithsonian Magazine *and* Airways Magazine. *He keeps in shape flying a World War II B-25 bomber, "Show Me." John presently works for the FAA as an Aviation Safety Inspector in St. Louis, MO where he resides with this wife, Carla.*

WHITE HOUSE CHARTERS A TO Z

By William Frisbie

Pan Am and the White House Charters

Pan Am had a long relationship with the White House, acting as the "unofficial" charter carrier for the press corps who accompanied the President on his flying journeys outside of Washington—whether for a short domestic hop or a trip around the world....from a 727 to a 747.

In fact, the very first President to fly while in office was Franklin Roosevelt, who in 1943 flew from Dinner Key in Miami to Casablanca on a secret mission during WWII—on a Pan Am flying boat—the Boeing-314. He celebrated his 61st birthday on the return trip.

Pan Am Archives

President Roosevelt and aides aboard a Pan Am Clipper en route to Casablanca

I first began flying White House charters in 1984 when President Reagan made a trip to China. The White House knew I had flown all the proving and initial flights to Beijing, Shanghai, and Canton, starting in 1978 as the bamboo curtain began to fall. The White House wanted the benefit of my China experience as China's air traffic system was unbelievably backward, mostly ADF approaches, altitude measured in meters not feet, wind speed in meters per second, and although the charters carried five crew members, they were all pilots who had no knowledge of navigation in the area. Also, in those days, the de-icing of a 747 was accomplished by opening the over wing emergency exits and having the Chinese beat the ice off the wings with bamboo sticks.

A Presidential trip overseas is an enormous undertaking. The Presidential staff does not want the public to know the size and cost of these trips. Advanced teams go to each stopover with operations, security and place support people and special vehicles—all bullet proof—in each city to await the arrival of Air Force One.

Many aircraft are involved. In addition to Air Force One, there is usually a backup Air Force One in case of a mechanical problem. Then there is the White House press plane, other passenger jets including 707's, Gulfstreams, Lear Jets, and countless cargo and rescue aircraft.

On the White House press aircraft, we carried cabinet staff members, security personnel, and secret service members. We even took along our own customs and immigration staff so we could clear US government formalities onboard. We also carried our own medical personnel.

Air Force One is the call sign for whatever airplane in which the President is travelling. The tail number of the 747, which the President currently flies, is 28000. The Office of the President acquired the airplane in 1990, during the administration of George H. W. Bush. Immediately behind the cockpit on the upper deck is a highly technical communication center, equal to anything on the ground. Behind the communications center is the President's office with bedroom quarters downstairs in the front of the aircraft, including a bathroom with a shower. Galleys are state-of-the art with all food prepared to order by US Air Force personnel—no frozen meals for this crowd of VIPs. There is even a hospital room with surgical capability onboard. When the President travels by helicopter, the call sign is Marine One, as it is a US Marine Corps operation.

Pan Am cockpit crews and cabin attendants, who had security clearances processed in advance, flew the press charters. It was necessary to have a reservoir of such pre-cleared employees so as not to jeopardize a mission. When we flew a charter, we had an open cockpit door policy and the flight attendants, who not only excelled at providing superb service, doubled as comic relief for the journalists. They often dressed in outlandish costumes such as a gondolier shirt or Mao tunic. We even had crazy Halloween outfits during the final week of a Presidential campaign.

Flying with President Bush was much different from flying during President Reagan's administration. President Reagan took a much more leisurely approach to getting to destinations, while President Bush was always a man in a hurry. For example, when Reagan went to China in 1984, we stopped and rested in Honolulu and again in Guam before arriving in Beijing, allowing the President to adjust to time zones as we went along. In contrast, in February of 1989, President Bush flew from Washington (Andrews Air Force base in Maryland) straight to Tokyo with a fuel stop in Alaska. In any case, the President's schedule is published in advance to the exact minute and one can set a watch as to when Air Force One blocks in.

The longest duty day I remember was returning from Asia following Emperor Hirohito's memorial services. We left Tokyo before dawn for Seoul, South Korea and stayed at the airport all day during the President's meetings. We then left Seoul around dusk for Washington and while en route, we saw a sunrise and another sunset before landing in Andrews, well before dark—and then we had to ferry the aircraft back to JFK.

On most flights, we flew an interchange with Air Force One. The media would observe the departure and then board our flight and depart afterwards. During the trip, our aircraft would pass Air Force One in order to arrive first and allow the media to cover the Air Force One arrival. Sometimes this interchange can be challenging—especially on short flights, or when the winds are adverse. The White House press wants to make sure they record every trivial piece of history, even catching the President slip on the stairs—as they did with President Gerald Ford.

Communications is top notch when traveling with the White House. At every stop, a telephone was brought onto the aircraft and when dialed 0, a White House operator would answer and connect you anywhere in the world. En route, we used a discreet VHF frequency to communicate with Air Force One sharing all sorts of information. On one occasion, a female journalist became extremely ill en route to China. She was nearly comatose with a very low heart rate and blood pressure. A tent was fashioned on the floor of the aircraft for privacy while a White House nurse onboard attended to her and came to the cockpit to talk to the President's doctor onboard Air Force One. Rather than choose to divert to Okinawa, we elected to attempt to continue to Shanghai, but were prepared to land if her condition worsened. This journalist had very little sympathy from her fellow White House press travelers, as this crisis had happened once before. It was caused by an experimental drug she used to combat acne – all at the price of vanity.

A representative usually accompanied our flight attendants from the catering department, often Jimmy Leahy, and they always prepared their own menus, based on what the White House press corps liked to eat. It was always elaborate—eggs benedict, lobster, steaks and plenty of goodies, snacks and candy bars everywhere. But often, they wanted hamburgers, chili, or Mexican food. Nothing was denied. The bar was always open and the press clearly earned their reputation as hard hitting drinkers. The White House paid Pan Am for the charters and then billed each news organization on board. The Press Office did the seating chart, careful not to seat rivals together.

All of our trips were exciting as we were witnesses to history. I especially remember the 1987 economic summit which was held in Venice—what a beautiful and romantic place. We also included a side trip to Rome. Then we left for Berlin, where President Reagan delivered an address at the Brandenburg Gate in front of the Berlin Wall exhorting President Gorbachev of the Soviet Union to, "Tear down this wall." The flight to Berlin was a challenge, as we landed at Templehof Airport, the airport used in the Berlin airlift following World War II. We had to fly between the apartment buildings on landing and had only 4,300 feet of runway with no glide path aids. The runway was actually longer than 4,300 feet, but was only 143 feet wide so the 747 could only use the first 4,300 feet to permit a turn-around.

Shortly before leaving office in December 1988, President Reagan invited our crew to meet with him and have lunch at the White House in appreciation for the support the White House received from Pan Am. This was a great thrill and remains, to this day, one of my greatest memories from my flying days.

My last trip was with President Bush to Helsinki for another summit with the Russians. This was the first time the White House flew the 747 on a presidential trip and it was one of my last trips before my retirement. President Bush invited my wife Joan to go along. It was her first experience travelling with the White House press corps and she was the first "civilian" to tour the new Air Force One. During my seven years flying the White House press corps, I became very close friends with the crews of Air Force One. They are great pilots and friends with whom I still stay in touch. I also marveled at how our super flight attendants handled the difficult, egotistical press.

Today, I am still flying, but I am buying my own gas.

Courtesy of the Author

William Frisbie

WHITE HOUSE PRESS TALES

By Nancy Scully

Flying With Presidents

Looking back over my many photo albums, I realized they contained family events followed by photos of one of the US Presidents visiting a city in the US or a fabulous destination somewhere in the world. There were pictures of Air Force One and photos of places that the President had visited on the campaign trail or at a summit with world leaders. The memories come flooding back at the amazing opportunities that

Courtesy of the Author

Nancy Scully, left, with President Reagan

205

I had been given as a flight attendant for Pan American World Airways and one who was chosen to fly on the White House Press Charters.

Many times people asked me how the company chose me for the prestigious opportunity to accompany the White House on the Press Charters. I believe I came to the attention of Pan American World Airways due to my performance during the hijacking of Flight 64 in 1980. It was the beginning of the most exciting travel anyone could experience, as a flight crewmember.

Flight 64 was on its third leg (flight to a destination) of a one day trip between Miami and San Juan and the crew was about to be over the contractual legal limits for a duty day. The captain had the wheel chocks removed and we were holding at the gate for final baggage loading. The flight attendants were seating the passengers and securing the galleys. We were tired and ready to start our final leg for the day with a layover in San Juan. Shortly after take-off, two passengers, one tall and one short, Laurel and Hardy look a-likes, stood up from their seats and poured gasoline on the seats in front of them. They threatened to light a gasoline-filled Top Job bottle with a lighter. They then said, "Cuba!" This was the beginning of one of the many hijackings between Miami and Cuba in the early '80s. The captain flew to Cuba and the hijackers were taken off in hand cuffs as the passengers waited for the Swiss Embassy to negotiate the release of the plane and crew to fly to our original destination. But that is a story for another time.

Several months after the hijacking, I received a phone call from crew scheduling asking if I would be interested in working a White House Press Charter to accompany President Carter to the Sugar Bowl to view his beloved Georgia Bulldogs. I accepted the offer and following the trip, they asked me to join the press charters on future trips. The press charters carried the reporters and press staff who were not part of the pool traveling on Air Force One. The White House Travel Office would arrange each trip and work with the advance teams to assure travel comfort, gourmet meals, and what turned out to be memorable trips in the course of writing history. We made the trips fun and the press and staff several times claimed they would rather travel on the Pan Am plane rather than Air Force One because they had more fun and better food. On foreign trips, we would dress in a costume representing the place we had visited. We had hula skirts over our uniforms, babushkas, or an apron with pictures of sushi from Japan. Each morning, we greeted the press before departure with orange juice, Dunkin' Donuts, and steaming cups of coffee. Some of the reporters' children nicknamed us the Donut Ladies when they traveled with us for long summer visits to the Western White House in Santa Barbara. Many times, we prepared Eggs Benedict and or lamb chops for the short morning trip between Andrews and NYC. This was a hurried service. One time we were rushing so quickly that the plate of eggs, bacon and hash browns flew off my tray and onto a White House correspondent's lap as she tried to read her newspaper in the front row of the 727.

The charter crew and the press were like family. This was a time when the press plane was the reporters' time to be away from all their company assignments; a place to relax before the hurried and sleepless days ahead of them as members of the traveling press.

As the crew, we were witnesses to history. For thirteen years, we were at the economic summits in Venice and England and at the meetings of Presidents Reagan and Gorbachev in Moscow and Reykjavik, in the negotiation of the end of the Cold War and limiting nuclear armament. We were invited to climb into the huge transport cargo planes that carried the armored limos in which the Russian President rode. It was like being in a Tom Clancy novel. The airplane nose had a two story window of small panes of glass. One could imagine a gunner sitting there while approaching a target.

I recall a trip with President Reagan, returning from China, when we made a stop in Anchorage on May 2, 1984 to meet with Pope John Paul II. The President met him again, a few months later in Miami. It has been reported these two men shared a common bond with their deep religious beliefs, their commitment to human rights, especially with regard to Poland, and the coincidence of having both been victims of assassination attempts.

One particular trip President George Bush made to China was a prelude of things that would unfold a few months later. It was the evening of China's farewell dinner for President Bush in Beijing. While in Beijing, we, being crewmembers, regarded the world as our mall and went shopping. As we were returning to our hotel in a taxi, packages in hand to prepare for our departure the next morning, we were kept from entering our hotel. Prior to the dinner, the Chinese placed restrictions on movements in and out the hotel until all the guests had arrived. As the Chinese were in charge of protection, with the Secret Service secondary as in most host countries, they had us trapped in the middle and we had to obtain permission to enter the hotel.

Outside the hotel, students were protesting the hosting of the dinner by the Chinese Vice Premier Wu Xueqian. President Bush invited astro-physicist Fang Lizhi to the dinner. According to the students outside the hotel, the Chinese government was not pleased with the invitation.

I encountered an impassable line of Chinese police in their khaki green uniforms with the red star on their hats preventing us from getting back to our hotel. The students started speaking to me in perfect English, explaining the trouble that may occur due to the banning of Lizhi's attendance at the dinner. They were concerned he would be turned away from the event.

Courtesy of the Author

On foreign trips the crew would dress in local costumes

Suddenly many police vans sped into the area in which I was speaking to the students. I watched as the police clubbed and dragged them into police vans. I found myself standing alone, as if there had not been anyone there but my crew and our van. It was the strangest feeling.

I was not touched or harmed, and yet everyone vanished. Two months later, the events of Tiananmen Square unfolded. I believe many of those same students speaking to me that evening were part of the tragedy that unfolded as students protested and lost their lives.

There were many occasions when we were invited to the White House Press Office if we were in town before or during a trip. We watched the election returns and would often be in the Rose Garden for a visiting dignitary's meeting with the President. On one particularly cloudy afternoon, we were in the Rose Garden when President Reagan presented Mother Teresa with the Medal of Freedom.

As President Reagan towered over this tiny woman, she became larger than life. All of a sudden, the sun appeared and her presence displayed a magnitude of brightness. She stated her unworthiness in accepting the Medal and we stood in awe of the moment.

The memories are still fresh, in recalling touring the winding streets of Venice during an economic summit and catching views of PT boats, SEAL teams, and helicopters flying overhead for security precautions. Several crewmembers were in Normandy for Reagan's famous speech and on the first 747 to ever land in Berlin Templehof Field before his, "Tear Down This Wall" speech.

We tapped on the door of the unassuming wooden building in Reykjavik to see where Reagan and Gorbachev would summit, as the world waited to see if we would finally see the end of the "Evil Empire." We traveled to Saudi Arabia to visit the troops of Operation Desert Shield on Thanksgiving in November 1990. President Bush and Barbara stood on a fighter jets wing and greeted the sea of desert beige khaki dressed soldiers on that holiday far from home. The military officials allowed one of the press charter crewmembers to climb inside of one of the fighter jets. We practiced wearing gas masks in case of an attack.

Courtesy of the Author

Press Plane Crew with President and Mrs. Bush

How can anyone explain the excitement in climbing the Great Wall for the first time to view the miles of one of the few sites recognizable from outer space? Or the surreal experience of walking on the Saudi's red carpeted pathway after landing on the airstrip in Dhahran that appeared as acres of glistening white ground? A friend of mine once said, "We traveled like kings and queens on a pauper's salary."

I was blessed and most thankful to all at Pan American World Airways and the White House Travel Office to have been an eyewitness to world history. Finally, having come from Ohio, it was exciting for me to ride the train on Reagan's whistle stop campaign and have my parents greeting us on arrival in Toledo to the sounds of "I'm Proud to be an American."

Nancy, her husband Pat, and daughter, Brianna, live in Stuart, FL.

THE LAST CLIPPER

By Mark S. Pyle

Any pilot's final flight is traumatic, but when it's the last
for an American icon, it becomes a part of history

At one time, I subscribed to Aviation Quarterly, which was remarkable in its quality, its appreciation of aviation, and its unrelenting pursuit of excellence. It was hardbound and worthy of being perused in my favorite lounge chair as I enjoyed a snifter of choice brandy. I was a life-time charter member, but it is now defunct and belongs to history.

Nothing is forever!

Courtesy of Airline Pilot

The *Clipper Goodwill*
blocks in at Miami after making its final passenger flight for Pan Am

209

My airline now belongs to the past, as surely does my aging lot of forgotten magazines. Pan American World Airways is lost--lost to corporate ineptitude, governmental indifference, and an inability to change with the world it helped to bring together.

"It looks like a beautiful day to go flying," First Officer Robert Knox of Greensboro, N.C., said as we began our ritual of checking the weather along our route of flight. Flight 219, bound for Bridgetowne, Barbados, was one hour from departure. We completed the paperwork that would ensure that the trip would meet all legal requirements for performance and weight and balance. We were more than businesslike, because CNN had reported the night before that Delta Air Lines had withdrawn its support for our newly proposed company.

On most occasions, we would have made a comment or two about sports or hobbies at a predeparture briefing. Individuals who had not flown together before would use such small talk to break the ice of unfamiliarity.

This morning was certainly different--an air of finality hung about everyone at our counter. The fact that it was 6 a.m. further depressed the atmosphere. The engineer, Chuck Foreman of Washington, D.C., was poring over the fuel figures. He had just returned to the Boeing 727 from its much larger cousin, the jumbo B-747.

We walked briskly to our aircraft, ship No. 368, one of the newest B-727s in the fleet and quite a pleasure to fly with its more powerful engines and spirited performance. Pan Am had many B-727s, but most were older. Their engines were always adequate but would not produce the kick in the seat of this newer model. I stowed my gear in the cockpit with a feeling of quiet pride, generated by command of such a machine. I then walked aft to greet the flight attendants who would complete our ship's company on this beautiful New York morning.

Immediately, the purser raised the question of Delta's withdrawal, and my answer was the same as it would be to my cockpit crewmembers: "Whatever the day holds, we will make it a good trip." All agreed that it would be, whether as the first of many, as the promised "born again" Pan Am with roots in Miami, or as the last of many.

We acknowledged the pushback clearance from our ground team, or what had been our ground team. Now that they were attired in their Delta uniforms, we felt a sense of unreality as we left the gate. Our aircraft responded in its usual marvelous manner--the engines whined to life as though longing to push onward into the promise of this cloudless morning. The ground team gave us a salute, and we were off. The navigational computer engaged, and we took our place on the runway as the final checklist items, routine with years of repetition, were completed.

Clipper Goodwill

As we gathered speed, I marveled at what fine engines the wonderful folks at Pratt and Whitney had provided for us. Gently, I eased the nose of this beautiful airplane skyward. The sound of rushing wind and whirring instruments added to what is always a magic moment in every pilot's life. The ground fell rapidly away, and the sky above beckoned. Both man and machine were happy to oblige. We turned away from the familiar Manhattan skyline and pointed the nose of Clipper Goodwill south--toward Barbados.

After leveling at 31,000 feet, the routine of monitoring powerplant and navigational instruments settled in. The conversation once again turned to what we felt to be the abandonment of our airline by what we had all thought was a corporate good guy. Not a visionary by any means, I had detailed my fears along these same lines from the day the agreement was finalized. "The Delta promises were necessary to cement the agreement and nothing more," I had said, and all along I had hoped I was wrong! I, like many of my friends, was not fortunate enough to transfer, or more correctly, I was not on the right airplane--the Airbus A310. (Delta wanted only certain groups of pilots, based primarily on airplane qualification.)

We flew over Bermuda, that incredible 21-square-mile piece of volcanic rock, where I had spent my last Christmas on layover. I have many happy memories of Bermuda and of other places--all associated with destinations on what had been a world carrier. Tokyo, Seoul, Bangkok, Manila, Beijing, Berlin, Frankfurt,

London, Venice, Oslo, Istanbul, and many other cities--destinations previous Pan Am employees largely pioneered--all hold memories for many more Pan Am employees.

Only a few puffy cumulus clouds--airborne cotton balls--blocked our way to Bridgetowne as we began our descent. The approach along the western coast of Barbados is surreal. The island is truly a multicolored jewel set in a background of turquoise sea. We landed to the east, as the trade winds nearly always dictate, touching down 4 hours 30 minutes after our departure from New York. We taxied to the gate and shut down our engines as we had done hundreds of times before. This time there would be a difference, a notable difference! In the four and onehalf hours of our flight, tragic history had been made.

Pan Am ceases operations

The station manager approached as he always did and greeted the inbound passengers. He then stepped into our office (the cockpit) and greeted us cordially, explaining he had some bad news. I quickly responded that I thought we could guess the nature of his grim tidings. He produced a message from New York operations in a very familiar format. This content, however, had never before in its 64-year history been inscribed on any Pan American document. Pan Am, as of 9 a.m. on Dec. 4, 1991, had ceased operations. None of our flight attendants could restrain their emotions, or their tears. All were at least 20-year veterans with Pan American or National Airlines. They vented their disbelief and their resentment of the Delta decision; consoling them prevented those of us in the cockpit from showing our own pent-up feelings.

Our station manager asked us if we would operate the trip to Miami. He would find a way to buy fuel. Many passengers were stranded, and some Pan Am employees were packing to leave their stations and their jobs.

We informed our station manager that we would delay as long as possible. This would ensure that all those wishing to return to Miami had time to board. We waited more than two hours in mostly silent thought while the passengers gathered from their hotels and employees packed their belongings.

At one point, the local airport employees who had served Pan Am so well, and whom Pan Am had so well served, came to the aircraft. A tearful ceremony followed. Flowers and good wishes were exchanged. The local television news media requested interviews. Airport employees barraged the Clipper Goodwill for last pictures, which would adorn family scrapbooks.

At 2 p.m. EST, the wheels came up on Clipper 436, hailing from Bridgetowne, Barbados, and bound for the city of Pan Am's birth. We flew with silent thought, exchanging few words as time passed. San Juan Center cleared our flight direct to Miami, and I punched in the navigational coordinates for Miami International a final time. Little could be said in the face of a solemn reality--the certain knowledge of dead-end careers. What happened can best be described as a death in our immediate family. Pan American was my family in every sense. It was the corporate family to thousands.

The engineer interrupted my thoughts as we began our descent into Miami: "Should I call in range?"

"Yes," I said, "someone will surely still be there. The airplanes must be put to bed."

The engineer spoke again in my direction very softly, so softly I could not understand.

"Pardon me?" I said.

This veteran engineer of more than 25 years choked back tears through clouded eyes. He said, "Mark, we're the last flight--the final flight." That circumstance had not occurred to me. He continued, "They want us to make a low pass over the field."

I said, "You're kidding, right? They're joking!" Privately, I thought it might be a friend who had landed before me, now pulling my leg.

211

"No joke," he said, "they are going to be there to meet us--some kind of ceremony."

Miami lay before us. A cold front had just passed, and fog followed the coastline, extending out to sea almost to the Bahamas. Miami sat on the other side of the fog bank, eerie and beautiful at the same time. Dinner Key lay nestled in the fog. My mind raced at the finality of what I was doing. This wasn't just the end of my career! This airline's fading into history far surpassed the end of any individual's career. Franklin Roosevelt had left from that same Dinner Key aboard Dixie Clipper, bound for Casablanca in 1943, the first American President to fly while in office.

Pan Am had not been just a part of history; it had made history for all of its 64 years. It was always there when the government needed it. Indeed, Pan American Clippers had many scars as mementos from encounters with enemies of the United States. From Japanese bullet holes a lumbering clipper received as it evacuated key military personnel from Wake Island during the early stages of World War II, to the terrorist bombing of "Clipper 103." More recently Pan Am pilots and airplanes aided in Operation Desert Storm. A Pan American Clipper brought me home from Vietnam. Now Pan Am had only Clipper Goodwill and this last crew--this final flight.

With the passengers briefed carefully as to our intentions, I called for flaps 15. We descended on the electronic glideslope that had so often guided me to Miami. We now executed the requested low pass--my first since I left the Navy many years ago. As we flew down the centerline of Runway 12, I noted the lineup of American Airlines aircraft that would soon take our place. As we completed the low pass, the tower issued a final statement: "Outstanding, Clipper!"

Pulling up and turning downwind for our final approach and landing, I looked at the beautiful Miami Airport and the city it serves. We all realized this would be the last time. Again, the finality of the moment slammed my senses. Our wheels touched for the last time in a Pan American aircraft --the last time for a scheduled revenue flight of any kind for this historic airline.

Approaching the taxiway, we began to see the reception that stretched before us. Airport vehicles of every description--police and security vehicles, port authority and fire equipment--lined the taxiway, and video cameras abounded. Lines of individuals in semi-military formation were everywhere.

Salute to history

As we taxied past the first formations, men and women came to brisk attention and saluted "the last of the Clippers." Tears welled up in my eyes then for the first time. Many rows of people and machines--all smartly formed--all saluted. I returned the salute just as crisply, fully knowing that their salutes were to this "machine" and to all the "machines" that bore the title "Clipper" for 64 years. Their salute was to the history that this ship represented and to all that had gone before.

We passed the line of fire equipment, and the water cannon was fired over the aircraft. My emotions reeled under the weight of this tribute to Pan Am's last

Courtesy of the Author

Mark Pyle

flight. I engaged the windshield wiper to clear water that was on the windscreen, but that did little good for the water in my eyes. My first officer fought back his tears. He had worn Pan Am blue for 23 years.

One final formation--all Pan American ground personnel--tendered their last salute. We approached the gate and set the brakes for the last time. We shut down systems for the last time and secured the faithful engines. Sadly gathering our belongings, we shook hands. Our final fight was over. No eyes in the cockpit were dry. Many of the departing passengers shared our moment of grief. The tears for Pan Am will continue.

Upon returning to my home, our 13-year-old son presented me with a letter. Through his own tears, he named me Pan Am's greatest pilot. For one brief moment, on one tearful occasion.

Note: This article reproduced with the permission of the Airline Pilots Association.

AWARE

By Mary Goshgarian

Pan Am Aware

Born and raised in Massachusetts, I left rustic New England to come to glamorous Miami in 1956 and began working for Pan American in the traffic and sales department. After a few other airport jobs, I was lucky to get an assignment at the Miami Clipper Club and through the years met some of my favorite movie stars including Sophia Loren and Burt Reynolds---he even gave me a kiss!

Courtesy of the Author

Mary Goshgarian in the Store at the Pan Am International Flight Academy, Miami

214

As I gained seniority, I was able to hold an afternoon shift and had time a few days of the week to help with my friends who were involved with Aware. Started by Berlin pilots, this group of employees would rally political and civic support for the company during our difficult days in the mid seventies. My good friends Helen Dodd and Dave Abrams would sell small promotional items, literally out of their desks, to raise money to support Aware. My schedule allowed me to volunteer and help them, a labor of love I continue to this day, in my 88th year.

After the company ceased operations, we set up a little store where we sold a selection of Pan Am nostalgia such as original Pan Am dishes, silverware, water pitchers and clothing such as jackets, tee shirts, sweatshirts. We even have commemorative key chains, calendars, umbrellas, beach towels, clocks and a large selection of Pan Am books.

Along with Nellie Koch, Sybil Holder and Tony Lutz, we keep the store open 3 days a week from 11am to 3pm. Due to the generosity of Vito Cutrone, a Pan Amer who now runs the center, we have a lovely store on the 2nd floor of the Pan Am International Flight Academy right off of 36th Street next to the Miami Airport. Vito most kindly provides this space to us free of charge and that helps us make a few dollars each year that we are putting aside for a Pan Am Museum to be located in Miami.

You can say that managing the store, ordering the inventory and talking about Pan Am with our customers keeps me young. The Pan Am Flight Academy is always busy with aviators from around the world as well as maintenance and flight attendants who use the facility. Some of our best customers are from Nigeria, Iraq, and we even get correspondence from such far and away places such as Australia and Japan, writers anxious to buy Pan Am souvenirs.

When you are in Miami, please stop by – I'll be happy to give you a ten percent "Pan Am" discount!

A PILOT'S SALUTE

By Buck Clippard

Thoughts of a Veteran Pilot abut Pan Am

In Martin Scorsese's 2004 movie *The Aviator*, Scorsese portrayed Howard Hughes as an airline pioneer. While being an interesting story about the quirky boss of TWA, the movie failed to give credit where credit is due: The role of Juan Trippe's Pan American World Airways in shaping international commercial aviation and Mr. Trippe's extraordinary leadership.

Juan Trippe was truly a visionary and a genius. From humble beginnings in 1927, he created the greatest international airline in history. In addition, he also fashioned the Inter-Continental Hotels chain of worldwide luxury hotels, the World Services Division (Cape Kennedy housekeeping and tracking stations), and the Pan Am Building. When finished, the Pan Am Building was the world's largest commercial office building. He facilitated worldwide travel, and along with Boeing, was responsible for developing the 707 and first wide-body, two-aisle aircraft, the famous Boeing 747.

Pan American was unique among US airlines. It was the "Chosen Instrument," the airline selected to operate the international air routes of the United States and the airline of choice for Americans traveling overseas. Pan Am also operated a world-wide air cargo system, and in response to competition, established a charter operation with global reach.

Pan Am achieved many "firsts" during its time. One of its timetables said it all: "First in Latin America, first across the Pacific, first across the Atlantic and first around the world." There were other firsts, as well, including, to list just a few, radio communications, instrument flying, cabin attendants, meals aloft, Tourist Class service, US-flag jet service, ILS landings, business class, and many more.

The Company's advertising boasted of "Serving All Six Continents" and that it was "The World's Most Experienced Airline." This was no exaggeration. The airline was everywhere. Sales offices opened in the best locations in the US and in the world capitals served by the airline. A traveler visiting a Pan Am ticket office could purchase a ticket to anywhere around the globe. In addition, the ticket offices provided full service, including assistance with visas, hotels, and even information on the political situation around the world. It was once said Americans overseas could get more accurate and timely information on events in the world at the Pan American ticket offices than at the US embassy! Pan American's travel brochures, posters, books, and maps were legendary—published in its own in-house printing department, and provided as a service to the traveling public.

One could not overlook Pan American's operating and technical staffs: those who flew the aircraft and those who kept them flying. It was not an exaggeration that Pan American pilots were the best in the world. It was a fact. And it was not an exaggeration Pan American set the standard for aircraft maintenance. That, too, was a fact. What is the standard today was set by Pan Am over sixty years ago. This expertise was recognized the world over and as a result, Pan American sent experts around the globe to assist developing airlines with its Technical Assistance Program (TAP). Pan American pilots and stewardesses were legendary for their heroism in voluntary support of the United States. If Americans were in trouble, Pan American was there to fly them to safer harbors.

In the industry, all knew Pan American for its operation of many charter and special flights. Among them were the Sukarno Charters (Indonesia), flights for the Shah of Iran, and the Presidential Press Charters. Pan Am flew many military charters, including over three hundred Boeing 747 charters hauling troops to Desert Storm, Hajj Charters from Tehran and Jakarta, industry charters (Fedders and Carrier air conditioner companies), cargo charters (printed money, gold, the Vatican Art, exotic animals), and the charters I was most familiar with, the Olson charters.

There was a saying, "If you want a good tour, go with American Express, but if you want a great tour, go with Harvey S. Olson." Olson annually chartered a Pan Am Boeing 707 to team up with the QE2 for an "Around the World Air-Cruise," a thirty-seven day trip on the jet and ship with 83 VIP passengers, cruise directors, and a hand-selected crew. I was fortunate to be included on these trips for four consecutive and memorable years.

With Deregulation, fortunes began to change for Pan American. Domestic carriers with large domestic networks won international routes, which infringed on Pan American's route structure. Ironically, Pan Am could fly daily trips starting around the world from both the east coast and west coast, but was not allowed to fly across its own country carrying paying passengers to make it a complete around-the-world flight.

Pan Am's sovereign route system also began to crumble. Newly empowered foreign flag carriers, awarded either new US-access or additional US-gateways, became fierce competitors. There were other things that contributed to the demise of Pan American. First and foremost was terrorism. Other contributing factors included the tragic accident at Tenerife, the sale of the Pacific Routes, the Pan American/National Merger or other management decisions. I'll leave that to the historians to debate.

Since Pan American ceased operations in 1991, my fellow former employees have maintained a close family relationship through reunions, luncheons, and cruises. We have organizations such as the Clipper Pioneers (former pilots), World Wings International (former stewardesses), the National/Pan American Alumni Association, and the Pan Am Historical Foundation. There is a newsletter, "PanAmigo," published out of Miami, that keeps members in touch. And recently, a hosted family reunion for 600 Pan Amers which was featured in the *Wall Street Journal* story, "Return of Pan Am, for a weekend," written by Scott McCartney, the *Journal's* aviation correspondent. Pan Am memorabilia continues to sell Pan Am items in Miami (the AWARE store).

It's always good to become reacquainted with old friends and colleagues at reunions and other occasions to re-hash memories of our times together. Pan Am may be gone, but hopefully, never forgotten. After the 2011 Pan Am family reunion, it was said, "You may take Pan Am out of the skies, but you cannot take Pan Am out of these guys and girls."

May this spirit continue until the last one remaining turns out the lights.

Courtesy of the Author

Buck Clippard

Buck spent over 28 years as a pilot with Pan American, based in Berlin, Hong Kong, Sydney, Los Angeles, New York, and Miami, with a temporary assignment in Tehran, He retired in 1991 when the company went out of business. He commutes between Tucson and Fort Lauderdale.